AN INTERNATIONAL PERSPECTIVE ON ECONOMIC EDUCATION

AN INTERNATIONAL PERSPECTIVE ON ECONOMIC EDUCATION

Edited by

William B. Walstad
University of Nebraska-Lincoln

Kluwer Academic Publishers
Boston/Dordrecht/London

Distributors for North America:
Kluwer Academic Publishers
101 Philip Drive
Assinippi Park
Norwell, Massachusetts 02061 USA

Distributors for all other countries:
Kluwer Academic Publishers Group
Distribution Centre
Post Office Box 322
3300 AH Dordrecht, THE NETHERLANDS

Library of Congress Cataloging-in-Publication Data
An international perspective on economic education / edited by William B. Walstad.
p. cm.
Includes index.
ISBN 0-7923-9437-2 (alk. paper)
1. Economics -- Study and teaching (Secondary) I. Walstad, William B.
HB74.5.I58 1994
330'.071'1 -- dc20 93-42732
CIP

Printed on acid-free paper.

Printed in the United States of America

CONTENTS

VI. THE ROLE OF ECONOMIC EDUCATION IN A TRANSITION TO A MARKET ECONOMY

LIST OF FIGURES AND TABLES

FIGURES

TABLES

LIST OF CONTRIBUTORS

William J. Baumol is Professor Emeritus of Economics at Princeton University and Director of the C. V. Starr Center for Applied Economics at New York University, U.S.A.

Klaus Beck is a Professor at the Institute for Economics Education, University of Nurnberg, Germany.

William Becker is Professor of Economics at Indiana University, U.S.A., and Editor of the *Journal of Economic Education*.

Lucien Ellington is Professor of Education and Associate Director of the Center for Economic Education at the University of Tennessee at Chattanooga, U.S.A.

William Greene is Professor of Economics at New York University, U.S.A.

Dimitrina M. Ispirodonova is a graduate student in the Department of Economics at the University of Cincinnati, U.S.A.

Kyung-Keun Kim is a Fellow at the Center for Economic Education at the Korea Development Institute, Seoul, Korea.

Volker Krumm is Professor of Education at the University of Salzburg, Austria.

Kevin McKenna is Professor of Economics at Curtin University of Technology, Australia.

Anthony Myatt is Professor of Economics at the University of New Brunswick, Canada.

Sherwin Rosen is Professor of Economics at the University of Chicago, U.S.A.

Francis W. Rushing is Professor of Economics and holds the Bernard B. and Eugenia A. Ramsey Chair of Private Enterprise at Georgia State University, U.S.A.

Phillip Saunders is Professor of Economics and Director of the Center for Economic Education at Indiana University, U.S.A.

Ruth Shen is Professor of Economics and Director of the Center for Economic Education at San Francisco State University, U.S.A.

T. Y. Shen is Professor of Economics at the University of California-Davis, U.S.A.

Tadahisa Uozumi is Professor of Education at Aichi University on Education, Japan.

George M. Vredeveld is Professor of Economics and Director of the Center for Economic Education at the University of Cincinnati, U.S.A.

Charles Waddell is Associate Professor of Economics at the University of New Brunswick, Canada.

William B. Walstad is Professor of Economics and Director of the National Center for Research in Economic Education at the University of Nebraska-Lincoln, U.S.A.

Michael Watts is Professor of Economics and Director of the Center for Economic Education at Purdue University, U.S.A.

David J. Whitehead is Senior Lecturer in Education (Economics) at the Institute of Education, University of London, United Kingdom.

ACKNOWLEDGMENTS

No book is published without help from many people and organizations. This volume is no exception. The book was made possible by the hard work of the chapter authors, whose names are listed in the table of contents. These authors should be recognized for their chapter contributions.

The Calvin K. Kazanjian Economics Foundation, Inc. provided financial support to cover some costs associated with the book. I am especially grateful to Mike MacDowell, Managing Director of the Kazanjian Foundation, for his genuine interest in the volume and encouragement of my work in economic education over the years.

Recognition should also be given to the *Journal of Economic Education* and the *Journal of Economic Literature* for permission to use material from articles. Chapters 6 and 7 are revised and updated versions of articles that originally appeared in those journals.

My associates at the University of Nebraska-Lincoln gave me great assistance in the final phases of the project. Sharon Nemeth spent many hours working on the text and tables. Her typing skills and attention to detail were invaluable in preparing the manuscript for publication. Tammie Houser offered ideas on text organization and layout. Kevin Clark worked on the index. Syed Ali reformatted figures. Mike Wranik and Jeanette Iwasa proofed the manuscript. I greatly appreciated all of this effort because it was critical for the timely completion of the volume.

Finally, I am indebted to Zachary Rolnik, Senior Editor at Kluwer Academic Publishers. He encouraged my idea for this volume from the beginning and was instrumental in turning an idea into a book.

William B. Walstad

AN INTERNATIONAL PERSPECTIVE ON ECONOMIC EDUCATION

CHAPTER 1

AN INTRODUCTION TO AN INTERNATIONAL PERSPECTIVE ON ECONOMIC EDUCATION

William B. Walstad

Economics is taught in some form in the secondary schools of nations throughout the world. Economics instruction is essential at this level of schooling for the development of the economic understanding of students (and future citizens). The subject is rarely taught in elementary schools, and when it is, the content coverage is quite limited. Although economics courses are offered in universities, the majority of students end their formal education with secondary school, and those students who continue their education at a university are unlikely to take an economics course. The fact is that the best opportunity for the economic education of the youth of a nation occurs in secondary schools. This book examines economic education at this critical level of the educational system.

The teaching of economics in secondary schools varies across countries. Some nations give strong emphasis to economics and teach it as an academic subject, while others consider the subject to be less important and treat it as part of vocational education. These differences occur because of history, the structure of education, and other national factors. At the same time, there are common elements in the economic education of many countries, especially in content coverage. This contrast between the common features and the uniqueness of economic education in secondary schools of major industrial nations exemplifies the international perspective presented in this book.

The international perspective is developed in the six sections of the volume. The first section discusses why nations should include economics in school curricula, and presents a framework for teaching economics that should have global appeal. Dissension and consensus on economic issues among North American and European economists are examined in the second section, and implications for instruction are drawn based on the identified areas of agreement and disagreement in economists' thinking. The third section surveys the U.S. research literature on precollege economic education and assesses the current state of economics instruction in U.S. schools.[1] The economics curricula and educational practices in seven other nations – the United Kingdom, Canada, Japan, Germany, Austria, Korea, and Australia – are described in the fourth and fifth sections.[2] The fifth section also presents international comparisons of economic understanding based on national testing in six of those nations. The sixth and final section explores the role of economic education in centrally planned economies, and its effects on the transition to a market economy, using Russia, Bulgaria, and China as case studies. The remainder of this chapter describes these section themes and the chapter contents.

I. THE RATIONALE AND FRAMEWORK

The rationale for economic education is a compelling one and explains why economics is taught in secondary schools. This rationale was perhaps best stated almost a quarter century ago by George Stigler (1970), an American Nobel laureate in economics.[3] His justification for the special position of economics instead of other subjects was that it contributed to one of two classes of knowledge:

> 1. As a means of communication among people, incorporating a basic vocabulary or logic that is so frequently encountered that the knowledge should be possessed by everyone.
> 2. As a type of knowledge frequently needed and yet not susceptible to economical purchase from experts. (p. 78)

Economic education has found a place in the secondary school curricula of many countries primarily because it contributes to the first type of knowledge. People like to think and to talk about the economic issues that affect them in the roles that they might assume over a lifetime – as consumers, workers, producers, or as citizens. Basic economic literacy helps people understand the economic concerns that directly affect them in their economic and civic roles. Nations benefit from economic education because it improves the public's ability to understand critical economic issues that affect a nation. For example, the effective transition to a market economy for the nations of Eastern Europe and for the new nations established in the former Soviet Union will require extensive economic education among the citizenry. Even countries with developed market economies, such as the United States or Japan, benefit when citizens are educated in basic economic principles and apply those principles to issues, whether they concern taxes, trade policy, health care reform, or government budget deficits.

Economic education also contributes to the second type of knowledge. For some economic decisions, such as personal investing in the stock market, it is possible to hire professional or technical help. In most cases, however, it is neither practical nor economical for an individual to hire a professional every time a decision needs to be made. Even when outside opinions are given, the final decision must made by the individual, not the advisor. Each person, therefore, must ultimately serve as his or her own *economist* in making many economic choices. Economic education is likely to improve the competence of each individual to be a good economist when making personal and social economic decisions about issues encountered over a lifetime.

In Chapter 2 of this volume, William Baumol, a distinguished U.S. economist, offers a case for economic education based on the first class of knowledge identified by George Stigler. He reviews five major developments that illustrate the "radical change" in the U.S. and in other major economies over the past 50 years: the economic growth boom of the postwar period for major nations; the internationalization of domestic markets; the convergence of standards of living among leading industrialized nations; the collapse of centrally directed economies; and, other changes affecting inflation, business cycles, and the price of basic services such as health care or education. Baumol states that "if graduates of secondary education emerge from school ignorant of these crucial developments the world they inhabit will be incomprehensible" (p. 19). He believes that economic education has an obligation to provide students with "at least the beginnings of an analytical framework" (p. 31) for comprehending the economic world. Baumol thinks that studying economics is important because simple common sense is an unreliable guide for analyzing economic events. To illustrate this point, he concludes with six examples of misunderstandings and misconceptions that economic education can correct.

The strength or weakness of the case for economic education ultimately depends on how government leaders and educators in a nation perceive its contribution to the economic understanding of the public. Some nations will see economics as a relatively basic dimension of a student's education, perhaps not quite as basic as reading, science, or mathematics, but close in order of importance. Other nations will assign a lower priority to the teaching of economics because of uncertainty about the effects of economic knowledge on students. Whatever the emphasis, the next question that must be answered is what should be the "analytical framework" for teaching economics?

Phillip Saunders offers a global response to this question in Chapter 3. The answer is based on the *Framework for Teaching the Basic Concepts* that he helped write for the National Council on Economic Education. The *Framework* describes 22 basic economic concepts and sorts them into fundamental, microeconomic, macroeconomic and international categories. It recommends that these concepts be taught to students before they graduate from senior high school. It also suggests that a problem-solving or decision-making approach be used for the teaching of economics to students.

The advocacy of the U.S. *Framework* as the basis for a global framework is obviously a normative one, of which Saunders is well aware, but the proposal deserves careful consideration. This document represents over thirty years of development work by distinguished U.S. economists, and has withstood major criticisms (see Chapters 4 and 7). The *Framework* also receives positive reviews from economic educators in other nations, as discussed in Chapters 11, 12, and 14. These comments suggest that the *Framework* has validity as a global statement of the content and approach for economics in the schools of the world.

II. DISSENSION AND CONSENSUS IN ECONOMICS

Economists are both respected and ridiculed by the public. The respect comes from the recognition that economic problems are worthy of careful study, and that economic analysis can offer insightful, if not always politically palatable, answers to perplexing problems. The prime example of the respect is the Nobel Prize in economic science. The ridicule comes from the confusion created by conflicting opinions that economists express about the economic issues that they study. Many in the public and the press perceive economists as divided on economic issues and unable to agree on the answers to economic problems. This sentiment is illustrated by a newspaper cartoon of two people talking with a caption that reads: "which economist should we listen to today?"

In Chapter 4, Michael Watts discusses the historical and current reasons for the ideological conflicts in the economics profession that produce differing positions on economic issues. As Watts explains, the conflicts and debates among economists (and noneconomists) that are evident today are not new, but can be found throughout the history of economic thought beginning about the time of Adam Smith's *Wealth of Nations*. The dissension in contemporary economic thought can also be traced to the intense debates and self-evaluations among economists in recent years over whether economic methods are "scientific," or whether they, and the analysis and conclusions based on those methods, are best characterized as ideology.

The points and counterpoints in Chapter 4 are unsettling to read because the intensity of the disputes calls into question the basic content and approach to economic education that seemed so settled in Chapter 3's *Framework*. These concerns cannot be ignored given the public perceptions of divisions among economists, and the historical and contemporaneous evidence that only reinforces the perceptions. They create serious doubts about whether economics can be meaningfully taught below the college level. Watts concludes that it can be, but offers the following guidelines:

> In areas where most economists agree, it only seems reasonable that the burden of proof in any argument that proposes teaching concepts and ideas outside that consensus lies with those who would do so. Conversely, in areas where dissension rules, or is at least writ large within the profession, those who want to ignore these debates must offer strong arguments to justify any one-sided presentation on such topics; and they should recognize that normally to do so in programs for precollege students will lead to serious charges of intellectual or even ideological bias. (pp. 61-62)

These guidelines should help economic educators resolve the dilemmas from the content debates in the economics profession.

Chapter 5 switches focus from dissension among economists to consensus among economists. In the first part of that chapter, William Becker, William Walstad, and Michael Watts review survey studies of the opinions of North American and European economists on economic issues. Contrary to public and press comments, the surveys show substantial evidence of a general consensus among economists in their views on many economic topics. The consensus varied somewhat by the country-origin of the economists, but there were more similarities than differences.

The second half of the chapter uses the survey data from U.S. economists as a benchmark measure of what it is like to "think like economists" because this is an often-stated goal for economic education. The authors employed three different methods to compare the economists' opinions with opinions collected from other U.S. groups. The results showed that economists and economic educators thought alike on economic issues. High school economics and social studies teachers and journalists thought alike. The correspondence, however, between the thinking of economists (or economic educators) and teachers or journalists was limited. Thus, there are significant gaps in the transmission of economic information and ideas from economists and economic educators to other key groups in American society.

III. RESEARCH AND ASSESSMENT IN THE U.S.

Other transmission gaps that result from the teaching of economics raise curriculum and instruction questions. How is economics taught to students in the schools? What do students understand about economics as a result of coursework or the infusion of economics into other subjects? How can student learning be measured? What student, teacher, or school factors contribute most to economic understanding? Which technological innovations or instructional materials best increase economic knowledge? What are the lasting effects from economics instruction? Similar questions have been addressed in research studies of precollege economic education in the U.S. for over thirty years. The results from that body of research were reviewed in two major surveys in recent years (Becker, Greene, and Rosen, 1990; Walstad, 1992). Both reviews have been updated for this volume.

The survey of research studies of high school economics in the U.S. in Chapter 6, by William Becker, William Greene, and Sherwin Rosen, examines four issues. The first section discusses the measurement of economic knowledge with standardized tests and the problems that the authors perceive with the interpretation of test scores in research studies. The second and longest section assesses the findings from studies of special curriculum projects, attitudes, teacher effects, coursework, technological innovations, student characteristics, and the lasting effects of instruction. The third section returns to testing issues and argues that test scores are of limited value as measures of learning. What is more important, according to the authors, is to show the connection between what students learn and its effects on decision-making, or observable market outcomes such as wages. The fourth section discusses sample selection bias in research studies, and gives examples of procedures that can be used to correct this problem.

In Chapter 7, William Walstad evaluates the changes in economic education in U.S. secondary schools, using the 1961 recommendations of the National Task Force Report on Economic Education to structure the assessment.[4] The improvements over the past thirty years include: (1) a significant increase in the percentage of high school graduates completing an economics course (from 16 percent in 1961 to 44 percent in 1990); (2) more instructional time devoted to economics; (3) teaching that is more analytical and less descriptive; (4) better content preparation of teachers; (5) the availability of higher quality textbooks and many useful supplementary materials; (6) a national network of college and university economic educators to provide teacher education in economics; and, (7) a large number of research studies. Although the progress has been great, the chapter calls for further work because economics is not a *universal* subject in the education of U.S. secondary students.

IV. ECONOMICS INSTRUCTION IN DIFFERENT NATIONS

Economics is a term that describes different types of courses and a range of content in secondary schools. From a strict perspective, an economics course would focus on basic principles of microeconomics and macroeconomics as defined by academic economists. From a broader perspective, topics in business education, consumer education, vocational education, or entrepreneurship would constitute the "economics" that should be taught to students. A curricular decision that each nation must make is whether to treat economics as a separate academic subject, as a broader set of topics to be taught in various subjects, or some combination of the two choices.

Other curricular decisions differ across nations and sometimes by educational units within nations. One decision concerns when students should be learn economics. Some nations begin economics instruction in elementary school while others teach it at the end of secondary school. Other decisions involve how many and what type of students will be taught economics because it can either be a required subject taken by all students or an elective subject taken by a select group. In addition, decisions must be made about the amount of course preparation that teachers must have before teaching the subject.

The majority of the chapters in this volume address these decisions when they discuss how economics is included in the school curricula of eight industrial nations – the United States, the United Kingdom, Canada, Japan, Germany, Austria, Korea, and Australia. Brief descriptions of economic education in each nation follows, beginning with the U.S. because it serves as the basis for cross-national comparisons.

United States. As discussed in Chapter 7, the academic view of economics has dominated the teaching of economics in the U.S. because of the influence of economists, first through the National Task Force report and later through the *Framework.* A separate semester economics course is taken by about 44 percent of American high school graduates. This course is usually offered in the twelfth grade as an elective, although more states and school districts have made economics a required course for students and some offer economics courses at other grades. The alternative to a separate course is the inclusion of economics lessons in other subjects. The infusion strategy has been widely used by U.S. schools because of state legislation. Not all students, however, receive the same type or a high quality of economics instruction through infusion because the legislation differs by state and instruction varies by teacher.

United Kingdom. In Chapter 8, David Whitehead describes economic education in the U.K. The U.K. adopts a more academic approach to the content of economics at the upper secondary level (students aged 16-19 years old) than that found in American schools. There is no *Framework*-type document used in the U.K. that is designed to limit the economic concept load to a minimum to make a course more manageable for teachers to teach or for students to learn. Instead, teachers typically follow a common core syllabus that covers what would be taught in a college principles of economics course in the U.S.

The reason that economics is taught more intensively and for longer periods (up to two years) in the U.K. is in preparation for subject examinations that affect entrance to the university. The Advanced Level examinations are graded by external examiners, not by teachers. By contrast, separate economics courses in the U.S. typically last just a semester, do not follow a common syllabus, and are not tied to external exit examinations that affect university entrance. U.K. teachers are also specialists who have the equivalent of a master-degree in economics, whereas U.S. social studies teachers mostly study history or other social sciences because they are more likely to teach those subjects. Few U.S. teachers hold the equivalent of a master's degree in economics.

Only the high ability U.K. students qualify for A-level studies. These students study three of nine possible subjects (biology, business studies, chemistry, economics, English, geography, history, math, and physics). Whitehead estimates that economics, together with business studies, a course that also includes some economic content and is viewed as a complement to rather than a substitute course for economics, are the most popular options among 16-18 year olds still in school. Together these subjects are studied by about 25 percent of the A-level school population.

Canada. The Canadian experience with economic education is explained by Anthony Myatt and Charles Waddell in Chapter 9. In Canada, the number of course offerings and course content in economics vary by province in much the same way as they do by state in the U.S. The approach to economics is an academic one that focuses on basic principles of economics, and thus the content coverage is closer to that found in an American high school course than in the A-level (university-type) courses of the U.K. The authors report that only 3 percent of Canadian high school students, aged 15-19 years old, take economics, significantly less than in other industrial nations.[5]

Chapter 9 also addresses an additional topic – the lasting effects of economic education in high school. This topic was first discussed in Chapter 6, and is important for assessing the value of high school economics, especially for students who take economics at a university. Myatt and Waddell first review the past research studies that showed some lasting effects of taking a high school course on student achievement in university economics courses in both the U.S. and the U.K. They then present their findings that showed positive effects on grades in a university economics course from having taken a Canadian high school economics course.

Japan. In Chapter 10, Lucien Ellington and Tadahisa Uozumi discuss the major features of the Japanese school system. This system was established from 1947 to 1950 using the U.S. as a model, which means that economics is included as part of the social studies curriculum. The social studies curriculum is set at the national level by the Ministry of Education and does not vary by prefecture (i.e., state) as in the U.S. Consequently, all Japanese students are taught the same economic content in courses.

Economics is included in three different courses in the social studies curriculum in Japanese secondary schools. Economic concepts represent about a third of the required ninth-grade civics course, which covers such topics as prices, savings, taxes, consumer education, occupations, unions, employment, and the role of government and business in the economy. Economics also accounts for about 20 to 33 percent of the required tenth grade course on contemporary society. This course would discuss comparative economic systems, the national economy, business cycles, and international economics (trade, the balance of payments, and exchange rates). The third course, politics and economics, is an elective course that is taken in the twelfth grade by perhaps one-third or one-half of students. It covers material similar to that found in the contemporary society course but in more depth.

Germany and Austria. Klaus Beck and Volker Krumm describe the system for educating students in economics in Germany and Austria in Chapter 11. The U.S. has a comprehensive high school system that educates all students, both the college and non-college bound, but in the German system students are separated at an early age into different schools based on projected ability and career path. The five types of German upper secondary schools are: (1) general secondary schools that prepare students for university entrance; (2) senior vocational schools that provide career training and a business degree for entry into higher-level jobs, and also preparation for university entrance; (3) intermediate vocational schools that prepare students for middle-level jobs, but not for entrance to the university; (4) secondary schools that provide general education for those who are not interested in the university or a career; and (5) dual vocational schools that offer part-time vocational or technical training in school and part-time apprenticeships in businesses as preparation for entry into middle to lower-level jobs.

The educational system in Austria has the same hierarchical structure based on ability and career path as found in Germany. In Austria, however, there are only four types of schools because there is no school that provides education for students not seeking a career or entrance to the university. Also, the senior vocational schools have higher qualifications for the business degree or for preparation for the university than in Germany.

The curriculum analysis by Beck and Krumm show that German and Austrian high school students do not take a separate course in economics as students can in the U.S. Rather, economics is infused in the curriculum of each type of school to varying degrees, but the extent of instruction depends on the school, which in turn depends on the ability of the student and career-orientation. The most economics is included in the senior vocational schools that prepare students for entry into higher-level jobs or the university. In these schools, economic concepts would be taught in combination with other subjects such as accounting, business, and management. For the small percentage that are university-bound, economics would be taught primarily in combination with history, social studies, or geography courses. Although these university-bound students would be comparable in ability to the students in A-level economics courses in the U.K., they receive much less direct economics instruction.

Korea. The Republic of Korea requires a course in "politics and economy" before high school graduation according to Kyung-keun Kim in Chapter 12. Half of this course is devoted to economics. Students enrolled in regular high schools take the politics and economy course for four semesters, and thus receive about one year of economics instruction, while students attending vocational high schools take the course for two semesters, and receive a semester of economics instruction. The course content is contained in a required national textbook and it covers material comparable to that in a college principles textbook in the U.S.

Kim finds there are problems with economic education in Korea that may limit the effectiveness of student learning. Few economics items (1.5 percent) are on the university entrance exams. Students may not take economics seriously as a subject because their efforts are directed to learning material more central to the university exam. Economics is also taught superficially because there is too much content to be covered in a course. Compounding these problems are the inadequate preparation of teachers and the use of a single textbook that presents too many economics concepts in a dry and uninteresting manner.

Australia. The structure of economic education in secondary schools in Australia would be closest to that found in the U.K. based on the descriptions of Kevin McKenna in Chapter 13. Those students who decide to take economics spend two years of concentrated instruction on the subject, often in preparation for university examinations. The content coverage is extensive and would be similar to that found in an A-level economics course in the U.K or in a college principles of economics course in the U.S.

McKenna estimates that about 27 percent of Australian students study economics in the last two years of high school. For these students, the study of economics would account for one-fifth or one-sixth of all coursework. The percentage of students who complete the final two years of high school in Australia, however, is a group of more mixed ability than that found with students in A-level economics in the U.K. because more students continue their education after age sixteen in Australia than in the U.K.

V. ECONOMIC UNDERSTANDING ACROSS NATIONS

The *Test of Economic Literacy* (TEL) is a nationally normed and standardized multiple choice achievement test designed for use with eleventh and twelfth grade high school students in the U.S. (Soper and Walstad, 1987). The 46 items on the two forms of the test assess student understanding of basic economic concepts as outlined in the *Framework*. Psychometric studies with the 8,205 students (4,235 form A and 3,970 form B) who took the TEL showed that it is a reliable and valid measure of economics achievement. The TEL has a long history of use in U.S. research in economic education, as described in Chapters 6 and 7.

The TEL has become the standard for international comparisons of the economic understanding of high school students. In 1989, for example, the TEL (form A) was administered to 7,549 students in the U.K. and the results compared with the U.S. norms (see Chapter 8). Three other cross-national comparisons using the TEL are reported for the first time in this volume. Chapter 11 presents data from the administration of a German translation of the TEL to 9,149 students (4,612 form A and 4,537 form B) in Germany and to 3,354 students (1,664 form A and 1,690 form B) in Austria in 1991. Chapter 12 describes the results from translating the TEL into Korean and giving it to 4,334 students attending Korean high schools in 1992. The Australian TEL data discussed in Chapter 13 were collected in 1991 from 939 students enrolled in West Australian high schools.

The average scores and the standard deviations for the TEL data for the U.S., U.K., Germany, Austria, Korea, and Australia are reported in Table 1.1. No assertion is made that these data represent a scientific international comparison of economic understanding. There are differences in the composition of the groups in terms of ability and other characteristics, the sampling procedures vary, and the data were collected in different years. There may be unknown language or cultural problems, especially with the translation of the TEL questions into German or Korean. Despite the differences and potential problems, the TEL means are suggestive of what would be expected based on the description of the schools of each nation and the ability of students.

Students in the U.K. showed the highest level of performance with an average score of 36 points on the 46-item TEL. This result was expected given that U.K. students had two years of economics instruction and were higher ability students. Australian students in the twelfth grade followed next with an average score of 31 points. These students had two years of high school economics, but the ability level of this group was more mixed than were the A-level students in the U.K.

Significantly lower levels of performance on the TEL were found among U.S., German, and Austrian secondary students. The probable reason was less economics instruction. American students took only about a semester of economics, and the specific content varied depending on school or state mandates, the teacher, and other factors. German and Austrian students learned about economics in the context of such courses such as history, geography, or business and management, but they did not take a separate course in economics.

TABLE 1.1: Results on the *Test of Economic Literacy* (form A) By Nation

	Mean	S.D.	N
United States			
Overall	22.06	8.33	4,235
With Economics	23.33	8.45	3,153
Grade 11 (1 semester)	21.26	7.99	633
Grade 12 (1 semester)	24.04	8.47	2,168
Without Economics	18.37	6.71	1,082
Grade 11	17.20	5.91	408
Grade 12	19.78	7.14	463
United Kingdom			
Overall	30.09	7.78	7,549
With Economics (A-level)			
Grade 11 (1 year)	31.84	5.52	2,169
Grade 12 (2 years)	36.87	4.74	1,814
Without Economics (A-level)			
Grade 11	23.53	6.40	1,713
Grade 12	25.62	6.12	1,084
Germany			
Overall	22.06	7.28	4,612
By School Type			
General Secondary Schools	24.34	6.14	671
Senior Vocational/Technical	25.14	5.55	716
Intermediate Vocational/Technical	15.02	4.92	711
Dual Vocational/Industry	23.80	6.49	632
Dual Vocational/Retail, homemaking	15.90	5.53	757
Austria			
Overall	22.48	7.23	1,664
By School Type			
General Secondary Schools	22.34	6.01	513
Senior Vocational/Technical	25.33	5.97	655
Intermediate Vocational/Technical	19.68	6.23	164
Dual Vocational/Industry	15.58	4.32	55
Dual Vocational/Retail/homemaking	14.30	4.91	169
Republic of Korea			
Overall	23.77	7.25	4,334
With Economics	24.42	7.58	3,025
Without Economics	22.25	6.18	1,309
Australia			
With Economics			
Grade 12 (2 years)	31.11	6.40	571
Grade 11 (1 year)	26.90	7.16	368

Sources: United States (Soper and Walstad, 1987); United Kingdom (Chapter 9; Whitehead and Halil, 1991); Germany (Chapter 11); Austria (Chapter 11); Korea (Chapter 12); Australia (Chapter 13).

Their performance also depended on the type of school and the ability of the students. Students in the university-bound schools or senior vocational schools performed somewhat better than students in other schools.

Korean students with economics scored somewhat better than U.S. students with economics, but the average Korean students also had a year of instruction compared with less than a year for high school students in the U.S. As explained earlier, this lower than expected level of performance in Korea may have occurred because of a lack of motivation to study economics given that few economics questions are included in the university entrance exam. This motivational factor combined with teaching and textbook problems may have limited student learning and may explain the achievement level of Korean students in economics.

VI. ECONOMIC EDUCATION AND THE TRANSITION TO A MARKET ECONOMY

A significant event in the past few years was the demise of the Soviet Union and its replacement with independent nation-states now oriented to economic and political reforms designed to create market economies from one centrally directed economy. The former Soviet satellite nations of Eastern Europe are also making the difficult and radical transition from a command economy to a market economy. Even China, though still under the central control of the Communist Party, has experienced stronger economic growth in recent years because of the reintroduction and expansion of markets within its borders. These developments in Europe and Asia represent an economic transformation *and* an educational opportunity of major proportions.

The final three chapters of this book describe the role of economic education in the economic changes in the nations of the former Soviet Union, Eastern Europe, and China. Students and teachers in these emerging market economies need to understand how a market economy works. They need education and training in basic economic concepts and decision-making skills that will enable them to comprehend the required economic reforms, the problems that occur in the transition, and the economic institutions of a market economy. This education should enable teachers to provide effective classroom instruction, and it should help students learn how to participate in a changing economy.

Francis Rushing examines economics instruction in Russia in Chapter 14. He first describes the basic features of the educational system that existed in the Soviet Union until its breakup. Under this system, Marxian ideology and the precepts of the Communist Party were infused throughout the curriculum, especially in history and in geography, and the material was taught to students as dogma, not to develop analytical thinking or decision-making skills. This long history of indoctrination is an obvious barrier to the emergence of market economies in nations created from the former Soviet Union. In the second part, he assesses how serious this attitudinal barrier is based on data from survey studies. He concludes that Russians, especially the youth of the nation, are more sympathetic and favorable to economic reforms and to a market economy than might be expected from past education and history. He also reports initial evidence that economics instruction for precollege students will improve both the understanding of and the attitudes towards markets, thus indicating the potential for economic education to contribute to economic reform in the nation.

The next three sections of Chapter 14 are devoted to Rushing's suggestions about the economic content and the implementation of economic education programs in Russia. In the fourth section, he presents his list of economic concepts and discusses the decision-making skills that should be taught in the schools. The recommended list of concepts and the decision-making approach are based on the U.S. experience with the *Framework* (see Chapter 3), but give more emphasis to microeconomics rather than macroeconomics, and also stress entrepreneurship. The fifth section offers specific ideas, based on what are considered to be relevant U.S. projects or experiences, of how economic education should be included in Russian curricula and how teachers should be educated in economics. The last section describes activities by organizations and individuals in the U.S. to prepare materials and textbooks for Russian schools and to conduct workshops and seminars in economics for Russian teachers. In his conclusion, Rushing strongly recommends that economic education be given a central place in Russian school curricula, and warns of the dire consequences if the nation fails to educate its youth about economics.

Chapter 15 provides further illustrations of the themes raised in Chapter 14. George Vredeveld and Dimitrina Ispirodonova use Bulgaria as a case study in Chapter 15 to describe the role of economic education in nations of Eastern Europe. They first explain the history of the socialist education system that existed in Bulgaria until 1989 and describe how Marxist principles were taught in the schools. The authors then examine the philosophical and structural changes that occurred in the schools with the fall of the Communist Party. In this section of the chapter, they give special attention to the work of economic educators from the U.S. to change the economic education in Bulgaria through teacher education and curriculum reform. They also report results from an administration of a Bulgarian version of the TEL to 97 high school students and compare those results to U.S. norms.

Vredeveld and Ispirodonova observe, however, that economic education in Bulgaria faces severe difficulties. Among the difficulties that they experienced in their teacher training and curriculum work were: popular sentiment against features of a market economy; a weak commitment to educational reform by teachers and administrators; teacher vulnerability in a changing society; problems with poor translations or adaptations of economics lessons; the lack of textbooks; and, teacher resistance to the use of instructional strategies that directly involve students. They believe that these difficulties eventually can be overcome, especially if resources are used to educate younger teachers and school administrators.

In the last chapter of the book, Ruth Shen and T.Y. Shen evaluate economic education in China, a nation with only a limited market economy because the overall economy is still dominated by the central control of the Communist Party. Three goals for economic education are examined in their evaluation – the enhancement of knowledge, the preparation for citizenship, and the development of decision-making skills. The authors conclude from their analysis of contents of three high school economics textbooks that economic education contributes little to the three goals and is largely "political thought education," a description applicable to the Marxist education in the former Soviet Union and Bulgaria in past years (see Chapters 14 and 15).

Despite state indoctrination, Shen and Shen find that Chinese students are quite knowledgeable about how a market economy works and hold values that support a market-oriented rather than a state-controlled economic system. This conclusion is based on the survey evidence that they present in the chapter that compared the responses of high school students in China and northern California on questions of economic knowledge (including TEL questions), and on questions about attitudes and values. They believe that Chinese students develop their view of the world from many sources, not just from classroom preaching. Student knowledge and appreciation of a market economy is shaped by world awareness, by positive personal experience with markets, and by contradictions between the centrally planned and market segments of the Chinese economy. Should the Chinese government move toward true democracy and economic reform in the future, these findings suggest that political thought education will soon be forgotten by Chinese youth and that the implicit understanding of markets will dominate economic thinking, thus smoothing the transition to a market economy.

VII. CONCLUSION

Economic education is essential in all nations to prepare students for the changing world economy. The increased volume of international trade makes the global economy more interdependent and complex. Domestic economic policies in powerful economic nations have worldwide consequences that must be considered by policy makers. Competition among businesses for shares of international markets is intense and significantly influenced by global events and national economic policies. Less developed countries are struggling to improve living standards and economic performance. Nations that formerly relied on central economic planning to direct their economies are being transformed into market-based economies. Students will need more economic knowledge to comprehend and to participate actively in the changing global economy.

This volume offers a description and an assessment of economic education in the secondary schools of major industrial nations near the end of the 20th century. The conclusion that can be drawn from chapters in this book is that more needs to be done to improve economic education around the world so that students will be able to understand economic developments of today and those they are likely to experience in the next century. Economics should be taught more intensively in the school curricula of all nations. Teachers will need more education in economics and better preparation in how to teach the subject in a meaningful way in the classroom. New instructional materials should be developed that increase student understanding of basic economic concepts and at the same time give insights into local, national, or international economic events. What must be recognized in all nations is that economic education is now a necessary and vital part of the general education of citizens.

NOTES

1. U.S. authors and materials are given noticeable weight in this volume. The reasons are because of history, resources, and the international influence of American economists, not because of national bias. The U.S. has a longer history with formal economic education than perhaps any other nation, as is evident from the 25-year record of the *Journal of Economic Education*, and from over 40 years of economic education articles in the *American Economic Review* (Hinshaw and Siegfried, 1991). The U.S. has the largest national network of college and university faculty in economic education, who provide teacher education, develop curriculum materials, and prepare standardized tests (Walstad and Soper, 1991). This history and experience makes the U.S. the most likely candidate as a standard for national comparisons as described later in this chapter.

2. Only seven nations are included in sections five and six because of space limitations. Those selected were primarily major industrial countries that represented regions of the world. Each nation had a history of economic education, past publications about the teaching of economics in these nations, and a knowledgeable author or authors willing to prepare chapters. The countries in this book are probably representative of the range of experiences with economic education in industrial nations, but no claim is made that their descriptions apply to less developed countries. Too little was known or has been written about economic education in LDCs to be included in this book.

3. For further discussions of the case, see Walstad and Soper (1991).

4. This influential report, written by well-known economists drawn from the American Economic Association, described the basic economics that was considered to be essential for good citizenship and also understandable to high school students. It served as the major content statement for American economic education until it was replaced in the mid-1970s by the *Framework* (see Chapter 3).

5. This percentage is lower in part because of the divisor in the calculations. The Canadian percentage uses all students aged 15-19 years old as the divisor rather than high school graduates for a year as was the case in the calculation of the U.S. percentages.

REFERENCES

Becker, W. E., Greene, W., & Rosen, S. (1990). Research in high school economic education. *Journal of Economic Education, 14*(1), 10-17.

Hinshaw, E. C., & Siegfried, J. J. (1991). The role of the American Economic Association in economic education: A brief history. *Journal of Economic Education, 22*(4), 373-381.

Saunders, P., Bach, G. L., Calderwood, J., & Hansen, W. L. (1993). *A framework for teaching the basic concepts*. New York: National Council on Economic Education.

Soper, J. C., & Walstad, W. B. (1987). *Test of economic literacy: Examiner's manual*. New York: Joint Council on Economic Education.

Stigler, G. J. (1970). The case, if any, for economic education. *Journal of Economic Education, 1*(2), 77-84.

Walstad, W. B. (1992). Economics instructions in high schools. *Journal of Economic Literature, 30*(4), 2019-2051.

Walstad, W. B. & Soper, J. C. (1991). *Effective economic education in the schools*. Washington, DC: Joint Council on Economic Education and National Education Association.

Whitehead, D. J., & Halil, T. (1991). Economic literacy in the United Kingdom and the United States: A comparative study. *Journal of Economic Education, 22*(2), 101-110.

CHAPTER 2

ECONOMIC EDUCATION FOR A HALF-CENTURY OF RADICAL CHANGE

William J. Baumol

The fact that our lifetimes coincide, at least in part, with the half-century that has followed World War II distorts our perspective and makes the remarkable economic developments that have pervaded the period seem routine and commonplace. Perhaps the clear exception is the collapse of the centrally directed economies of the Soviet Union and Eastern Europe and their attempt to transfer control to the market mechanism. Probably all of us are astounded by that particular turn of events, but it is, in fact, only the latest and most visible of a set of historically unprecedented manifestations that have brought the world economy to its present state. The postwar era has been characterized by widely enjoyed increases in economic output and productivity whose like has never before been experienced for any protracted period, by a remarkable expansion in international trade, and by a dramatic convergence of per-capita incomes and productivity levels in the wealthiest industrialized countries, permitting a number of them nearly to catch up to the world's economic leader, though many poorer countries have meanwhile fallen even further behind.

These facts by themselves, and what we know of their explanation, surely deserve to be taught to precollege students, for if graduates of secondary education emerge from school ignorant of these crucial developments the world they inhabit will be incomprehensible. The reasons for teaching about these phenomena go beyond the imparting of information for its own sake alone, because these extraordinary developments put a new complexion on many policy issues. For instance, the U.S. loss of leadership in some industries can be viewed with more equanimity if we believe that a better world includes many countries all about equally prosperous, rather than one in which all other nations are far behind America. Similarly, the postwar developments call for a reevaluation of some of the criteria of U.S. antitrust policy – if the market for a particular product is open to foreign invasion, then the fact that a single American firm is responsible for an overwhelming share of the *domestic* output of that commodity is much less likely to confer market power upon it.

This chapter will review the postwar economic developments that have just been mentioned, as well as a number of others, and will provide some pertinent evidence. Then I will examine some of the policy implications, and describe misunderstandings that are likely to arise among the electorate of the future if their economic education is incomplete.

I. THE GROWTH BOOM OF THE POSTWAR PERIOD

In a society habituated to economic growth the slowdowns and relatively brief retreats that accompany periodic recessions understandably constitute traumatic deviations from the natural state of affairs. But it was not always so. Economic historians suggest that per-capita real income in eighteenth century Britain had barely reattained its magnitude in Rome of the third century A.D., thus implying that in those one and a half millennia the average growth rate of per-capita output was approximately zero. Even the Industrial Revolution did not change matters much. It has been estimated that the first half-century of the Industrial Revolution (between, roughly, 1770 and 1830) produced a growth rate in real per-capita income on the order of just 0.3 percent per year (e.g., Williamson, 1984). It was only gradually that economic progress began to speed up, and in most of the developed world it reached its peak (at least so far) in the first two decades after the Second World War – the era Angus Maddison (one of the world's leading authorities on historical international comparisons) has dubbed the "Golden Age."

Figure 2.1 shows for five of the world's wealthiest countries (France, Germany, the United Kingdom, Japan and the United States), Maddison's estimates of growth in real per-capita incomes for 1950 through 1973, compared to the earlier period 1900 to 1929 (perhaps the last period before World War II in which the state of the world economy can be considered to have approached some degree of normalcy). The superiority of the postwar growth rates should be clear enough. Except for the U.S., the later growth rate for each of the countries was well over twice as high as in the earlier interval.

Figure 2.1: Growth Rates, Per-Capita GDP

Five Countries, 1900-1929 vs. 1950-1973

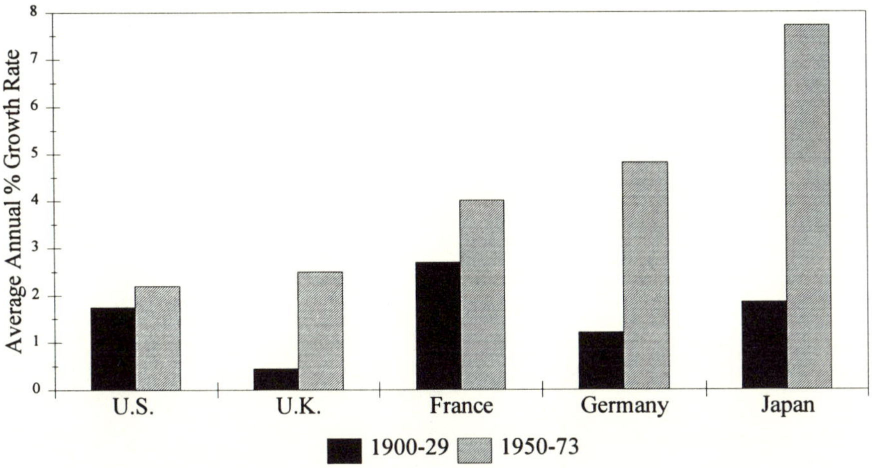

Figure 2.2 undertakes to suggest how these growth rates have affected living standards, comparing, at the beginning and end of the postwar period, this time, the *level* (rather than the growth rate) of real per-capita income of each of the countries included in the previous graph. We see that over the 40-odd years between 1950 and 1989, average incomes rose by a factor ranging from 2.1 for the U.S., to 7.8 in the case of Japan. Japan's eightfold increase in per-capita income is clearly spectacular, but dispassionately considered, even the datum for the U.S. is impressive.

This extraordinary economic progress did not consist of just an expansion in the sheer quantity of output per person. Technological innovation revolutionized not only production processes, but also added dramatically to the variety of products available to consumers. Color television, the VCR, the jet airplane, the dishwasher and clothes dryer, the personal computer, and the photocopier are only among the most obvious in the list of items that have transformed the pattern of consumption, and have done so in many countries besides the U.S.

These facts belie the view sometimes expressed that long-term economic growth throughout the world is evaporating, or the more common conclusion that the American economy has reached a stage of long-term stagnation. We will return to the latter issue presently.

Figure 2.2: Real Per-Capita GDP

Five Countries, 1950 and 1989

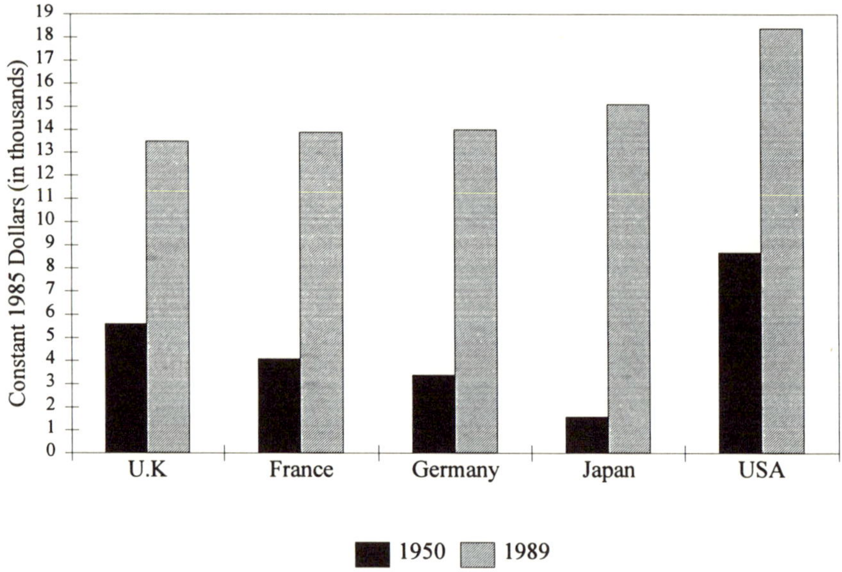

II. EXPANDING INTERNATIONALIZATION: WORLD MARKETS VS. DOMESTIC MARKETS

Increasingly, markets for economic goods have grown international. Producers ever more commonly find their prime competitors to be foreign firms, and sell larger shares of their outputs to foreign buyers. Much of this is ascribable to improvements in transportation that have lowered the cost and sped the transmission of products across national boundaries. Not only the improvements in ocean shipping and air transportation play a role here. The international linkup and the declining real cost of use of the telecommunications and computer networks have also have played an important role, for reasons we will note.

It has been estimated that over the course of a century the share of GDP of the industrialized countries that goes into exports may well have trebled. Figure 2.3 shows that share for the United States over the course of the postwar period. We see that though U.S. exports fell from 6.3 percent of total GDP in 1949 to 4.6 percent of the total in 1959, since then they have risen steadily, to 10.5 percent in 1991. Though the growth in the share of exports in U.S. sales may have been larger than that in other countries which were already exporting a considerable proportion of their outputs, the increasing internationalization of the market was nevertheless pervasive.

Figure 2.3: U.S. Exports as Percent of GDP

1949-1991

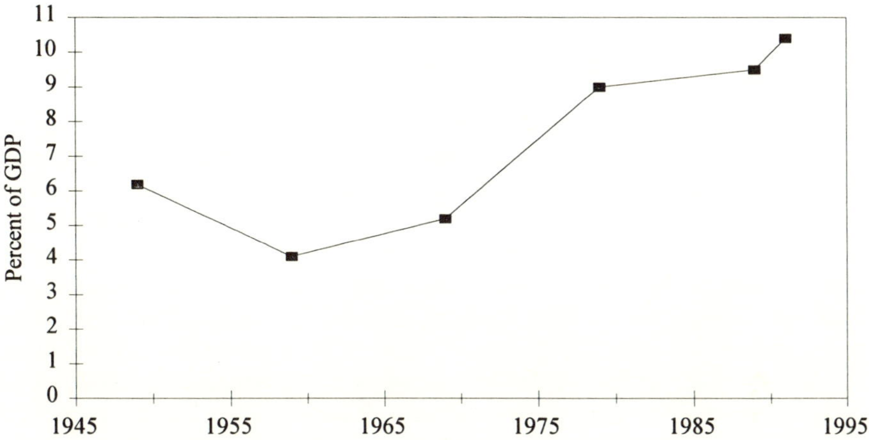

Source: Council of Economic Advisors (1989, 1992)

The magnitude of the shift toward export-bound production is surely impressive, but one is hardly surprised to find such expansion in international trade of tangible items such as computers, airplanes, automobiles, wheat and radios. However, there are many other products that are virtually never traded. These include services such as haircuts, housecleaning and the like. Indeed, the outputs of the service sector are often taken to be inherently unexportable, or very nearly so, because of their intangible character. In fact, modern technology is increasingly changing this. The compound technology that encompasses both telephones and computers permits financial markets in country A to sell ever more of their services to investors and other individuals in country B. Engineers in country C increasingly obtain services such as blueprint preparation in country D, to which the required specifications have been transmitted by telephone or fax, and from which the required drawings are promptly retransmitted by similar means. The performing arts provide another illustration of the increasing ease with which services are now exported. In the past, there were occasional visits by a theater company of one country to another country fairly distant from home. However, transporting an entire company is a costly and difficult operation. The mass media have changed all that, and now American films and television programs constitute one of our more significant exports, to the distress of rivals in the importing countries whose screens and airwaves these products of the U.S. often dominate.

Thus, there appear to be ever fewer sectors of any country's economy that are immune from invasion from abroad and which do not turn at least partly to other nations for portions of their markets. Increasingly, then, the economy is growing to be just one world.

III. THE CONVERGENCE PHENOMENON

In the middle of the nineteenth century the United Kingdom was the undisputed economic leader of the world. Half a century later the leadership position was taken over by the U.S. In both cases, there was little question as to the identity of the occupant of the vanguard position, with virtually all other countries well behind the leader. In the first half of the twentieth century the U.S. was indeed the golden land, to whose standards other countries could only look up. Today, all this has changed. Though, contrary to what is widely believed, the U.S. is still in the lead in terms of average standards of living and levels of productivity (*particularly* in manufacturing), there are now a half-dozen other countries following closely on America's heels. Those friendly rivals have dramatically narrowed the gap both in terms of output per capita and productivity levels. Figure 2.4 illustrates the phenomenon. For each of the 5 countries

Figure 2.4: Real Per-Capita GDP as Percent of U.S.
Five Countries, 1950 and 1989

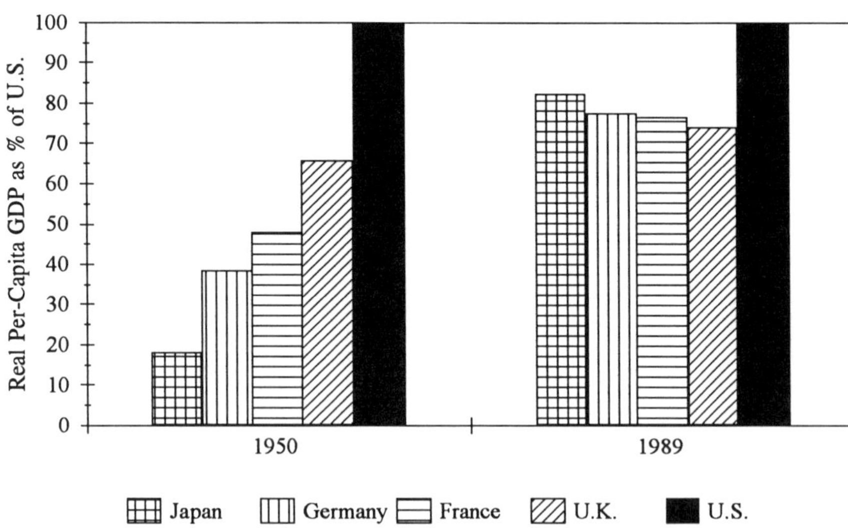

reported upon in Figures 2.1 and 2.2, the graph shows per-capita GDP as a percentage of the U.S. level, both in 1950 and in 1989. While in 1950 per-capita GDP for the other countries averaged only 33 percent of the U.S. level, by 1989 (though none of the others had nearly caught up with the American figure), it averaged 79 percent of U.S. GDP per capita.

This convergence probably began in a small way in the last two or three decades of the nineteenth century. However, it really took off after 1950, with some slowing (and, perhaps, some partial reversal) since the mid-1970s. We have just seen how dramatic the convergence phenomenon has been. This closing of ranks has, however, largely been confined to fewer than two dozen industrialized countries, the members of what I have elsewhere referred to as the "convergence club." Not only the less developed countries, but even the middle-income countries, as a group, have failed to come closer to the standards of the leading economies.[1]

Economic historians ascribe the convergence phenomenon to several sources. The two influences that are probably cited most often are scale economies and technology dissemination. On the first of these, it is often suggested that many of the industries which led in the technological progress that underlay the growth in productivity of the past two centuries were large enterprises, which characteristically have had an advantage in terms of cost and other areas relative to their smaller rivals. Strict scale economies and the costliness of R&D (along with the fact that R&D's results are at least as applicable to large enterprises as they are to small) are but two of the sources of this advantage. It has been suggested by acute observers such as Moses Abramovitz (1986) and Richard Nelson (forthcoming) that this fact alone enabled the U.S., with the unparalleled size of its domestic market, to forge ahead in the nineteenth century. On this view, two phenomena eventually eroded the American advantage and enabled other countries to begin to catch up to it. First, after some point in almost every industry, the benefits of further increases in size of operation begin to exhaust themselves, and many business enterprises in the U.S. may have attained that scale. The business enterprises of Europe and the Far East still typically have a way to go in that direction, and this has facilitated rapid growth in those regions. Perhaps more important, the growth of international trade has given business firms in smaller economies access to markets far larger than those offered by the United States alone. This, too, enabled the typical enterprise abroad to move toward an American scale of operations with whatever productivity and competitive advantages that offers.

Technology transfer is the second source of convergence frequently cited by economic historians. Innovation does not derive from any one nation alone. In fact, at any given time in a "typical" country of the approximately 25 nations that constitute the world's industrialized core, probably more than 90 percent of the techniques in use in the production processes of that country derive from foreign sources. This is almost a tautology, because if all of these economies were employing the latest techniques and product designs and therefore sharing the same technology, for the "average" country among these 25 it is true by definition that only 1/25th of the technology will have derived from domestic sources. Thus, imported techniques are probably far more important for this "average" nation's economic performance than is its own success as an innovator. Every country in this group does import technology from many others but the trade is generally not in balance. The economic laggards usually have far more to learn from the leaders than the leaders can learn from the laggards. As a result, the technology exchange process contributes more to the growth of the economies that are slightly behind than it does to those in the vanguard. Those that are far behind, the LDCs, typically also gain less in the process because they generally possess few of the skills – in the form of engineers, scientists and technicians – needed to make effective use of these opportunities; also, the product mix of the industries in LDCs often offers relatively little scope for the benefits of technological sophistication. All this means that the technology transfer process makes for slower growth in the economies at the apex of the pyramid, comparatively fast growth in the second-level economies, and slow growth at the bottom of the economic hierarchy. Hence, this may go far in explaining why the countries in this second echelon have been converging upon the leading economy, while the LDCs as a group have failed to do so.

If either or both of the explanations offered above do account for the bulk of economic convergence, then a second implication follows. The logic of the argument implies that, as the mildly laggard countries come close to catching up with the leaders, the convergence process can be expected to tend to run out of steam. The sizes of business firms and product markets in those countries will have approached those of the former leaders, so that this source of what have been described as the "advantages of (moderate) backwardness" will tend to become exhausted. Similarly, the favorable technology trade balance of these countries will have brought the sophistication of their technology abreast of the economic leaders' so that the former will no longer have less to offer in this trade than the latter. Thus, as the convergence process continues, and countries approach more closely to one another in performance, the superior rapidity of growth by the mild laggards will tend to erode. We can perhaps expect a future with a number of countries close together at the front of the economic race, i.e., a regime of shared leadership.

There is some evidence that this is happening, as is indicated by the next two figures. The first (Figure 2.5) shows the history of overall productivity levels in four countries over the postwar period, using the U.S. as reference point, so that in every year we set U.S. = 100. The graph indicates that France, Germany and Japan are all still behind the United States, though France and Japan are still moving up toward the U.S. level. But the graph suggests that the catch-up process may be slowing and that the other nations may only be approaching the American time path as asymptote (never to surpass it). The time path of German

Figure 2.5: Productivity Levels as % of U.S.

France, Germany, Japan, 1950-1990

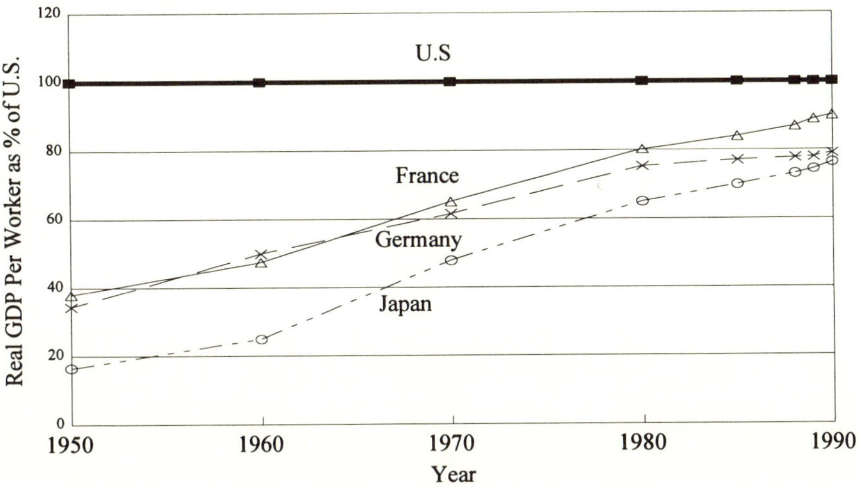

productivity for well over a decade suggests that Germany is no longer even moving up toward the U.S. level. The next graph (Figure 2.6) shows the *growth rate* (rather than the absolute level) of *manufacturing* productivity for Germany, Japan and the U.S. over the same postwar period. This figure shows that in the early postwar period the output-labor ratio grew far more quickly in Japan and Germany than it did in the United States. But, since then, the American growth rate has exhibited no downward trend, while that in the other two countries has fallen sharply. The growth rate of German manufacturing productivity, contrary to widespread belief, is now well below that of the U.S. and has been for a number of years sufficient to indicate that this development is not a cyclical manifestation or a fortuitous blip. Japan's manufacturing productivity is still growing faster than America's, but the difference in the rates is now very small and, arguably, within a range that does not permit it to be distinguished with confidence from statistical error.[2]

To summarize, the past half-century has, indeed, brought with it a process of convergence in the living standards and productivity levels of the world's leading economies, with the gaps among them narrowing sharply, but with that between them and the LDCs becoming larger. One cannot predict with any degree of confidence where this process will lead another half-century into the future. However, both the theory and some empirical evidence suggest that the process may not presage a radical change in the identity of the economic leaders, but rather a move toward group leadership, in which a number of countries with high records of accomplishment share similar living standards and productivity levels.

Figure 2.6: Manufacturing Productivity Growth

U.S., Germany, Japan, 1950-1990

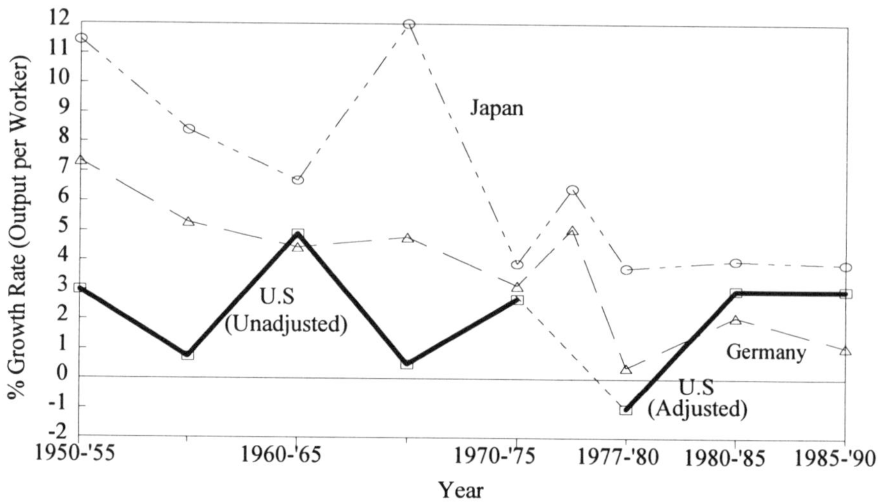

IV. COLLAPSE OF THE CENTRALLY DIRECTED ECONOMIES

Though it is only very recent and did not occupy the bulk of the postwar period, the collapse of the centrally directed economies of the Soviet Union and Eastern Europe is one of the most striking developments of our era and one that is likely to be most significant in its effects upon the world economy in the more distant future. There is no need to document this development here, as has been done with the other issues discussed so far, because it has had so much publicity and its outlines are certain to be familiar to the reader. The pertinence of this upheaval for my purposes will become clear in the second half of this chapter, when I discuss the implications of world developments for economic education and the way in which they increase the urgency of this educational activity.

V. OTHER POSTWAR ECONOMIC DEVELOPMENTS

There were, obviously, many other significant postwar developments that merit more than a passing reference, but that cannot really be examined with the care they deserve in an essay of this size. I will discuss only a few examples to illustrate the sorts of phenomena involved.

On the macroeconomic side, one can cite the rise in what is considered a "normal" rate of inflation, along with the decline in the severity of recessions.

It is true that spectacular inflations have been experienced before, notably after World War I in Germany, Hungary and elsewhere. But perhaps never before has an inflation rate of some 3 or 4 percent per year been accepted for nearly half a century as an indication of price *stability*. This is suggested by the observation that, despite the inflation of the Napoleonic wars and the American Civil War, the nineteenth century as a whole was probably one in which price levels actually declined. Or, to take another example for contrast, probably the most severe and protracted period of price rise in English history before the 20th century was the great Tudor inflation which lasted some 140 years, from the accession of Henry VIII to the establishment of Cromwell's Commonwealth. In that period, the price level has been estimated to have increased about eightfold. Yet the average annual rate of price increase during those years was, roughly, a mere 1.5 percent per year – minuscule by the standards of the second half of the 20th century.

If the performance on the inflation front has been poorer than that in the past, the record in terms of the business cycle is far more felicitous. Recent recessions have, of course, been painful enough, and there is no reason to suggest that the problem shows any signs of disappearing. Yet the fact that the downturns of the postwar period have been referred to as "recessions" rather than "depressions" is no mere change in terminology. After World War II periods of poor business conditions have often entailed a sharp *slowdown* in growth rather than an actual and substantial decline in output, as occurred during the Great Depression of the 1930s. Postwar unemployment rates have rarely approached even half the percentage figures manifested during the Depression. All in all, we seem, either by luck or sound policy, to be coping better with business downturns than we did before.

Turning to developments on the microeconomic side, we may note that the postwar period has been plagued by persistent and relatively rapid increases in prices of several of the service industries, notably in health care and education. From 1947 to 1986 the average annual rate of increase in the price of a visit to a general medical practitioner (the price charged by the doctor to the patient) was nearly 5.5 percent, compared to an average increase of 4.2 percent per year in the Consumer Price Index, according to the Bureau of Labor Statistics. This 1.3 percentage-point difference may not seem very large, but over the 39 years in question it was enough to raise the cost of a physician visit approximately 750 percent in nominal terms, or 150 percent in dollars of constant purchasing power.

Over the years 1947-1986 the price per patient-day at a hospital increased even more rapidly, by a considerable margin, than the cost of a visit to a physician. The cost of a hospital stay is reported by the U.S. Bureau of the Census to have risen at an average annual rate of 11.7 percent compounded, which over the 39-year interval cumulated to more than a 9,000 percent increase. This amounts to a 1,750 percent rise in terms of dollars of constant purchasing power.

Education costs have shown patterns very similar to those of medical care. Cost per pupil-day of elementary schooling has also risen steadily and cumulatively at a rate markedly outstripping that of inflation, intermediate between that of a physician visit and that of a hospital stay, according to the reports of the U.S. Department of Education.

The long-term significance of real and persistent price increases of these magnitudes is indicated dramatically by a simple projection. Assuming that current trends in their real prices continue and that the share of their real outputs in the total real national product continues, a 50-year projection yields the following results: Medical expenditures, instead of constituting 11 percent of total national output, as they did in 1987, must rise to more than 35 percent of the total in the year 2040. And the share of expenditure devoted to education will have risen from under 10 percent of the total at the beginning of the period to more than 20 percent at the end. In other words, if current relative price trends and output proportions continue as they are now, by the time four decades of the next century have passed, education and health care alone will absorb well over half U.S. gross domestic product!

These disturbing price trends are often attributed to avarice or inefficiency. For example, the growth in health care costs is blamed on the greediness of physicians and their unscrupulous overcharging. But the evidence indicates that there must be far more to the explanation. While the ethics of doctors are probably no better than those of professors, or the members of any other profession, the temptation to attribute the problem to villainy is surely misguided. The fact is that over much of the post-World War II period the real (inflation-adjusted) earnings of doctors in the U.S. have been virtually constant. The 1991 U.S. *Statistical Abstract* reports the trends in median net physician incomes for the years 1975-1988. During this 13-year period medical doctors saw their nominal median incomes approximately double, from $58,400 to $117,800 (not adjusted for inflation). However, because at the same time the Consumer Price Index also doubled, real (inflation-adjusted) *physician income at the end of the period was almost exactly where it had begun.*

There is obviously no single influence to which one can attribute this disturbing trend in the prices of health care, education and a number of other services such as street cleaning, police protection, repair of automobiles and other equipment, legal services and the live performing arts. But their one common and distinguishing characteristic is that each of them is to some extent a personal, handicraft activity, whose production depends on human labor and cannot be completely mechanized or standardized, and which, consequently, is relatively slow in comparison with the rest of the economy in terms of the productivity growth it is able to achieve. Other things being equal, if productivity growth in an activity such as education is, by the nature of what may be considered its production technology, condemned to grow more slowly than that in computer manufacturing and other sectors of the economy, it follows that the cost and, hence, the price of education must grow persistently and cumulatively faster than the average for the economy. This technological imperative, surely, is a major contributory influence accounting for the disturbing course of the prices of health care and education, among other services, that has persisted throughout the postwar period, and has become a major political issue throughout the developed world.

VI. ECONOMIC EDUCATION: TOPICS FOR THE CURRICULUM

One of the crucial components of an economic education program is the lesson that unaided common sense is not always a reliable guide for economic decisions. So many economic phenomena and relationships are either not obvious or are altogether counterintuitive that education in the discipline is needed by the nonspecialist. The distressing shibboleths and the perverse economic programs sometimes supported by politicians and by wide segments of the general public are attributable to their dependence on what appears to be common sense, even though, on occasion, it turns out to be common nonsense. It seems to me, therefore, that one of the crucial obligations of economic education is to provide the student with at least the beginnings of an analytical framework as well as any ancillary materials needed to avoid such misunderstandings, with all of their serious consequences for society.

The postwar developments that have been described in earlier sections of this chapter provide us with a number of observations or implications that are either far from obvious to those who have not studied the matter carefully, or that contradict common judgments and common intuition. The remaining pages of this chapter undertake to provide examples of the sorts of misunderstanding and misconception that economic education can rectify.

1. General Misinformation. Most of the developments of the postwar period that have just been described are unrecognized by students and by the public generally. Of course, most people are aware of the threat of inflation, the rising cost of health care and, perhaps, that of education. However, they generally do not know how substantial the longer-term economic growth rate has been, or how much international trade has grown, or that the industrial economies have undergone marked convergence, or that recessions have grown distinctly less severe. These, of course, are hardly peripheral developments, and merit inclusion in the curriculum simply as important pieces of knowledge. One may well judge that any adult who is unaware of the bulk of these developments is ill-informed. This alone is sufficient to warrant a place for them in the teaching program, and helps to strengthen the argument for wider dissemination of education in economics.

In addition, as will be seen in the following paragraphs, failure to recognize and begin to understand such postwar economic developments can lead to misconceptions about appropriate policy, which can easily transmit their distorting influence to the political arena. As has been said, one of the major contributions to be hoped for from economic education is to make the public better informed about such matters in order to make them better citizens and to improve their role in the political process. The observations that follow are intended only to be illustrative and are neither meant to exhaust the list of pertinent issues nor even to focus upon all of those that are the most important for public policy.

2. Political Pressures for Emergency Measures to Enhance Long-Term Growth. Effective measures to stimulate the growth of productivity and per-capita income are usually desirable, almost by definition. But the policies that are appropriate if there is reason to fear that those growth rates are undergoing catastrophic decline are very different from the policies called for when there is no such emergency. The programs needed under emergency conditions are apt to be more precipitate, extreme and, in a real sense, very much more costly.

Current political rhetoric often implies that we are in the midst of such a crisis, or that it is imminent. Perhaps fortunately, political stalemate has so far prevented these cries from being translated into ill-considered and hasty action. The lack of evidence that long-term growth in the United States and the other industrial nations is undergoing such a crisis should lead to calmer and more painstaking consideration of the growth issue. This does not necessarily mean that growth developments are best left to take care of themselves, or that measures to encourage growth are ill-advised. But the evidence that, despite shorter-run recession problems, longer-run prospects are far from grim can surely give society time to deal with this issue in a considered manner that is likely to be more effective and less costly than one that only a crisis can justify.

3. Growth of International Trade and Antitrust Issues. The strength of the market power (if any) that is possessed by the business firm that is under scrutiny in an antitrust investigation is usually studied with the aid of data intended to measure the share of the domestic market constituted by the company's output and the ease of entry by prospective rivals if monopoly profits make the arena sufficiently attractive to newcomers. It is generally agreed that either small market share or extreme ease of entry deprive the firm of market power and therefore should generally exempt its pricing practices and other related actions from the scrutiny of antitrust watchdogs.

Both of these pertinent pieces of evidence have in many industries been affected substantially by the postwar internationalization of markets. For example, in earlier periods the American automobile industry was populated by four firms, all of them U.S. companies. Today, foreign cars constitute a substantial share of the American market. A number of Japanese firms, as is only all too obvious, have become formidable competitors. In addition, Swedish, German, Korean and other foreign vehicles are readily available and seem comfortably entrenched in our market. Their rise also confirms that the market is hardly characterized by impenetrable barriers to entry.

All of this means that a contention that U.S. auto makers possess considerable market power has lost much of its plausibility. The story can be repeated for a number of other industries, and it would seem to mean that for such industries one cannot justify the devotion of nearly as much attention by the antitrust authorities as one could immediately after World War II.

4. The Loss of World Leadership By a Number of U.S. Industries. Immediately after the war it was not inappropriate to think of the U.S. as an island of wealth surrounded by other lands *all* of which were substantially poorer. Many observers believe that such a state of affairs is hardly ideal, even in terms of the self-interest of the United States. Poor countries are poor customers for American products and, besides, they are apt to be troubled by instability which ultimately becomes a problem for the United States as well. Thus, the convergence process, which brought perhaps ten other countries within hailing distance of American standards of living and productivity levels, is something that should be considered a "good thing," not only for our competitors but for the United States as well.

However, it is impossible to achieve such convergence if these other countries do not each achieve proficiency in *some* fields and even take over leadership in those lines of endeavor. The manufacturing sector of the U.S. economy has been classified into 13 subsectors for which one can obtain fairly comparable data on relative productivity in several countries.[3] These figures indicate that in the early postwar period the U.S. led in each and every one of these subsectors. But in a convergence process such ubiquitous superiority could hardly be expected to last. And, indeed, recent data indicate that American industries have lost their productivity lead in four of the thirteen subsectors, but retain it in the remaining nine.

Looked at in this way, the diffusion of leadership may be taken as a development far less damaging to American interests than it is generally interpreted to be. While it is undoubtedly painful to the employees and investors of the affected industries, the appropriate response may not be a desperate effort to shore up the declining enterprises, but a program to ease and facilitate the transition, with, perhaps, training grants and other forms of assistance to the affected work forces. It is, of course, not the object here to digress into a careful study of suitable policy, but only to suggest how knowledge of these economic developments may well influence the way the issues should be thought about.

5. The Rising Cost of Education and Health Care. Only a few words need be said here about what may perhaps be called the permanent crisis of health care costs. If the primary source of the problem is technological, as has been argued here, then the search for villains on whom to blame the problem is hard to defend. Moreover, it must then be recognized that the commonly proposed remedy – price controls of greater or lesser severity or subtlety – can only exacerbate the real social damage. If the real costs of providing these services will continue to rise, then price controls, as we know, will necessarily end up reducing the quantity and quality of the services supplied; and that, surely, is not the remedy we are seeking.

6. The Collapse of Central Economic Direction. Finally, I offer a few remarks on some lessons drawn from the collapse of the centrally directed economies of the Soviet Union and Eastern Europe. The most pertinent and most obvious lesson is, of course, the superiority of the market mechanism as an engine of production. Many of us believed it before, but few of us may have realized quite how great is the loss of productivity that can result from departure from a market regime.

A second lesson is one in environmental economics. Before the disintegration of the Soviet Union, there were many who were prepared to attribute the bulk of the damage to the world's environment to the activities of capitalist enterprises and their unswerving devotion to the pursuit of profits. The mind-boggling desecration of the environment in the Soviet empire that was revealed when it was opened to the world's inspection indicates that central control is hardly a panacea in this arena, and lends strength to the arguments of economists that market mechanisms may well be the best instruments to use in overcoming the environmental shortcomings of the unregulated market.

A third lesson of the Eastern European experience is that a well-functioning market mechanism cannot be created overnight, and that the process can be costly and painful. Overoptimism about the transition may well backfire when it results in disappointed expectations and exacerbates popular resistance to necessary steps for the creation of a market economy.

Finally, the experience of the former Soviet Union brings out a lesson for us all. We must not forget that the market mechanism, with all its virtues, is not without its shortcomings. Already, the first steps toward its creation in Eastern Europe have brought unemployment where little had been experienced before, introduced more visible income inequalities and incentives that made high-priced goods available, but affordable almost exclusively to those who were able to outdo the others in this newly competitive world. The moral is not that the market mechanism should be viewed with suspicion and hostility, but that its shortcomings should be recognized forthrightly so that some effective measures to deal with them can be designed and instituted.

VII. CONCLUDING COMMENT

This has been an exciting half-century, one of relative peace and of unprecedented prosperity. For students whose entire life has been encompassed by this era it is not easy to recognize how different it is from earlier periods, or how significant those differences are for our understanding of the workings of the economy and the design of rational economic policy. All this is grist for the mills of economic education. This brief essay can hardly begin to cover all there is to be said on the subject; but perhaps enough has been said here to indicate how rich a field it is.

NOTES

The author is grateful to the Alfred P. Sloan Foundation, the Price Institute for Entrepreneurial Studies and the C.V. Starr Center for support of this work.

1. There is a sense in which this statement is not quite true. A multitude of very recent studies have shown consistently that if one uses regression analysis to test for convergence, but includes in the regressions separate pertinent variables such as investment in machinery, expenditure on education, and so on, for the countries in the sample, then the residual – the portion of real per-capita GDP growth not accounted for by these variables – shows that convergence extends to perhaps 90 percent of the world's economies. This result has an important interpretation. It suggests that if the middle-income countries that are not members of the convergence club spend enough on machinery, education, etc., they can expect to gain admission to the club, because they too enjoy the benign influence of the economic forces underlying convergence that will be discussed presently in the text. In other words, the recent studies provide clues about what these excluded countries can do to join the group of converging countries.

2. Earlier data provided by the U.S. Bureau of Labor Statistics did, in fact, indicate that these two growth rates have been virtually the same for about a decade. A recent conservative revision by the U.S. has reduced the American growth rate estimate and its result is shown in Figure 2.5. It has been argued by some observers, however, that while some such downward adjustment was called for, the one actually carried out by the BLS may have gone slightly too far.

3. Actually, the U.S. classification includes a greater number of subsectors, and the German data contain a still greater number. However, the smaller number of subsectors in the Japanese data can be used in the process of comparison that we carried out, by combining of a number of American subsectors and doing the same for the German figures.

REFERENCES

Abramovitz, M. (1986). Catching up, forging ahead, and falling behind. *Journal of Economic History, 46*(2), 385-406.

Baumol, W. J., Nelson, R. R., & Wolff, E. N. (Eds.). (forthcoming). *International convergence of productivity and the evidence of history.* New York: Oxford University Press.

Maddison, A. (forthcoming). Explaining the economic performance of nations, 1820-1929. In W. J. Baumol, R. R. Nelson, & E. N. Wolff (Eds.), *International convergence of productivity and the evidence of history.* New York: Oxford University Press.

Nelson, R. R., & Wright, G. (forthcoming). The rise and fall of American technological leadership: The postwar era in historical perspective. In W. J. Baumol, R. R. Nelson, & E. N. Wolff (Eds.), *International convergence of productivity and the evidence of history.* New York: Oxford University Press.

U. S. Bureau of Labor Statistics. (various years). *Consumer price index for general practitioners' office visits.* Washington, DC: U.S. Government Printing Office.

U. S. Bureau of the Census. (various years). *Statistical abstract of the United States.* Washington, DC: U.S. Government Printing Office.

U. S. Department of Education. (various years). *Digest of Education Statistics.* Washington, DC: U.S. Government Printing Office.

Williamson, J. G. (1984). Why was British growth so slow during the industrial revolution?" *Journal of Economic History, 44*(3), 687-712.

CHAPTER 3

A GLOBAL FRAMEWORK FOR TEACHING ECONOMICS

Phillip Saunders

The Committee that developed the National Council on Economic Education's *A Framework for Teaching the Basic Concepts* (Saunders et al., 1993) sought to present a concisely stated set of economic concepts for teaching economics in United States schools below the college level. How appropriate are these concepts for teaching economics in other countries? Are there concepts in economics that are as universal as the basic concepts in, say, mathematics or physics, or are economics concepts country specific? Could an appropriate international committee develop a global framework of basic concepts that could be used to teach economics below the college level throughout the world? We can't get a specific answer to the latter question until it is tried, of course, but in this chapter I will argue that, subject to a few important caveats mentioned below, the basic answer is "yes." Indeed, switching from a "positive" analytical mode to a "normative" advocacy mode, I will argue that such an attempt should be made, and that the National Council's existing *Framework* offers a useful starting point from which such an international committee could launch its deliberations.

In the remainder of this chapter I will first outline the basic structure of the National Council's existing *Framework*, then discuss the important caveats mentioned above, and conclude with some personal comments on what the most important economic concepts in a still-to-be-developed global framework for teaching economics might be.

I. THE NATIONAL COUNCIL'S FRAMEWORK

Table 3.1 lists the National Council *Framework's* 22 basic economic concepts. These concepts are subdivided into: fundamental economic concepts; microeconomic concepts; macroeconomic concepts; and international economic concepts. Also contained in the *Framework* and shown in Table 3.1 are seven measurement concepts and methods, and seven broad social goals for evaluating economic performance and policies.

Table 3.1: Basic Concepts

Fundamental Economic Concepts

1. Scarcity
2. Opportunity Cost and Trade-offs
3. Productivity
4. Economic Systems
5. Economic Institutions and Incentives
6. Exchange, Money, and Interdependence

Microeconomic Concepts

7. Markets and Prices
8. Supply and Demand
9. Competition and Market Structure
10. Income Distribution
11. Market Failures
12. The Role of Government

Macroeconomic Concepts

13. Gross National Product
14. Aggregate Supply
15. Aggregate Demand
16. Unemployment
17. Inflation and Deflation
18. Monetary Policy
19. Fiscal Policy

International Economic Concepts

20. Absolute and Comparative Advantage and Barriers to Trade
21. Balance of Payments and Exchange Rates
22. International Aspects of Growth and Stability

Table 3.1: Basic Concepts Continued

Measurement Concepts and Methods

Tables
Charts and Graphs
Ratios and Percentages
Percentage Changes
Index Numbers
Real vs. Nominal Values
Averages and Distributions Around the Average

Broad Social Goals

1. Economic Freedom
2. Economic Efficiency
3. Economic Equity
4. Economic Security
5. Full Employment
6. Price Stability
7. Economic Growth
8. Other Goals

Source: Saunders et al., 1993, p. 14, pp. 51-54.

The concepts and goals shown in Table 3.1 were selected to achieve a broad overriding educational objective to "enable students, by the time they graduate from high school, to understand enough economics to make reasoned judgments about economic questions." The *Framework* committee noted that these economic questions:

> ...include personal economic questions as well as broader matters of economic policy that students will face as members of democratic society. Learning to make reasoned judgments about economic questions will help students become more effective decision makers and more responsible citizens. Indeed, the most important step toward understanding in economics – as in other branches of knowledge – is the replacement of emotional judgment by objective, reasoned analysis. (Saunders et al., 1993, p. 3)

As this quotation implies, there is a heavy emphasis in the *Framework* on economics as a way of thinking rather than a set of answers. The emphasis on systematic, objective analysis that encourages a reasoned approach to evaluating various alternatives with respect to specific criteria is illustrated with use of a formal decision making grid. The general format of such a grid is shown in Table 3.2.

Table 3.2: Sample Decision-Making Grid for Systematic Evaluation of Each Alternative With Respect to Each Goal or Criterion

	GOALS OR CRITERIA			
ALTERNATIVES	Goal or Criterion 1	Goal or Criterion 2	Goal or Criterion 3	Goal or Criterion 4
Alternative 1				
Alternative 2				
Alternative 3				
Alternative 4				

Source: Saunders et al., 1993, p. 10.

The intersection of the rows and columns in a decision-making grid creates boxes or "cells" which match up each alternative with each goal or criterion. Evaluation marks such as pluses or minuses or some form of numeric evaluation scale can be placed in the cells to indicate how each alternative, including a "do nothing" alternative, helps meet each goal or criterion. Often in personal and social decision-making situations, no single alternative meets all of the goals or criteria, and all criteria are not regarded as equally important. But, even in situations where goals conflict and evaluations differ, the systematic use of a decision-making grid can help clarify the issues and make the evaluation process a more reasoned one. By highlighting the costs, benefits, and trade-offs of different choices the economic way of thinking helps equip students to evaluate alternative courses of action or inaction in personal economic situations involving their roles as consumers, members of the work force, savers and investors, and in social situations involving their roles as citizens and voters.

II. BACKGROUND CAVEATS

The concepts that might be emphasized in a global framework for teaching economics depend crucially on the broad educational objectives to be achieved. The National Council's *Framework* is a useful starting point only if one accepts the ultimate goal of developing students' ability to make reasoned judgements about personal and social economic questions. The assumption that students will become "members of a democratic society" is explicitly stated in the *Framework*, and it is crucial in deciding which economic concepts to teach below the college level.

Another important consideration that must be kept in mind in discussing the nature and number of concepts to include in a global framework for teaching economics is the amount of time to be devoted to the teaching of economics at different grade levels and different parts of the curriculum. In this regard it is important to note that the existing *Framework* was ***NOT*** intended to be the outline for a single high school course in economics. Many students in the United States and other countries end their formal schooling before reaching this level. If possible, attempts should be made to teach some basic economic concepts and the economic way of thinking before the high school level. The success of attempts to "infuse" economics into the curriculum below the high school level, of course, depends crucially on the availability of appropriately designed materials and appropriately trained teachers. Experience with the *Trade-offs* film/video series, which was designed to improve the economic understanding and decision-making skills of 10-to-13-year old students in the United States and Canada, provides perhaps the best documented case of a successful and widely used example of infusion. However, this experience also emphasizes the importance of appropriately designed materials and appropriately trained teachers.[1]

The success of *Trade-offs* lead to the development of the *Give & Take* series for older students and the *Econ and Me* series for younger students. A 1985 study of the *Give & Take* series by Chizmar and others found that

> using economics as an instructional vehicle in the classroom does not detract from an improved performance in broader social studies skills and other, more basic, learning. In fact, the findings of this study indicate that student performance in these latter areas is improved as a result of the instruction in economics." (Chizmar et al., p. 99)

A final caveat concerns the obvious point that different countries have different languages, different cultures, different values, different institutions, and different "mixes" of the basic production and distribution mechanisms of tradition, command, and market prices which will no doubt make it considerably more difficult to develop a global framework for teaching economics than the by-no-means easy task of developing such a framework in a single country.[2] If one is willing to establish appropriate parameters with respect to the previous caveats, however, I believe that a global framework of basic economic concepts can be developed. The examples and the materials developed to teach the concepts can be and should be different in different countries, but the basic concepts themselves can be the same.

III. PERSONAL OBSERVATIONS

My belief that a global framework of basic economic concepts can be developed, if one focuses on enhancing student decision-making skills in countries that are willing to develop materials and train teachers to teach economics at various grade levels in addition to providing at least a one-semester course (and preferably a one-year course) at the senior high school level, is based more on personal opinion than hard evidence. But my experience with the *Trade-offs* and *Give & Take* series in the United States and Canada plus some recent projects in Russia and Ukraine leads me to believe that an appropriate international committee could indeed reach agreement on a limited set of basic economic concepts. I observed the use of translated versions of some *Trade-offs* and *Give & Take* videos and the accompanying teacher's materials in intensive workshops with school teachers in Moscow, Russia and Kharkov, Ukraine in August and September, 1992, in St. Petersburg, Russia in December 1992, and in Novisibirsk, Russia in July 1993. Even in this environment of rapid and confusing changes in the economic systems of these countries I was impressed with the ability of the participating teachers to come up with examples and situations that they could use in their own classrooms to illustrate and explain the basic concepts illustrated in the videos, including teaching activities that made explicit use of decision-making grids. The same thing is true of other simulation games and activities that were used to illustrate specialization and productivity, exchange and interdependence, supply and demand, market-clearing prices and changes in market-clearing prices, the effects of price ceilings and price floors, and the effects of large increases in the money supply on the price level.

Two problems with simply listing concepts as is done in Table 3.1 are that not all of the concepts are equally complex or equally important, and the same concept can be learned with different degrees of sophistication. Experience to date, however, indicates that it is generally easier for teachers and curriculum developers to come up with examples and activities dealing with the concepts classified as fundamental economic concepts and microeconomic concepts in Table 3.1 than it is for those classified as macroeconomic concepts and international economic concepts.

Space constraints prevent me from elaborating in detail all of the concepts I would advocate for inclusion in a global framework, but there are seven concepts in particular that I would identify as the most important for teaching below the high school level. If these concepts are effectively taught before students reach high school, less time will have to be devoted to them in separate high school economics courses, and this will allow more time for focusing on the important macro and international economic concepts that now appear to get short shrift in the economics teaching materials with which I am familiar. In selecting the seven concepts elaborated in the next section, I have tried to choose only those that have the most to contribute to the development of critical thinking and decision-making skills of students less than 15 years of age. The degree of sophistication that I think is necessary in this context is indicated by the brief explanations following each concept.[3]

IV. THE SEVEN MOST IMPORTANT ECONOMIC CONCEPTS FOR EARLY DEVELOPMENT OF CRITICAL THINKING AND DECISION-MAKING SKILLS

Opportunity Cost. This is the most valuable opportunity that is lost when a decision is made to do one thing instead of another. This•concept is crucial in evaluating alternatives. It is a key component in developing critical thinking and informed decision-making skills in a variety of contexts.

Marginal Analysis. Many decisions do not involve all-or-nothing choices. It is often possible to substitute a little more of one thing for a little less of something else. Comparing *additional* costs and *additional* benefits of various choices *at the margin* is an important aspects of critical thinking that often helps one make better decisions.

Interdependence. Decisions in one situation often affect decisions in other, sometimes seemingly unrelated, situations. Like marginal analysis, an awareness of possible indirect (interdependent) effects is an important aspect of critical thinking that often helps one make better decisions.

Exchange. Either directly through the often cumbersome process of barter, or indirectly through the use of money, exchange helps increase productivity and expand choices. In turn, increased productivity and expanded choices make decision-making and opportunity costs less painful than they would otherwise be.

Productivity. Productivity is the amount of output (goods and services) produced per unit of input (resources) used. An increase in productivity means producing more goods and services with the same amount of resources, producing the same amount of goods and services with fewer resources, or a combination of both. As indicated above, increased productivity expands choices, and expanded choices make decision-making and opportunity costs less painful.

Money. Money, either in the form of currency or checking deposits, serves both as a medium of exchange and a unit of account. As a medium of exchange, money facilitates specialization and the division of labor, which are among the main ways of increasing productivity. As a unit of account, money facilitates the comparison of the costs and benefits of alternatives. Such comparisons lie at the heart of critical thinking and effective decision-making.

Markets and Prices. Markets are institutional arrangements that enable buyers and sellers to exchange goods and services. Prices are the amounts of money that people pay in exchange for a unit of a particular good or services (e.g., $2.00 a pound, $12.00 an hour, $.50 a liter, etc.). The ratios that exist between various prices are called relative prices. Relative price ratios facilitate the comparison and evaluation of alternatives, and thus enhance critical thinking and effective decision-making.

V. OTHER IMPORTANT ECONOMIC CONCEPTS FOR CONSIDERATION IN A GLOBAL FRAMEWORK

If the concepts described in the preceding section are taught in earlier grades as important tools in personal decision-making, more public policy-oriented concepts can be taught at the high school level in the context of social decision-making. The broad concept of the role of government, for example, might be used as an overall organizing devise for the consideration of concepts that are concerns of public policy in all democratic countries. These include micro concepts such as competition and market structure and income distribution, macro concepts such as monetary policy and fiscal policy, and international concepts such as comparative advantage and barriers to trade. Institutional details and cultural values will differ from country to country in many of these areas, but a global framework might be able to specify the basic underlying economic concepts that should guide the development of teaching materials in policy-oriented high school courses.[4]

My own candidates for inclusion in such a global framework are the remaining concepts identified in Table 3.1. Since these concepts are elaborated in the National Council's *Framework* at the level of sophistication that I think is attainable in a well-taught high school course, I will not take the space to repeat that material here. As indicated at the beginning of this chapter, however, I do this only in the spirit of a tentative first step to focus the discussion of an appropriate international committee.

Hopefully, such an international committee can be convened in the near future to begin the serious, thoughtful, and exciting work necessary to see if it is indeed possible to develop an agreed-on global framework for teaching economics below the college level.

NOTES

1. At its peak the 15-program *Trade-offs* series was broadcast by more than 180 public television stations and was widely distributed by the 53 member agencies of the original consortium. The series was supported by an unprecedented number of teacher training programs throughout the United States and Canada, and over 200,000 teachers were trained in these programs. In 1981 the Agency for Instructional Television (now the Agency for Instructional Technology) published a summary of 15 independently conducted studies that concluded that:

- the series significantly improves students knowledge of and attitudes toward economics
- the series significantly improves teachers' attitudes toward economics
- student cognitive and attitudinal gains were further increased with teacher inservice training
- teacher attitudinal gains were further increased with inservice training.

2. In this regard it should be noted that the National Council's existing *Framework* has been criticized precisely because it is a "mainstream," consensus document. [*Ed. note*: For a discussion of the history and criticisms of the *Framework*, see Chapter 7.]

3. These seven concepts were first specified by me in a prospectus prepared for the Agency for Instructional Technology (1991).

4. Examples of some existing teaching materials that might be adapted to accommodate different institutional contexts are contained in the National Council's *Capstone* document. *Capstone: The Nation's High School Economics Course* is a curriculum package that emphasizes "preparing students to function successfully as citizens of a national and world economy" (Reinke et al., 1989, p. v). Several lessons in this document are directed at understanding the role of government in the economy, monetary policy, and fiscal policy.

REFERENCES

Agency for Instructional Television (1981). *Trade-offs: What the research is saying.* Research Report 82. Bloomington, IN: Agency for Instructional Television. [Now available from the Agency for Instructional Technology, Box A, Bloomington, IN 47402-0120.]

Agency for Instructional Technology. (1991). *Prospectus: Critical thinking and decision-making skills through economic education.* Bloomington, IN: Agency for Instructional Technology.

Chizmar, J. F., McCarney, B. J., Halinski, R. S., & Racich, M. J. (1985). 'Give and take,' economics achievement, and basic skills development. *Journal of Economic Education, 16*(2), 99-110.

Reinke, R. W., Schug, M. C., & Wentworth, D. R. (1989). *Capstone: The nation's high school economics course.* New York: Joint Council on Economic Education.

Saunders, P., Bach, G. L., Calderwood, J. D., & Hansen, W. L. (1993). *A framework for teaching the basic concepts* (3rd ed.). New York: National Council on Economic Education.

CHAPTER 4

ECONOMISTS' IDEOLOGICAL CONFLICTS AND CONSENSUS ON ECONOMIC ISSUES, AND THEIR IMPLICATIONS FOR ECONOMIC EDUCATION

Michael Watts

From the time national economic education organizations were first formed in the United States and in other nations, usually in the decade or two following World War II, one fundamental issue they have faced is deciding exactly what economics to try to teach at the elementary and secondary levels. In some countries – especially those where the market system was rejected in favor of central planning, or at least severely circumscribed by an extensive system of government planning and regulation – that question was often restated as "What *kind* of economics will be taught in the nation's schools?"

Economic educators trying to answer either form of this question looked hopefully to academic economists at colleges and universities in their respective nations, seeking guidance in the form of widespread professional agreement on content, basic methodology, and even some public policy recommendations. At least in democratic nations, they usually found that their hopes were only partially fulfilled. Some journalists and other social commentators have suggested that is due to the complexities of modern life in industrial societies, but in fact the same problem would have been found even if the economic education organizations had been founded 50, 100, or 150 years earlier, because for as long as there has been a recognized academic discipline of economics, the field has been characterized by consensus in some areas, dissension in others, and a great deal of introspective study on the sources and ultimate desirability of such agreement and disagreement. Briefly reviewing the history and substance of this consensus and dissension is, therefore, a useful exercise both for economists and economic educators.

I. IDEOLOGY AND CONSENSUS IN THE HISTORY OF ECONOMIC THOUGHT

Long before economics came to be accepted as an autonomous social science, economic concepts and issues were widely discussed by political and moral philosophers, by princes and legislators dealing with public policy issues, and by those involved with practical issues of commerce and production. How the individual concepts discussed by such writers might fit together to form an economic system, or how their proposed policies might work themselves out in the context of an economic system, were topics not extensively discussed before Adam Smith's *Wealth of Nations*, or at least until a few of Smith's most important and most immediate precursors. But once the *Wealth of Nations* was enthusiastically received by large numbers of scholars and statesmen from many different countries, later economists regularly aspired to answer such questions and to make economics a true social science, built on propositions that were internally consistent and tested, whenever possible, by both deductive and empirical methods.

The problems facing the first few generations of professional economists were daunting. Then, as now, they weren't the only people writing about economic problems and public policies, nor were non-economists often willing to defer to them either for the analysis of economic problems or, especially, for policy prescriptions to cure these problems. As a result, the most prominent early economists found themselves simultaneously engaged in several kinds of debates. Most pleasantly and productively, perhaps, they argued with other leading economists who disagreed with specific propositions put forth in their papers or books. (The most notable example of this is the long, amiable correspondence between David Ricardo and Thomas Malthus.) But they also dealt with writers and lesser economists who sought to popularize economics. (For example, Ricardo and John Stuart Mill generally approved of tracts by such writers as Janet Marcet and Harriet Martineau; a bit later, Alfred Marshall decidedly did not.)[1] And they sparred with other writers and public figures who wanted to dismiss all or part of the "received wisdom of political economy" for pragmatic and mundane reasons (including Robert Owen and William Cobbett, authors and public figures quite popular with groups of workers being organized into fledgling trade unions).

On purportedly higher planes, the early economists also crossed pens and ideas with literary and religious leaders who were often shocked by the hard-minded methods employed by the upstart proponents of this new discipline, and frequently repelled by the conclusions economists reached on such topics as subsistence wages, "positive and negative" checks to population growth, and future prospects of England and Europe *vis a vis* the New World. (Thomas Carlyle, who succeeded in labeling economics "the dismal science," was the most voluminous and perhaps most enduring antagonist in this group of critics. But much of his position was anticipated by Jonathan Swift's satire of cost-benefit analysis, "A Modest Proposal," and none of these critics got off a better line or put the stakes any higher than Cardinal Newman, who described economics as "a science at the same time dangerous and leading to occasions of sin.") A. W. Coats (1988) summarizes this period by noting "Early nineteenth-century British economics provides a wealth of examples of economists' desire for unity, the difficulties of achieving it, and their concern to protect the intellectual authority of the *cognoscenti* against criticism from the lay public."[2]

Although the outcome of such disputes wasn't easily foretold by those engaged in them, these challenges were eventually weathered while the discipline's status grew, measured by such outcomes as the number of courses and professorships in economics being offered at colleges and universities, and the opportunities for publishing economic books and articles in respected journals. But then a new kind of challenge arose in the mid-nineteenth century, starting from within the discipline but soon leading to suspicion and criticism from without. A new school of economic analysis was announced with the appearance of "scientific socialism" (in contrast to the "utopian" socialism of writers such as Charles Fourier), and especially by the writings of Karl Marx and his collaborator Frederick Engels, who argued that certain phases of economic history were foreordained due to changing patterns in the ownership of the means of production and the development of new production technologies. Among other consequences of those forces, Marx and Engels claimed, was the development of a pro-capitalist system of economic thought, represented most vividly by Adam Smith's notion of the invisible hand and his defense of the economic functions of profits (and losses, which are harder to explain than profits in a rigorous application of the labor theory of value – i.e., in Marx).

While the severity of the Marxist challenge to orthodox economics was unparalleled in the brief history of the discipline of economics, the idea of distinct schools of thought was not new. Even in the *Wealth of Nations* Smith discussed the French Physiocrats at some length, in benign but carefully measured and intellectually critical terms. And in England, several years before Marx the graduate student finished his dissertation, two businessmen and amateur economists, Richard Cobden and James Bright, formed the Anti-Corn Law League. Despite Disraeli's derogatory description of this group as "the Manchester School," it played a key role in ending the national policy of protectionism for agricultural products in 1846 (with Ricardo and J.R. McCulloch supporting the repeal, and Malthus opposing it on the grounds that agricultural interests were vital to England's national defense).

But there are schools of thought and then there are schools of thought, and unless one accepts the Marxist argument that mainstream classical and neoclassical economics was (and is) capitalism's *apologia*, clearly no other economic school of thought before or since has had the impact on world affairs that Marxism has. That impact was surprising in at least one respect because Marx's work was, for the most part, calmly received by the other (mainstream) economists of his day. Even if those economists didn't accept Marx's conclusions, policies, or politics, they generally saw him as highly intelligent, certainly well read in the discipline, and as a writer who was studying the right kind of economic problems and concepts (Hobsbawm, 1967). But looking back across the historical events of this century, the importance of Marxist thought and the dissension over it – both inside and outside of university departments of economics – is hardly surprising.

Even if it is granted that the former Soviet bloc didn't follow a pure form of Marxism – whatever that is taken to mean – and that the United States and other industrialized nations of the West didn't follow the exact prescriptions of any mainstream group of economists, from Adam Smith to almost any set of his modern descendants, ranging from Paul Samuelson and Robert Solow at MIT to Milton Friedman and George Stigler at the University of Chicago, the historical significance of both Marx and Smith's ideas is clear. Clearly the Cold War of this century was largely seen and decided as an economic competition between central planning on the one hand and market economies on the other (albeit with an extensive government sector providing a basic "safety net" and performing other important social and economic functions). Small wonder then that the debate by patriots and pensioners on both sides raged so long or so loud.

In academia, the contest between Marxist and neoclassical economics was waged on two broad fronts. Idealistically, the question was framed as which approach generated new theories and findings that advanced economic theory (pure and applied), or economists' empirical knowledge base. More immediately, to prudent and self-interested scholars worried about promoting their own careers the question was which approach would allow them to publish more in prestigious books and journals, and to hold positions at better universities. The answer to this latter question could, of course, depend strictly on the answer to the former; but it also admits the possibility that those who choose to adopt research agendas and methods that are not accepted as mainstream work will be penalized for their heretical views.

That is a plausible proposition because Marxian economic analysis never gained more than a small foothold in England or the United States – at least in economics departments – and its influence has waned in these two countries over this century. Furthermore, during the same period of time much the same fate befell the institutionalist school of economic thought, even though some of the most prominent economists working in the United States in the late-nineteenth and early-twentieth centuries were trained by the German historical economists or their followers, and rejected the "pure theory" associated with the marginalist revolution going on in England and Austria. Richard T. Ely, John R. Commons, Thorstein Veblen, and Wesley Mitchell all published influential works in this period, and all except Veblen served as President of the American Economic Association. Nevertheless, by the middle of this century both institutionalist and Marxist economists were openly labeled as members of dissident "fringe groups," and that was clearly reflected by such measures as publishing articles in top-rated journals, or holding positions and offering graduate training programs in leading universities.

Was this a sign of growing consensus in the discipline about the most effective research paradigms and methods, in terms of their ability to answer important theoretical, empirical, and policy questions? Or was it symptomatic of powerful pressures to conform, applied by the mainstream majority to small groups of persecuted minorities? Or was it perhaps simply the consequence of a dull complacency among most of those who became professional economists? As one would suspect, the answers offered and accepted for these questions depend a great deal on where the person offering or accepting them stands in the discipline – inside the mainstream looking out, or outside looking in.

II. IDEOLOGY AND METHODOLOGY IN CONTEMPORARY ECONOMIC THOUGHT

Different economists, critics of economics, and philosophers of science have reached different conclusions on the question of whether economics is, or can ever be, a true science. At one end of the debate are the positivists, who have long held more sway in economics than positivists now do in other disciplines, including the philosophy of science (on this point see Klamer and McCloskey, 1988; or from the fields of education and the philosophy of science, see Amundson, Serlin, and Lehrer, 1992).

The most influential modern book on positivism in economics remains Milton Friedman's *Essays in Positive Economics* (1953). Since that book appeared most Western economists have argued that economics is and can be scientific, to the extent that economists evaluate economic theories and models against the fundamental criterion of how well they predict real-world relationships involving variables included in the theories and models.[3] However, it is also recognized that when one theory or model is somewhat more accurate than another, but much more difficult or expensive to use and test, the less accurate model may be all that is required to answer some questions, which is to say develop certain kinds of predictions (Machlup, 1967). Under this methodological view, the science of economics advances as new theories and models are discovered which yield more accurate predictions, or less costly ways of deriving predictions that are as accurate (or nearly so) as those provided by current models, at least for certain applications.

At the other end of the debate about the scientific status of economic theory and policy prescriptions, some economists and critics of economics claim that it is impossible to develop a positive science of economics, or any other social science – and perhaps even any physical or natural science (e.g., see Gunnar Myrdal's 1973 *Against the Stream* or his 1953 *Political Elements in the Development of Economic Thought*; for similar arguments in the natural sciences see Georges Canguilhem's 1988 *Ideology and Rationality in the History of the Life Sciences*). Extreme pan-ideologists claim that all economic propositions and models reflect the interests and ideological bias of those who speak or write them,[4] and that people who set out to prove or disprove economic theories and models will regularly succeed or fail in doing that based on whether the failure or success of the test advances their own interests.

Such a claim is, of course, structured in a way that is difficult, if not impossible, to refute, because those who make it can always say that any evidence presented to refute the claim is itself biased and suspect. A cynic would say the pan-ideology argument is structured this way intentionally; and certainly a positivist would argue that if the claim isn't at least potentially refutable it holds no value as a scientific statement that is to be tested by its predictions, because a test that can't be failed isn't really a test. Moreover, the pan-ideology claim has been turned back upon the pan-ideologists themselves because if all statements reflect the interests and ideologies of those who make them, so does the claim that all statements are ideologically based (Klappholz, 1987).

Is this as far as we can go, then – square up against the stark choice between claims that statements in economics either can be and generally are, or are not and can never be, scientific, testable, and objective? Not entirely. Something of a middle ground remains, and has been identified most clearly in two of the premier histories of economic analysis, written by Joseph Schumpeter and Mark Blaug. Namely, even if we accept the idea that economists' decisions on what to write about and how to write about it are often or always influenced by current economic conditions, institutions, and economists' own values or ideological bias,[5] it is still possible to evaluate the validity of the theories and conclusions they put forward. To say this can not be done takes the extreme pan-ideology argument to yet a new extreme. To say it could be done but that, in practice, it rarely or never is, implies a cartel of mainstream economists that is larger, more powerful, and more stable than any cartel ever observed in the marketplace for goods, let alone ideas.

Few orthodox economists feel themselves to be members of such a cartel. In fact, many have publicly bemoaned the fact that so many people with little or no academic training in the discipline can pass themselves off as economists in the popular press, or hold positions in the Cabinet, the Federal Reserve System, and in 1993 almost as Chairperson of the Council of Economic Advisors. Appointments or near-appointments in these positions to people trained in journalism, accounting, and law – not economics – suggest a marketplace for economic ideas and policy proposals with very limited barriers to entry. That and the continued existence of "fringe groups" such as Marxist and institutionalist economists in U.S. universities, as well as more numerous schools of thought that operate within the mainstream perspective (including rational expectations, public choice, Keynesians, monetarists, Chicago-school microeconomics vs. "new industrial organization" game theorists, free traders vs. "efficient tariff" international trade theorists, and even supply-side economics) should offer considerable reassurance to anyone who fears that propositions made by leading economists will not be subject to sharp review and challenge from within the discipline, due either to deference to authority figures in the field or a pervasive ideological bias. Instead, the current state of the discipline seems closer to the status that F.Y. Edgeworth thought was most acceptable for economics over a century ago:

> We hold that for the mastery of a speculative and controversial science a certain multiplication of authorities is desirable. The false tendency of teachers to inculcate, and pupils to learn by rote, the very phrases and metaphors of a favorite author can only be corrected by dividing the allegiance of those who, like the Roman of old, 'rush to slavery.'
>
> History and literature, dialectics and all that the Greeks comprehensively called 'words,' seem the best correction of the narrow prejudices and deceptive associations which are sure to be contracted by those who have been confined to a single school or system.[6]

There are also three sets of evidence that offer insights to these methodological, ideological, and ultimately epistemological debates: First, some economists have conducted extensive reviews of work by historical and contemporary economists, and provided general (indeed sweeping) assessments about the practice of the scientific method in economics. Second, there is some new evidence about how the contemporary schools of economic thought that operate within the mainstream perspective, centered at major U.S. universities, are currently established and preserved. Finally, in the last 20 years several surveys of economists have been conducted to gather information on where there is a consensus of opinion among economists, where there is not, where the consensus has changed over time, and where it differs among economists from different countries.

The remainder of this chapter is a review of the first two sets of evidence, and a brief discussion of the importance of this general debate to the field of economic education. Namely, what practical outcomes and policy recommendations, if any, can legitimately be taught as part of the economic way of thinking in addition to the basic concepts and techniques that are used to analyze human behavior and social problems, and to develop those conclusions and recommendations? The survey literature on consensus is discussed in the next chapter.

III. WHAT'S RIGHT AND WHAT'S WRONG WITH ECONOMICS: A SAMPLING OF ECONOMISTS' SELF-EVALUATIONS

When prominent economists offer opinions on the status of the discipline of economics they frequently consider how large a role ideology plays in the theoretical and empirical work done by economists, and in their recommendations for public policy. The views expressed on these subjects are, to say the least, mixed. In fact, that economists so often feel it necessary to raise the issue of ideological influences in these assessments is itself a telling point, and makes the differences in their assessments less surprising. Once again, different economists' evaluation of the scientific status and progress of economics often depends on their own position as a mainstream member of the profession, or as a dissident.

For example, Joan Robinson published many important books and articles in traditional areas of economic theory, but nonetheless reveled in her role as a self-professed "heretic" as few have ever done. She concluded that "economics limps along with one foot in untested hypotheses and the other in untestable slogans," that "the leading characteristic of the ideology that dominates our society today is its extreme confusion," and only hoped that "economics can make an advance towards science" from its current "mixture of ideology and science," by clearing away "the decaying remnants of obsolete metaphysics" (1962, pp. 25, 147-148).

More recently, after comparing mainstream economics to numerous tests of what constitutes a science developed by Thomas Kuhn and other philosophers of science, Benjamin Ward (1972, p. 89) concluded that "Neoclassical economics is a full-fledged normal science: it passes all the tests. ...Economics is the very model of a modern major discipline." However, echoing Robinson, Ward also argued that

> (N)eoclassical economics has a strong class bias, ...its techniques discourage the endogenous treatment of political and social factors, however important they may be to a particular issue, and ...a positivist methodology prevents the serious discussion of values, which may be interpreted as a device for perpetuating existing value-prejudices.
>
> Marxist economics is not subject to the same class bias as neoclassical economics. Its practitioners are compelled by its framework to take broad interactive views of issues, and values play a central and substantive role as elements in the puzzles and techniques of analysis. Also, externalities and distribution play a central role in Marxist theory.

> However, Marxism, though it is a science, is a badly flawed one...
>
> One is tempted to sloganize: neoclassical economics is beginning to look like a case of techniques without relevance, Marxism of relevance without techniques. But that would be to ignore a really fundamental difference between the two...: their class bias. The neoclassical orientation might be called a using-the-institutions policy-orientation, Marxism a changing-the-institutions policy-orientation. (pp. 90-91)

From a different starting point and perspective, Donald McCloskey and Arjo Klamer have recently launched an extensive campaign to show that much of what passes as unassailable mathematical theory or statistical analysis in economics is, on closer inspection, flawed in design or execution, and rests on unrecognized and therefore inappropriate uses of "rhetoric." They want to abandon the "modernist" methodology of positivism, and reduce economists' reliance on mathematics and statistics in favor of clearer literary and historical discussions of many important questions and issues. By doing this, they claim, economics will become more scientific, because by adopting a more explicit and appropriate rhetoric it will have to face up to disagreements within the discipline *and* challenges from outsiders more directly. Methodologically, they would have the discipline incorporate additional techniques for resolving disputes that are old hat in the humanities, but new to economics (though they are, in fact, the same techniques described in Edgeworth's 1891 address, quoted above). McCloskey and Klamer claim that:

> An economics that does not recognize its own rhetoric can avoid facing the arguments of opponents indefinitely. That is how things have gone so far. Unrhetorical economics claims to 'test' its 'hypotheses' by confronting 'the facts' and scrutinizing 'the theory.' That this is not a persuasive description of economic discourse may be inferred from one decisive observation: Economists go on disagreeing violently about the degree of competition in American markets, the degree of dependence on international markets, the closeness of fit of rational models to ordinary people, and twenty other things.
>
> ...The ignorance of rhetoric leaves economists unable to confront doubts, really confront them. Run another regression that no one else believes. Deduce another consequence that no one else is persuaded by. Adduce another institutional fact that no one else sees as relevant. (Klamer and McCloskey, 1988, pp. 286-87)
>
> ...Economists have no rhetoric beyond the grunt of disbelief for articulating most doubts. The rhetorical situation is demoralizing. An economist asked why he goes on writing such dubious stuff will say with lame cynicism, 'I don't really *believe* it: I do it just for fun.'
>
> There is an opposite puzzle to that of doubt: It is the puzzle of scientific dogma. Economists march to and fro under different banners, raising huzzahs for different candidates for the Nobel Prize. Party loyalty provides a career. The young upwardly mobile economist always votes at his party's call. And

> never thinks of thinking for himself at all. Yet the existence of schools fits poorly with the received theory of science. The theory most economists espouse (although unlike their physicist heroes, they seldom carry it out) says that 'findings' will falsify the 'hypothesis,' and then of course everyone will change his mind. But nobody changes his mind. (McCloskey, 1988b, p.8 – his emphasis indicated)

Robinson, Ward, McCloskey and Klamer, and other dissenters have found some sympathy among the leading practitioners of mainstream, positivist-based economics. For example, Robert Solow (1988, p. 32) says that McCloskey and Klamer "are right to deflate the pompous methodology of economics as science ...because the practice differs so much and so openly from the prescribed method." And Mark Blaug (1978, p.726) says only that Benjamin Ward's critical book "is better in saying what is wrong [with economics] than in suggesting how to put it right." But Solow, Blaug, and other defenders of orthodox economics are also quick to praise the achievements of mainstream economists. For example, Solow (1988, pp. 32-33) worries that McCloskey and Klamer are "in grave danger of going too far" and argues that

> On the whole, ...logical or mathematical deduction from explicitly stated assumptions is better than reasoning by assertion, allusion, suggestion, or rough analogy, ...[and] formal statistical evidence – qualitative or quantitative – is better than anecdote.

And Blaug (1980) concludes that

> of all the contending economic doctrines of the past, it is only orthodox, timeless equilibrium theory – in short, the neoclassical [scientific research program] – that has shown itself to be willing to be judged in terms of its predictions. Orthodox economics can indeed boast that it has increased the economist's capacity for making predictions. (p. 262)

Other testimonials by mainstream economists from each of the competing schools encompassed in that label could be offered. No matter how much monetarists, Keynesians, or new classical economists may disagree with one another about particular models, empirical magnitudes, or policy prescriptions, they quickly close ranks in defending the value of economic analysis against a variety of popular, populist, and political abuses of basic economic reasoning. For example, reading a passage by Friedman, Solow, or most authors of economics textbooks (including McCloskey) extolling the virtues of basic price theory, one would be hard pressed to distinguish between the authors.

Reflecting that (limited) consensus, two final quotations will serve to close this section, taken from comments offered at the beginning and the end of a conference held at MIT in 1986,[7] in which economists challenging mainstream positions were asked to offer critiques of different section's of the Joint Council on Economic Education's *Framework for Teaching the Basic Concepts* (Saunders et al., 1984).[8] That document identifies the basic economic concepts and related skills that form the core of elementary and secondary economic education programs in the United States; and after listening to two days of criticisms of that document – which were usually criticisms of the mainstream economics included in the document – William Baumol (1988) rose to say:

> I am here to report that there is absolutely nothing wrong with the current state of economics and that, besides, the discipline's fundamental problems are being remedied as quickly as can reasonably be expected. ...(W)e in the establishment are by no means a homogeneous group. Our political views differ; our social goals differ. It is only our analyses that have a great deal in common.
>
> ...The mainstream economic approach succeeds so well in holding its position because it is a superb machine for finding out theorems. That is the source of its overwhelming dominance; that is why it rides so successfully, so roughshod, over all the alternatives that have been suggested. It is so nice to have a machine that can produce comparative static results, enable one to conduct econometric studies, and provide a variety of other such products. Critics repeatedly call for alternative constructs based on a richer psychology, with greater recognition of the role of history, with deeper nuances. They describe such a machine, but it turns out to be like an electric fork...: you plug it in, and it does absolutely nothing.
>
> My conclusion about the critics' paradigms, then, is that up to now they have not constituted alternative models capable of yielding substantial and concrete conclusions. So far, we have found no working alternatives to the mainstream approaches, with all their warts and blemishes. We have produced modifications and amendments, but in essence we have been forced to remain with the mechanism that goes back to Cantillon and Adam Smith. (pp. 323-324)

Before the formal conference proceedings began at MIT, Paul Samuelson (1987) addressed the participants and pronounced essentially the same verdict, though in somewhat more somber tones:

> From experience, I infer that some economics is better than some other. Kuhn was naively wrong in thinking that it all boils down to what school tie you've learned to wear. There is a reality out there that all too slowly reveals itself and forces the hand of the observing scientist.
>
> [M]y final word will be another lesson of experience. The shortcomings of a science ...more likely will be corrected from within than from without. Somehow, it is easier, apparently, to learn from one's friends than from one's enemies. Scientists ...are only human too! (p. 110)

IV. COMPETING SCHOOLS OF MAINSTREAM ECONOMIC THOUGHT: RELIGIONS, CLUBS, OR SOCIAL SCIENTISTS AT WORK?

At several points in this discussion the issue of schools of economic thought has been raised, either as something to be expected and perhaps even welcomed in considering controversial issues with models and data that don't answer all questions (as in Edgeworth's call for "a certain multiplication of authorities"), or as a sign of the failure of conventional economic models and methods (as in McCloskey's complaints that economists from one school of thought are rarely able to convince economists from competing schools).

In this section, a recent study that considered how competing schools of economic thought are perpetuated in leading U.S. graduate programs will be considered, together with statements and actions of representatives from these various schools in the public policy arena. In many ways, this evidence is most disquieting to those who praise the accomplishments of mainstream economics and point with pride to instances in which economists agree on issues more than their public reputation suggests, and more than the general public and its elected representatives do. The evidence is disquieting because it deals with how economists form their positions on public policy issues, especially in areas where economists disagree to the extent of establishing and joining competing schools.

In 1987, David Colander and Arjo Klamer studied "The Making of An Economist" in six top-ranked U.S. graduate programs: Chicago, Columbia, Harvard, MIT, Stanford, and Yale. They surveyed and interviewed over 200 graduate students, and concluded that "schools tend to reinforce previously-held positions...." Specifically,

> while some adjusting to the school view does occur in graduate school, unless the changes occur in the first year, the predominant factor in determining the beliefs of a graduate school student is self-selection. Graduate schools modify those beliefs somewhat but often reinforce previously existing views. (pp. 106-107)

That means different schools of economic thought persist because students with a certain set of views about the world, the economy, and economics go to one program, while those with different views go someplace else. In particular:

> Chicago students are most convinced of the relevance of neoclassical economics, and Harvard students least convinced. Apart from the Chicago students, the majority of graduate students question the possibility of separating positive and normative economics. In fact, three-quarters of those at MIT and five-sixths of those at Harvard deny the distinction between positive and normative economics.
>
> ...It seems to be a creed at Chicago that inflation is primarily a monetary phenomenon, with 100 percent agreeing with the proposition. At Harvard, 46

> percent disagree. Likewise, it seems a creed at MIT that fiscal policy can be an effective tool for stabilization, with no student disagreeing. At Chicago, 44 percent disagree.
>
> ...Chicago students have a significantly higher degree of confidence in the market than students at other schools. Harvard shows most variety in the answers with a significant number of the students skeptical of the market.
>
> ...Chicago students ...demonstrate the greatest commitment to neoclassical economics, with significant support for the rational expectations hypothesis and relatively less interest in the assumptions of price rigidity, imperfect competition and cost mark-up pricing. (One could also say that other schools demonstrate little support for Chicago ideas. As one third-year MIT student noted: 'There are no Lucas types [at MIT].'). It is particularly striking that not a single MIT student thinks the rational expectations assumption is very important.
>
> ...While Chicago definitely constitutes a specific school, there is less, but nonetheless some, evidence that other programs do too. ...Harvard students appear to be most skeptical, while Stanford students place themselves in the spectrum of opinions between Chicago and MIT students. (pp. 102-106)

Most disturbing were Colander and Klamer's conclusions about the graduate students' views on the profession and academic practice of economics:

> There was a strong sense that economics was a game and that hard work in devising relevant models that demonstrated a deep understanding of institutions would have a lower payoff than devising models that were analytically neat; the facade, not the depth of knowledge, was important. (p. 100)
>
> ...What students believe leads to success in graduate school is definitely techniques; success has little to do with understanding the economy, nor does it have much to do with economic literature. (pp. 109-110)

If this is how different schools of economic thought are maintained, it is quite reasonable to consider the hypothesis that disagreements between economists – especially on public policy issues related to competition, market power, and macroeconomic stabilization – will be eternal, with the proponents on each side of the issues drawn from a self-selection process that goes back to personal beliefs economists have formed no later than their first year of graduate school. The possibility that these debates can be ideologically rather than scientifically based is certainly plausible, if indeed not likely.

Moreover, the behavior of prominent economists who enter the policy arena long after they graduate does little to belay those concerns. For example, Robert Barro and Martin Feldstein, both at Harvard University, weighed in as supporters of Reagan-Bush proposals during those administrations and presidential campaigns, and later as critics of various proposals made by the Clinton administration. Alan Blinder, Laura Tyson, and other economists with MIT appointments or degrees dutifully line up on the opposing side. And just as

McCloskey says, nobody in the media, Congress, or the economics profession really expects one side to convince the other in the foreseeable future.

Other incidents signal even more serious disagreements about the content and appropriate practice of economics, in contrast to the more blatantly political disagreements associated with one political administration or another, and are waged with different degrees of civility and professionalism. For example, consider: (1) the debate between Milton Friedman (1962) and Paul Samuelson (1964) on the broad questions of correlation and causality in the relationship between political freedom and economic freedom; (2) the spate of decidedly low-toned articles in leading newspapers and popular magazines[9] condemning certain economists and the economics profession in general for its reactions to the appointments of Laura Tyson and Robert Reich to key positions in the Clinton administration; or (3) Robert Heilbroner's recent charges (1988) of ideological bias levied against Milton and Rose Friedman, Robert Lucas, Gordon Tullock, and Jude Wanniski.

These episodes, and many more like them, raise serious questions about the content, methodology, and scientific status of economics, and make it harder to judge whether economists currently have developed, or can ever develop, enough agreement among themselves to speak as a coherent discipline. In short, both the internal and external critics of mainstream economics can point to evidence indicating that consensus might rarely, if ever, evolve in such a contentious subject, at least as practiced by such a contentious group of people.

V. SOME INITIAL CONCLUSIONS ON THE QUESTION, "WHAT'S AN ECONOMIC EDUCATOR TO DO WITH ECONOMISTS' DISSENSIONS AND (LIMITED) CONSENSUS?"

The long-standing but all-too-contemporary dissension within the discipline of economics poses a fundamental challenge to those who work at planning and delivering economic education programs and curricula for elementary and secondary schools. In a subject where so little class time is available to begin with, and classroom teachers have so little coursework and training to draw on, what can we reasonably expect the teachers to learn themselves, and then teach to their students, without engaging in either deliberate or accidental proselytizing in areas where economists themselves have reached no professional consensus?

The first part of an answer to this question is itself debatable, but I would suggest that it is quite unreasonable to expect that any pre-college teachers – with the possible exception of those who regularly teach the high school economics course – will ever have the time, training, or inclination to know what most of the key areas of dissension among professional economists are. Granting that point, a key role for economists and economic educators who prepare curriculum materials and training programs for these teachers is to be well informed about what those areas are, and to make sure that if a controversial area is important enough to teach in these early grades that at least some flavor for the debate and dissension in the profession also comes through. It is one thing to offer Ph.D. programs that attract students who already take one side or another of such issues, and then reinforce that outlook or attitude. It is quite another thing, and much less defensible, to take that approach with younger, less informed, and less critically-minded students.

Presenting that level of depth and detail is, of course, inherently costly in an already crowded curriculum. Fortunately, most such episodes can currently be reserved for the full-semester high school course in economics, and even there in the second half of the semester. In most other grades and courses, the economic concepts and topics that are most suitable for coverage are, in practice, much more likely to come from areas where economists tend to exhibit relatively high degrees of consensus. (The key exception is in other secondary social studies courses, where public policy issues are frequently presented in textbooks, films, and other instructional materials with either little discussion of economic forces or a very one-sided presentation of some economists' views.)

How dangerous is it to present most economics prior to the full-semester high school course through what some critics have disparaged as a "consensual lens"? To those who work outside of the mainstream the practice will, no doubt, be seriously troubling. But it will also be quite similar in content, if not always in pedagogy, to the presentations on such topics as supply and demand, price controls, the role and functions of money, and the different types of unemployment that are found in virtually every principles of economics textbook (Walstad and Watts, 1990). The consistency in these principles courses and textbooks is, in fact, another key measure of consensus in the discipline that is an important standard and source of information to those who work in the field of economic education.

Finally, until a better standard emerges to determine when it is important to teach about dissension and debate within the profession, it is very comforting to have current survey evidence on where it is that economists typically agree – despite their many differences in values, politics, and personal philosophies – and where they do not. This survey data is summarized and discussed in the next chapter of this volume, but two guidelines which are grounded on the availability of that data, dealing with areas of consensus on the one hand and dissension on the other, are particularly relevant to the discussion and conclusions of this chapter. Namely, in areas where most economists agree, it only seems reasonable that the burden of proof in any argument that proposes teaching concepts and ideas outside that consensus lies with those who would do so. Conversely, in areas where dissension rules, or is at least writ large within the profession, those who want to ignore these debates must offer strong arguments to justify any one-sided presentation on such topics; and they should recognize that normally to do so in programs for precollege students will lead to serious charges of intellectual or even ideological bias.

Ultimately, these criteria are based on the tenet that what distinguishes academic-based economic education programs from business education and ideological or affective-oriented programs is this affiliation in program content with the current practice of academic economics, as established by professional economists at leading colleges and universities in the United States and around the world.

NOTES

1. This is discussed in J.R. Shackleton (1982).

2. See also Coats' 1964 article on "The Role of Authority in the Development of British Economics."

3. As McCloskey (1985, p. 9) notes, "It is odd that a group [Friedman and other Chicago-school economists] so annoying to other economists in most of its activities should have their assent in the matter of official method. Yet, a watered-down version of Friedman's essay of 1953 is part of the intellectual equipment of most American economists, and its arguments come readily to their lips."

4. This is sometimes called "the principle of sociologism." (Klappholz, 1987, p. 716)

5. Which Blaug (1980, p. 138) defines as "value judgments parading as statements of facts," recognizing that "value judgments themselves are not ideological statements, although all ideological statements are disguised value judgments...."

6. This quotation is used as a preface to Blaug's *Economic Theory in Retrospect* (1978). The second paragraph, but not the first, is from Edgeworth's inaugural lecture as the Professor of Political Economy at the University of Oxford in 1891, which was later published as "The Objects and Methods of Political Economy" (Edgeworth, 1925).

7. Papers presented at the conference were published in the Spring 1987 issue of the *Journal of Economic Education.*

8. [*Ed. note*: See also Chapters 2 and 7 for discussion of this document.]

9. In a "Commentary" piece published in the February 1, 1993 issue (p.59) of *Business Week*, the magazine's Economics Editor, Michael J. Mandel (who holds the Ph.D. in economics from Harvard), concluded that "[Tyson's] true sin, it seems, is apostasy, not incompetence: She is dangerous and offensive to the high priests of academic economics precisely because she, once one of them, no longer even gives lip service to their models and theories. ...(T)he shrill criticism of Tyson for being insufficiently analytical just makes academic economists seem even more out of touch."

REFERENCES

Amundson, R., Serlin, R. C., & Lehrer, R. (1992). On the threats that do not face educational research. *Educational Researcher, 21*(10), 19-24.

Baumol, W. (1988). Economic education and the critics of mainstream economics. *Journal of Economic Education, 19*(4), 323-330.

Blaug, M. (1978). *Economic thought in retrospect* (3rd ed.). Cambridge: Cambridge University Press.

Blaug, M. (1980). *The methodology of economics: Or how economists explain.* Cambridge: Cambridge University Press.

Canguilhem, G. (1988). *Ideology and rationality in the history of the life sciences.* Cambridge, MA: MIT Press.

Coats, A. W. (1964). The role of authority in the development of British economics. *Journal of Law and Economics, 7*, 85-106.

Coats, A. W. (1988). Economic rhetoric: The social and historical context. In A. Klamer, D. N. McCloskey, & R. M. Solow (Eds.), *The consequences of economic rhetoric.* Cambridge: Cambridge University Press.

Colander, D. C., & Klamer, A. (1987). The making of an economist. *Journal of Economic Perspectives, 1*(2), 95-111.

Edgeworth, F. Y. (1925). The objects and methods of political economy. In F. Y. Edgeworth, *Papers relating to political economy*, vol. 1. London: Macmillan.

Friedman, M. (1953). *Essays in positive economics.* Chicago: University of Chicago Press.

Friedman, M. (1962). *Capitalism and freedom.* Chicago: University of Chicago Press.

Heilbroner, R. L. (1988). *Behind the veil of economics: Essays in the worldly philosophy.* New York: Norton.

Hobsbawm, E. J. (1964). Dr. Marx and the Victorian critics. In E. J. Hobsbawm, *Laboring men: Studies in the history of labour.* Garden City, NY: Anchor Books.

Klamer, A., & McCloskey, D. N. (1988). Economics in the human conversation. In A. Klamer, D. N. McCloskey, & R. M. Solow (Eds.), *The consequences of economic rhetoric.* Cambridge: Cambridge University Press.

Klappholz, K. (1987). Ideology. In J. Eatwell, M. Milgate, & P. Newman (Eds.), *The new Palgrave: A dictionary of economics*, vol. 2. London: Macmillan.

Machlup, F. (1967). Theories of the firm: Marginalist, behavioral, managerial. *American Economic Review, 57*(1), 1-33.

McCloskey, D. N. (1985). *The rhetoric of economics.* Madison, WI: University of Wisconsin Press.

McCloskey, D. N. (1988). The consequences of rhetoric. In A. Klamer, D. N. McCloskey & R. M. Solow (Eds.), *The consequences of economic rhetoric.* Cambridge: Cambridge University Press.

Myrdal, G. (1965). *Political elements in the development of economic thought.* Cambridge, MA: Harvard University Press.

Myrdal, G. (1975). *Against the stream: Critical essays on economics.* New York: Vintage Books.

Robinson, J. (1962). *Economic philosophy: An essay on the progress of economic thought.* Garden City, NY: Doubleday and Company.

Samuelson, P. A. (1964). Personal freedoms and economic freedoms in the mixed economy. In Earl F. Cheit (Ed.), *The business establishment* (pp. 193-227). New York: John Wiley & Sons.

Samuelson, P. A. (1987). How economics has changed. *Journal of Economic Education, 18*(2), 107-110.

Saunders, P., Bach, G. L., Calderwood, J. D., Hansen, W. L., with Stein, H. (1984). *A framework for teaching the basic concepts* (2nd ed.). New York: Joint Council on Economic Education.

Shackleton, J. R. (1988). Why don't women feature in the history of economics? *Economics, 24*(3), 124-126.

Solow, R. M. (1988). Comments from inside economics. In A. Klamer, D. N. McCloskey & Robert M. Solow (Eds.), *The consequences of economic rhetoric.* Cambridge: Cambridge University Press.

Walstad, W. B., & Watts, M. (1990). The principles of economics textbook: History and content. In P. Saunders & W. B. Walstad (Eds.), *The principles of economics course: A handbook for instructors* (pp. 141-160). New York: McGraw-Hill.

Ward, B. (1972). *What's wrong with economics?* New York: Basic Books.

CHAPTER 5

A COMPARISON OF THE VIEWS OF ECONOMISTS, ECONOMIC EDUCATORS, TEACHERS, AND JOURNALISTS ON ECONOMIC ISSUES

William Becker

William B. Walstad

Michael Watts

One often-stated goal for economic education is to help people "think like economists."[1] But what does that mean? Economists obviously do not think alike on all economic issues. Sometimes dissension arises from different schools of economic thought, methods of analysis, or personal differences on normative goals; but sometimes there is general consensus among economists on issues that are controversial among other groups. For noneconomists to think like economists means recognizing both the dissension *and* the consensus within the economics profession on issues, and exhibiting similar responses to those issues. In fact, the degree of correspondence between the views of economists on economic issues and the views of a group of noneconomists is direct evidence of the degree to which noneconomists are thinking like economists. This chapter examines this correspondence – or lack of it – for several key groups of U.S. educators and journalists.

In the 1970s, several researchers sought to determine in which areas American economists showed the most agreement (or disagreement) on economic topics. In the 1980s, this line of survey research was expanded in three studies of economists residing in six other nations: Austria, Belgium, Canada, France, Germany, and Switzerland. In the early 1990s, the American results were revisited in a revised survey of U.S. economists, and a study of British economists was also conducted. Overall, the two decades of results show that there are many areas of consensus among economists – more than might be suspected from the portrayal of the disagreements among economists in the news media. Even across these nations, there is agreement on many issues, although the areas and the extent of agreement on many issues do vary across countries. A detailed review of these studies is provided in the first half of this chapter to identify what it means to think like an economist on a variety of public policy issues.

The second half of the chapter presents new survey data from groups of educators and journalists to assess similarities and differences of American economists' responses in the most recent survey. The new survey data presented here were collected first from economic educators – those offering university courses and workshops on methods of teaching economics for precollege teachers. High school economics teachers and social studies teachers were also surveyed, in part because of their role in providing most of the formal economics instruction that members of the general public will receive in the U.S., but also because support for economic education in the U.S. has often been based on the premise that teachers could be trained to think like economists by economic educators. American journalists were surveyed to find out what this influential group thought about economic issues, and to investigate the question of whether they had more influence on the secondary teachers than academic economists and economic educators.

I. FINDINGS FROM RESEARCH STUDIES ON CONSENSUS AMONG ECONOMISTS

In the 1970s economists were engaged in two, highly publicized debates on both sides of the Atlantic: (1) the dispute between monetarists and Keynesians, which touched on key theoretical, empirical, and policy issues, and (2) especially in Europe, a dispute about the net effects of Britain's proposed entry into the Common Market. In the U.S., the debate over monetarist and Keynesian policy prescriptions was played out before Congressional committees, in the financial press, and on the nightly news. In Britain, 154 economists signed a letter to the *London Times* arguing that Britain would gain by joining the Common Market, followed shortly by a letter signed by 142 economists saying Britain would lose.[2]

Reacting to these events and others like them, four economists (Kearl et al., 1977) surveyed several hundred U.S. economists in 1976 to determine in what areas, if any, there was a consensus of opinion. Although their article was titled "A Confusion of Economists?" they nonetheless concluded that there *was* a statistically significant degree of consensus:

> Consensus tends to center on micro-economic issues involving the price mechanism while the major areas of disagreement involve macro-economic and normative issues. The normative nature of many issues also allows ideological considerations to become important. However, it is clear from this analysis that the perceptions of wide-spread disagreement are simply wrong. On the other hand, it is true that for many outside the profession the questions of greatest interest are also those that generate the most disagreement within the profession. Hence a good deal of the sampling of economists' advice, which is in turn communicated to the public, comes from the weakest cell in our analysis – macro-economic policy. ...Put differently, the intersection of the greatest interest by the public and hence by journalists with what the profession 'knows' occurs in the weakest cell. (p. 36)

Europe. After the survey by Kearl et al. was published, the same basic survey was distributed to economists in four European nations (Belgium, France, West Germany, and Switzerland), translated and with additional questions added in some cases.[3] These results were compared to the U.S. findings in a paper by Frey et al. (1983). Nine statements were identified for which U.S. economists exhibited consensus (defined by Frey et al. as statements where 55 percent of respondents "generally agreed" or "generally disagreed," ignoring the "agree with provisions" response reported in Kearl et al.), but economists in at least one of the four European countries did not. Frey et al. concluded that:

> The general outcome of our analysis is that there exists a considerable amount of consensus among economists, but that there are also substantial differences between countries.... American economists seem to have the highest degree of consensus, followed by the German and the Swiss. More dissension was found for the French and the Belgians.
>
> As a general rule, economists seem to agree that government intervention should be reduced; it is not felt that the government should be an employer of last resort; except in Germany and Switzerland, economists think that the income tax rate structure should be indexed for inflation; with the exception of France, where they have been successful, it is felt that public enterprises are less efficient than private corporations and that the regulatory power of the government should be diminished; less than 30% of the European respondents think that government spending should not be reduced. (pp. 64, 68)

A unique feature of the study by Frey et al. was that it asked the European economists to indicate their "ideological position" on a continuous "left-right" scale, which was then used to split their samples into groups labeled "right," "centre," and "left." The resulting response patterns indicated that "approximately half of the 22 propositions are influenced by the ideological position of the respondent." The authors noted that "In many cases the influence of ideology can be expected because the propositions are normative with respect to content and/or phrasing (p. 67)." But that was not always the case:

> ...(T)here are some non-normatively phrased propositions to which 'left' and 'right' economists respond differently. This applies particularly to [the propositions] 'A minimum wage increases unemployment among young and unskilled workers'; 'A ceiling on rents reduces the quantity and quality of housing available'; and "consumer protection laws generally reduce economic efficiency.' These are topics on which the left-wing parties have taken a particularly firm stand. It is therefore not surprising but regrettable that economists also react to these propositions along the left-right spectrum. (p. 67)

A subsequent paper using essentially the same data sources, except for the addition of data from Austrian economists and the deletion of data on the Belgian economists, was published in the *American Economic Review* in 1984 by Frey et al., to compare the positions of the U.S. and European economists. The same entropy measures provided by Kearl et al. (1979) were used to identify consensus in this study, instead of the 55 percent "generally agree" or "generally disagree" rule used in the 1983 paper by Frey et al.; and all use of the "left " and "right" measures of economists' ideological positions was dropped. However, the conclusions in the 1984 paper were, not surprisingly, essentially identical to those developed in the 1983 paper by most of the same authors:

> The answers given to the 27 propositions by the over 900 economists in five countries exhibit the highest degree of consensus in one central aspect; namely, that the price system or market is taken to be an effective and desirable social choice mechanism. The propositions about which there is most disagreement were (a) those in which there is an abnormally high frequency of 'no answer' responses, which may be attributed to differences in economic policy traditions and unfamiliarity with the terms used; (b) outspokenly normative propositions about income distribution and government spending; and (c) propositions on at the present hotly debated issues such as monetarism or supply-side economics. In general, it could not be confirmed that positive and micro-propositions find a higher degree of consensus than normative and macro-propositions.
>
> The analysis further shows that a major cause for dissension are the differences in views between the economists in the five countries surveyed, attributable to the differences in culture and history as well as to the current economic and political conditions. Economists have had varying experiences with respect to the economic policies practiced in their countries, and therefore have different points of reference. The American, German, and Swiss economists tend to support more strongly the market and competition than their Austrian and French colleagues, who rather tend to view government interventions into the economy more favorably. (p. 994)

Canada. In 1988 Walter Block and Michael Walker surveyed all members of the Canadian Economics Association, using the same 27 items used in the earlier studies by Kearl et al. and Frey et al. Although more than a decade had passed since the Kearl et al. data had been collected, Block and Walker found that the Canadian responses were very similar to those of U.S. and German economists, and least like the responses from French and Austrian economists. Considering responses for the full set of 27 items, they found that "there seems to be no great difference in the extent of agreement between Canadian and U.S. economists" (p. 147). On individual items the U.S. economists were somewhat stronger in their support of free trade and anti-trust laws, but less supportive of the government's redistributive role. The U.S. economists were somewhat less in favor of reducing government spending, and a little less opposed to wage and price controls or to viewing the government as an employer of last resort. In short, even measured against the U.S. economists, the Canadians were "quite supportive of the price mechanism as an allocative device and convinced of the powers of market forces in determining outcomes" (p. 148). However, like the European economists and unlike the Americans, the Canadian economists exhibited no greater consensus on microeconomic topics than they did on macroeconomic questions (p. 143).

Comparing respondents with undergraduate, Masters, and Ph.D. degrees, Block and Walker found that: "The more highly educated the economist, the more likely he or she was to accept the role of markets" (pp. 148-149). And echoing several of the authors quoted earlier, they concluded that:

> True, there is discord on normative questions, but as to positive issues of price theory, there is great agreement. And why should this not be the case? Economists – like lawyers, plumbers, and doctors – have only their profession, and their specialized knowledge, in common. We would expect a core of agreement on matters of technical competency, but not on value judgments; this is the case, according to our findings. (p. 149)

Britain. In 1992, a comparable survey of British economists was published by Martin Ricketts and Edward Shoesmith. They found that the U.K. sample added "some evidence of international consistency between economists" (p. 211), but also found that "U.K. economists are more sympathetic with income-redistribution objectives and more willing to countenance government intervention to achieve them than are U.S. economists" (p. 212). As in the Canadian study, Ricketts and Shoesmith found more evidence of consensus on positive rather than on normative questions, but no support for the hypothesis that there is more agreement among economists on micro rather than macro issues.

The U.S. Revisited. Alston, Kearl, and Vaughan (1992) recently replicated and extended the survey by Kearl et al. (1979) among U.S. economists, to see whether there had been changes in the areas of consensus, and to explore the effects of different "vintages" of economists by comparing subgroups of economists who received their highest degrees prior to 1961, between 1961-70, 1971-80, or 1981-90. There were 21 propositions which appeared on both of the

U.S. surveys – the first conducted in 1976, the second in 1990. The authors statistically rejected the hypothesis that the overall distribution of responses on these 21 items was similar, and found significantly different responses on 10 of the 21 specific items. Three of those 10 statements dealt with the role of money in the economy, reflecting changes in the institutional framework for money creation and control in the U.S. between 1976 and 1990, and suggesting a decline in the support for monetarism. On the other seven items where there were significant changes in the pattern of responses, comparing the 1976 findings to those in the 1990 survey offered evidence that U.S. economists

> showed more disagreement with the Phillips trade-off between unemployment and inflation... and the claim that consumer-protection laws reduce efficiency..., [and continued but diminished agreement] that tariffs reduce welfare..., that cash payments are better than in-kind transfers..., that minimum wages increase unemployment..., that antitrust enforcement should be more rigorous..., and that the welfare system should be restructured along the lines of a 'negative income tax.' (p.207)

Many of these shifts move the U.S. economists somewhat closer to results found in the surveys of economists in other countries, but at least some of the movement probably reflects intervening historical changes in institutions and policy experience, and new developments in the professional theoretical and empirical literatures which may well have influenced economists' opinions in all of these nations. In fact, Frey and Eichenberger (1992) speculate that the differences in the views of American and European economists will "vanish" in future years as the academic market for economists in Europe becomes more similar to the U.S. market. Key international differences remain in 1990, however, particularly in comparing the U.S. economists (or Canadians) to European economists, and especially to economists in France, Belgium, and Austria. Although surveys in European countries and Canada could not find greater agreement on microeconomic topics than macroeconomic topics, that was still true for U.S. economists in 1990, as it had been in 1976.

Comparing the different vintages of U.S. economists, Alston, Kearl and Vaughan found significant differences on 16 of 40 statements (including several new statements that were not included in the 1976 survey). Specifically,

> a smaller proportion of respondents who received their highest degree prior to 1961 think tariffs reduce welfare..., and a larger proportion of this group tend to favor retaliation against subsidies and dumping in international trade.... A greater proportion of this group generally disagree that the trade deficit is caused by the inability of U.S. firms to compete....
>
> ...(T)hose who received their highest degree prior to 1961 or in the 1960's showed a greater tendency to disagree with the notion of a self-correcting economy... and the existence of a natural rate of unemployment.... There was

> also a higher proportion among these two groups who generally agreed with the stimulative impact of fiscal policy.... With respect to monetary considerations, the older one's highest degree the greater the tendency to disagree with the notion that inflation is a monetary phenomenon... and that the Fed should follow a money growth rule. (pp. 207-208)

Among a subgroup of economists working at top ten universities who were "presumably economists regularly engaged in research activities," however, these vintage differences were not significant; and there was a greater degree of consensus observed across the entire range of survey responses for these economists. The other subgroups included in the survey were random samples of members of the American Economic Association, government economists, business economists, teachers of principles of economics classes at four-year colleges and universities, and "evolutionary economists" (descendants of the U.S. institutionalist economists). Alston, Kearl, and Vaughan concluded that the pattern of vintage and consensus responses across these different subgroups of economists was "(w)hile not conclusive, ...consistent with the view that involvement in research does serve to change the perceptions of researchers and keep them abreast of the field" (p. 208).

II. SURVEY DATA FROM ECONOMIC EDUCATORS, TEACHERS, AND JOURNALISTS

The Alston, Kearl and Vaughan (AKV) study provides data on what it means to think like an American economist on a wide range of contemporary issues. The remainder of this chapter describes the procedures and the results from a survey assessment of whether other groups think like American economists. In particular, comparisons are made among economists, economic educators, high school teachers, and journalists to identify similarities or differences in their views on economic propositions.

A shortened form of the AKV survey that contained 29 of the 40 AKV items was used with each of the groups. Eleven items were eliminated from the AKV survey because they considered technical issues that were appropriate for Ph.D. economists, but too difficult or jargon-laden for use with teachers or journalists. Data from a twelfth item was omitted because a typographical error in the shortened survey changed the meaning of the question. Thus, the comparison among the groups was based on 28 of the 40 AKV propositions.

The teacher survey was sent to random samples of two groups of U.S. secondary teachers, using mailing lists purchased from Market Data Retrieval Inc. (MDR). The first list provided names and school addresses for 2,000 high school social studies teachers. The second list gave the same information for 2,000 high school economics teachers. Each year, MDR contacts each public school district to obtain a list of schools and teachers, then contacts every school to update its list of teachers and course/subject-area assignments. Those assignments can change over the year, and school offices may list someone who teaches a course in economics as a social studies (not economics) teacher, or show departmental chairs as having economics assignments even though they don't each economics. Therefore, although the MDR classification was used for initial identification, teacher responses from the survey were used to classify teachers as either economics or noneconomics ("other") for the analysis. A teacher was classified as an economics teacher if the teacher reported on the survey form that economics was the primary assignment or if the teacher taught an Advanced Placement economics course. Noneconomics teachers were social studies teachers who taught subjects other than economics, such as U.S. history.[4]

The survey of journalists was sent to all current members (1,189) of the Society of American Business Editors and Writers, and a random sample of 2,000 members of the Society of Professional Journalists (Sigma Delta Chi). This overall group of journalists was therefore a mixture of both business journalists and other journalists. Given the strong representation of business journalists in this sample, they were expected to be familiar with the business and economic issues addressed in the survey.

The economic educators who were surveyed were the 365 academic economists and educators located at state councils on economic education and college and university centers for economic education. These councils and centers are affiliated with the National Council on Economic Education. Most council and center directors hold Ph.D.s in economics or economic education, although some have graduate degrees in education and other areas. All are expected to be involved in teaching economics to precollege teachers.

All surveys were mailed by the Center for Economic Education at Purdue University in the spring of 1992. There were 4,000 surveys mailed to teachers. Of these, 871 were returned, for a response rate of 21.7 percent. Another 3,189 survey forms were mailed to journalists, but 106 were returned as undeliverable. Of those delivered, 655 were completed and returned, for a response rate of 21.2 percent. Economic educators were mailed 365 surveys, and 135 completed surveys were returned, for a response rate of 37 percent. The response rates are consistent with those in other consensus surveys. AKV, for example, reported response rates for economists in their survey ranging from a low of 28 percent for the 150 business economists to a high of 41 percent for 150 evolutionary economists, with an average response rate of 34.4 percent.

Table 5.1 provides the survey data on the percentage responses to the propositions for each group. Data from economists in the AKV study are included for comparison purposes. For each item, the respondents were asked whether they generally agreed, agreed with provisos, or disagreed with the proposition. The percentage of nonresponses to each item are not shown.[5]

Table 5.1: Survey Responses By Item and Group

1. Tariffs and import quotas usually reduce general economic welfare.

Groups	Generally Agree	Agree with Provisos	Disagree	Mean	N
Economists	71.3%	21.3%	6.5%	1.35	460
Econ. Educators	85.2	11.1	3.7	1.19	135
Econ. Teachers	65.5	18.6	14.1	1.48	174
Other Teachers	40.1	36.5	22.6	1.82	688
Journalists	54.8	30.4	12.7	1.57	641

2. A large federal budget deficit has an adverse effect on the economy.

Groups	Generally Agree	Agree with Provisos	Disagree	Mean	N
Economists	35.1%	47.6%	15.7%	1.80	457
Econ. Educators	46.7	46.7	5.9	1.59	134
Econ. Teachers	61.0	31.6	7.3	1.46	177
Other Teachers	70.5	22.8	6.6	1.36	693
Journalists	73.6	21.1	4.6	1.30	650

3. The money supply is a more important target than interest rates for monetary policy.

Groups	Generally Agree	Agree with Provisos	Disagree	Mean	N
Economists	34.3%	22.4%	40.1%	2.06	449
Econ. Educators	37.8	37.8	22.2	1.84	132
Econ. Teachers	40.1	29.4	29.4	1.89	175
Other Teachers	25.9	33.9	37.9	2.12	678
Journalists	24.6	33.4	34.7	2.11	607

4. Flexible and floating exchange rates offer an effective international monetary arrangement.

Groups	Generally Agree	Agree with Provisos	Disagree	Mean	N
Economists	56.0%	33.6%	8.4%	1.51	455
Econ. Educators	65.9	31.9	1.5	1.35	134
Econ. Teachers	61.6	31.6	5.1	1.43	174
Other Teachers	49.9	39.1	6.9	1.55	665
Journalists	52.2	35.3	5.2	1.49	607

Table 5.1: Survey Responses By Item and Group Continued

5. As the USSR moves toward a market economy, a rapid and total reform would result in a better outcome than a slow transition.

Groups	Generally Agree	Agree with Provisos	Disagree	Mean	N
Economists	27.2%	30.4%	40.1%	2.13	453
Econ. Educators	34.8	38.5	25.2	1.90	133
Econ. Teachers	19.8	28.3	50.9	2.31	175
Other Teachers	19.9	21.9	57.2	2.38	687
Journalists	22.8	30.1	44.3	2.22	636

6. Fiscal policy (e.g., tax cuts and/or expenditure increases) has a significant stimulative impact on a less than fully-employed economy.

Groups	Generally Agree	Agree with Provisos	Disagree	Mean	N
Economists	59.3%	30.6%	9.1%	1.49	459
Econ. Educators	40.7	51.1	7.4	1.66	134
Econ. Teachers	51.4	34.5	14.1	1.63	177
Other Teachers	45.1	38.5	14.8	1.69	683
Journalists	35.3	45.5	17.4	1.82	643

7. The distribution of income in the U.S. should be more equal.

Groups	Generally Agree	Agree with Provisos	Disagree	Mean	N
Economists	48.5%	24.4%	26.7%	1.78	462
Econ. Educators	23.7	40.0	34.8	2.11	133
Econ. Teachers	35.6	28.8	35.6	2.00	177
Other Teachers	40.1	31.7	26.8	1.87	684
Journalists	35.0	30.8	33.1	1.98	648

8. Antitrust laws should be enforced vigorously to reduce monopoly power from its current level.

Groups	Generally Agree	Agree with Provisos	Disagree	Mean	N
Economists	34.9%	36.9%	27.6%	1.93	461
Econ. Educators	24.4	50.4	23.7	1.99	133
Econ. Teachers	44.6	37.9	17.0	1.72	176
Other Teachers	46.4	35.3	17.0	1.70	685
Journalists	42.4	35.0	21.4	1.79	647

Table 5.1: Survey Responses By Item and Group Continued

9. Inflation is primarily a monetary phenomenon.

Groups	Generally Agree	Agree with Provisos	Disagree	Mean	N
Economists	39.7%	30.4%	28.5%	1.89	457
Econ. Educators	47.4	34.1	17.0	1.69	133
Econ. Teachers	35.0	33.9	29.9	1.95	175
Other Teachers	22.2	35.6	40.4	2.19	681
Journalists	18.5	25.7	50.7	2.34	621

10. The government should restructure the welfare system along lines of a "negative income tax."

Groups	Generally Agree	Agree with Provisos	Disagree	Mean	N
Economists	44.4%	34.1%	19.0%	1.73	452
Econ. Educators	48.2	34.8	15.6	1.67	133
Econ. Teachers	29.4	34.5	33.3	2.04	172
Other Teachers	26.5	35.7	30.1	2.04	641
Journalists	13.9	28.1	46.0	2.36	576

11. Wage-price controls are a useful policy option in the control of inflation.

Groups	Generally Agree	Agree with Provisos	Disagree	Mean	N
Economists	8.4%	17.7%	73.9%	2.66	464
Econ. Educators	1.5	8.2	90.4	2.89	135
Econ. Teachers	5.7	9.6	84.8	2.79	177
Other Teachers	10.8	21.3	67.3	2.57	690
Journalists	7.6	19.2	71.9	2.65	647

12. A ceiling on rents reduces the quantity and quality of housing available.

Groups	Generally Agree	Agree with Provisos	Disagree	Mean	N
Economists	76.3%	16.6%	6.5%	1.30	461
Econ. Educators	82.2	13.3	4.4	1.22	135
Econ. Teachers	72.3	20.3	6.2	1.33	175
Other Teachers	48.3	29.3	20.8	1.72	682
Journalists	51.3	27.0	20.0	1.68	644

Table 5.1: Survey Responses By Item and Group Continued

13. The Federal Reserve System should increase the money supply at a fixed rate.

Groups	Generally Agree	Agree with Provisos	Disagree	Mean	N
Economists	13.4%	30.6%	54.1%	2.42	455
Econ. Educators	11.1	37.8	50.4	2.40	134
Econ. Teachers	10.2	21.5	67.2	2.58	175
Other Teachers	11.1	25.9	60.2	2.51	675
Journalists	5.5	23.2	62.9	2.63	600

14. The level of government spending relative to GNP should be reduced.

Groups	Generally Agree	Agree with Provisos	Disagree	Mean	N
Economists	35.6%	19.0%	44.6%	2.09	460
Econ. Educators	43.7	27.4	28.2	1.84	134
Econ. Teachers	49.7	27.1	22.0	1.72	175
Other Teachers	51.7	31.4	15.7	1.64	686
Journalists	58.9	23.5	15.1	1.55	639

15. The Federal Reserve System has the capacity to achieve a constant rate of growth of the money supply if it so desired.

Groups	Generally Agree	Agree with Provisos	Disagree	Mean	N
Economists	25.4%	35.8%	36.6%	2.11	454
Econ. Educators	15.6	49.6	31.9	2.17	131
Econ. Teachers	38.4	35.0	26.0	1.88	176
Other Teachers	34.9	35.9	26.7	1.92	676
Journalists	22.8	31.6	37.3	2.16	600

16. Economic evidence suggests there are too many resources in American agriculture.

Groups	Generally Agree	Agree with Provisos	Disagree	Mean	N
Economists	48.7%	23.9%	21.3%	1.71	436
Econ. Educators	44.4	24.4	26.7	1.81	129
Econ. Teachers	20.9	20.3	54.2	2.35	169
Other Teachers	18.2	19.2	56.1	2.41	648
Journalists	14.2	16.2	57.1	2.49	573

Table 5.1: Survey Responses By Item and Group Continued

17. Reducing the regulatory power of the Environmental Protection Agency (EPA) would improve the efficiency of the U.S. economy.

Groups	Generally Agree	Agree with Provisos	Disagree	Mean	N
Economists	10.6%	25.4%	62.3%	2.53	456
Econ. Educators	11.1	37.8	48.9	2.39	132
Econ. Teachers	11.9	27.1	60.5	2.49	176
Other Teachers	15.1	21.8	62.3	2.48	688
Journalists	12.4	21.2	64.7	2.53	644

18. If the federal budget is to be balanced, it should be done over the business cycle rather than yearly.

Groups	Generally Agree	Agree with Provisos	Disagree	Mean	N
Economists	60.1%	24.8%	13.4%	1.52	456
Econ. Educators	54.8	31.1	11.1	1.55	131
Econ. Teachers	42.4	23.7	32.8	1.90	175
Other Teachers	30.8	32.4	31.6	2.01	658
Journalists	26.1	29.9	35.7	2.10	601

19. The cause of the rise in gasoline prices that occurred in the wake of the Iraqi invasion of Kuwait is the monopoly power of the large oil companies.

Groups	Generally Agree	Agree with Provisos	Disagree	Mean	N
Economists	11.4%	20.3%	67.5%	2.57	460
Econ. Educators	10.4	15.6	74.1	2.64	135
Econ. Teachers	40.7	22.0	36.7	1.96	176
Other Teachers	45.4	25.4	28.0	1.82	685
Journalists	30.8	19.5	47.6	2.17	642

20. In the short run, a reduction in unemployment causes the inflation rate to increase.

Groups	Generally Agree	Agree with Provisos	Disagree	Mean	N
Economists	17.7%	41.0%	39.4%	2.22	455
Econ. Educators	11.9	50.4	35.6	2.24	132
Econ. Teachers	33.3	31.1	35.6	2.02	177
Other Teachers	27.1	34.7	36.0	2.09	679
Journalists	20.2	35.1	40.6	2.21	628

Table 5.1: Survey Responses By Item and Group Continued

21. There is a natural rate of unemployment to which the economy tends in the long run.

Groups	Generally Agree	Agree with Provisos	Disagree	Mean	N
Economists	34.3%	34.1%	30.8%	1.97	460
Econ. Educators	51.1	34.8	14.1	1.63	135
Econ. Teachers	66.1	22.6	10.7	1.44	176
Other Teachers	62.1	28.2	7.8	1.45	681
Journalists	44.3	35.9	17.3	1.72	638

22. "Consumer protection" laws generally reduce economic efficiency.

Groups	Generally Agree	Agree with Provisos	Disagree	Mean	N
Economists	18.3%	23.9%	55.8%	2.38	455
Econ. Educators	23.0	36.3	39.3	2.17	133
Econ. Teachers	14.1	24.9	61.0	2.47	177
Other Teachers	13.7	23.9	61.2	2.48	686
Journalists	12.7	22.9	62.3	2.51	641

23. In the movement from a non-market to a market economy (e.g., Poland) it is important that the ownership of productive resources be privatized at the onset.

Groups	Generally Agree	Agree with Provisos	Disagree	Mean	N
Economists	35.1%	38.4%	23.7%	1.88	451
Econ. Educators	51.9	44.4	3.7	1.52	135
Econ. Teachers	33.9	50.9	14.1	1.80	175
Other Teachers	30.6	47.0	19.7	1.89	675
Journalists	34.2	45.5	16.0	1.81	627

24. A large balance of trade deficit has an adverse effect on the economy.

Groups	Generally Agree	Agree with Provisos	Disagree	Mean	N
Economists	26.3%	37.3%	33.8%	2.08	452
Econ. Educators	19.3	41.5	37.0	2.18	132
Econ. Teachers	56.5	31.1	11.9	1.55	176
Other Teachers	64.3	24.8	9.7	1.45	685
Journalists	58.6	28.2	10.4	1.50	637

Table 5.1: Survey Responses By Item and Group Continued

25. Lower marginal income tax rates reduce leisure and increase work effort.

Groups	Generally Agree	Agree with Provisos	Disagree	Mean	N
Economists	22.6%	32.8%	43.8%	2.21	460
Econ. Educators	20.7	41.5	34.1	2.14	130
Econ. Teachers	21.5	23.7	50.9	2.31	170
Other Teachers	13.0	24.1	54.3	2.45	634
Journalists	8.4	20.8	60.6	2.58	588

26. The trade deficit is primarily a consequence of the inability of U.S. firms to compete.

Groups	Generally Agree	Agree with Provisos	Disagree	Mean	N
Economists	18.1%	29.7%	51.5%	2.34	134
Econ. Educators	18.5	35.6	45.2	2.27	134
Econ. Teachers	35.6	35.0	29.4	1.94	177
Other Teachers	35.5	39.6	23.5	1.88	684
Journalists	25.2	37.4	35.6	2.11	643

27. Reducing the tax rate on income from capital gains would encourage investment and promote economic growth.

Groups	Generally Agree	Agree with Provisos	Disagree	Mean	N
Economists	21.1%	28.2%	49.8%	2.29	460
Econ. Educators	34.1	37.8	27.4	1.93	134
Econ. Teachers	44.1	33.3	22.0	1.78	176
Other Teachers	35.3	34.2	28.1	1.93	677
Journalists	40.0	33.4	25.3	1.85	647

28. The U.S. government should retaliate against dumping and subsidies in international trade.

Groups	Generally Agree	Agree with Provisos	Disagree	Mean	N
Economists	15.1%	35.1%	47.6%	2.33	454
Econ. Educators	7.4	35.6	56.3	2.49	134
Econ. Teachers	30.5	38.4	31.1	2.01	177
Other Teachers	35.7	40.4	21.0	1.85	674
Journalists	32.1	41.8	23.2	1.91	636

III. ANALYSIS

Three different methods were used to analyze the response patterns across groups to determine how much the groups differed from each other. The first analysis was conducted item-by-item to identify those items with similar responses between groups, and the count of items was used to assess group differences. The second method produced rank-order correlations between the set of responses of each group to all 28 items. The third method created an index score that indicated the extent to which each group was in agreement or disagreement with the views expressed by economists. The procedures and the results from each analysis are described in the sections that follow.

Item Analysis

The frequency distributions in Table 5.1 provide some insights into the thinking of each group. Item 1, for example, posed the proposition that "tariffs and import quotas usually reduce general economic welfare." There was general agreement on this item by the majority of respondents, with the exception of one group. The largest majorities came from economic educators (85 percent) and then economists (71 percent). Two-thirds of economics teachers (66 percent) and over half (55 percent) of the journalists generally agreed with the statement. Social studies teachers were the one group with less than a majority (40 percent) agreeing with the statement.

As a first assessment of similarities and differences among groups, a chi-square statistic was calculated for each item, assuming that groups are independent. This calculated chi-square statistic was used to compare each of the 28-item response frequencies for economists with the corresponding item responses for each of the other four groups.[6] If the value of the calculated chi-square statistic was not beyond the arbitrary critical value that puts five percent in the tail of the chi-square distribution, then the assumption of independence between the two groups was maintained. On the other hand, if the calculated value was beyond the critical then the two groups were assumed to be related.

Table 5.2 presents those items where group membership was independent of response type. The comparison of the economists with each group showed that the most item agreement occurred with economic educators, who had 10 items with common response patterns, followed by economics teachers with 8 items, journalists with 6, and other teachers with 4. The same ranking of groups by the number of items with insignificant differences in response sets occurred when economic educators were compared with the other groups. In these comparisons, economics teachers had 6 items with common response sets, journalists had 3, and other teachers had only 1.

Table 5.2: Survey Items with No Significant Difference in Response Patterns Between Groups

	Groups			
Groups	1	2	3	4
1. Economists	-----			
2. Economic Educators	10, 12, 13, 16, 18, 19, 20, 24, 25, 26	-----		
3. Economics Teachers	3, 4, 6, 9, 12, 17, 22, 25	3, 4, 11, 12, 14, 17	-----	
4. Other Teachers	4, 11, 13, 22	27	5, 6, 7, 8, 10, 13, 14, 15, 16, 17, 19, 20, 21, 22, 24, 26, 27	-----
5. Journalists	4, 5, 11, 15, 17, 20	21, 26, 27	4, 5, 7, 8, 13, 16, 17, 22, 23, 24, 27, 28	2, 3, 4, 8, 11, 12, 16, 17, 18, 22, 23, 24, 27, 28

The chi-square analysis also revealed that economics teachers thought more like other teachers or journalists than they did like economists or economic educators. There were 17 items with relatively little difference in patterns of response between economics teachers and other teachers. Economics teachers also shared 12 propositions in common with journalists, which was just two less than the number that the other teachers shared with journalists.

Rank-order Correlations

The item analysis identified those items with the most similarities in response patterns between groups, but a simple count of those items does not provide a precise measure of how much the groups differ from each other. Therefore, rank order correlations were calculated to assess group relationships. The frequency data in Table 5.1 were transformed into means for the correlation analysis. The mean responses are shown in the fourth column of Table 5.1. To calculate these means, individual responses were assigned a value of 1 for generally agree, 2 for agree with provisos, and 3 for a generally disagree. These values were averaged across all respondents in each group to produce item means for each group. A Spearman's rho correlation was calculated between each group using the means.[7]

Table 5.3 reports the results of the correlation analysis. The Spearman's rho for economists and economic educators was 0.892, confirming the high degree of concordance that is obvious from a visual inspection of the means rankings, and suggesting that there were only minor differences in the views of economists and economic educators on various economic issues. The concordance between the rankings of economics teachers and economists was lower, with a Spearman's rho of .623. This was about the same as the concordance between economics teachers and economic educators (.657), which was expected given the closeness in the views of economists and economic educators.[8]

There was much less agreement in comparing the other teachers to economists or economic educators. Spearman's rho was .468 between other teachers and economists, and .409 between other teachers and economic educators. These results suggest that the high school economics teachers hold opinions about economic issues somewhat closer to economists and economic educators than do social studies teachers who do not teach the subject. However, once again this analysis suggests that the secondary economics teachers think more like other teachers (correlation .883) than like either economists or economic educators.

The rank correlation between economists and journalists was slightly higher (.557) than the correlation between economists and social studies teachers (.468), but it was slightly lower than the correlation between economists and economics teachers (.623). More striking is the finding that journalists and teachers think alike about many economic issues: the rank order correlation between journalists and economics teachers was .932, and .926 between journalists and social studies teachers.

Table 5.3: Rank Order Comparison of Item Means by Group (Spearman's rho Correlations)

		Groups			
Groups	Description	1	2	3	4
1.	Economists	---			
2.	Economic Educators	.892	---		
3.	Economics Teachers	.623	.657	---	
4.	Other Teachers	.468	.409	.883	---
5.	Journalists	.557	.560	.932	.926

Index Scores

An alternative method to rank-order correlations for analyzing the degree of differences in thinking among these groups was the creation of an index score. The index score for each individual represents the degree to which a person's views were in agreement with the predominant view of economists across all issues. The score was created by first weighting the individual item responses (generally agree, agree with provisos, and generally disagree) based on the percentage responses given by economists for each category (see Table 5.1). That is, if an individual generally agreed on item 1, that item would contribute .713 toward to the index score because 71.3 percent of economists thought the same way. On the other hand, if the individual generally disagreed with the proposition, that opinion would only be worth a value of .065 because only 6.5 percent of economists were of a similar mind. After each item response was weighted according to the proportion of economists' responses, the values of the items were summed, divided by the number of items answered, and then multiplied by 100 to create an index score.

The means and standard deviations of the index scores for each group are given in the lower half of Table 5.4. The rank ordering of the score means is what would be expected based on the visual inspection of the item mean data and the rank-order correlations. Economists and economic educators had the highest index scores (39.9) followed by economics teachers (37.8), journalists (36.9), and social studies teachers (35.8).

The mean differences in index scores and the associated t-values calculated assuming no mean differences are shown in the upper half of Table 5.4. There was relatively little difference in the means of economists and economic educators ($t = -0.17$). All the other groups, however, showed relatively large differences in mean index scores. There was a two point difference in the index scores of economists and economic educators over high school economics teachers. The advantage doubled to four points when comparisons were made between economists or economic educators and social studies teachers. Journalists had index scores that were three points lower than economists and economic educators, but journalist scores were halfway between those of economics teachers and other teachers.

Explanations for the Results

The three different analyses showed the same basic relationships among the groups in their opinions about economic issues. Several plausible explanations can be given for these robust findings. Economic educators were the most similar to economists in their overall views probably because of similar education and training in economics among the members in each group. Most

Table 5.4: Mean Differences Among Groups on Index Scores (t-values in parentheses)

Groups	1	2	3	4	5
1. Economists	--- ---				
2. Economic Educators	-0.06 (-0.17)	--- ---			
3. Economics Teachers	2.08 (7.10)	2.13 (5.99)	--- ---		
4. Other Teachers	4.04 (19.77)	4.10 (12.89)	1.97 (6.89)	--- ---	
5. Journalists	2.99 (14.27)	3.05 (9.37)	0.92 (4.83)	-1.05 (-5.54)	--- ---
Means	39.86	39.92	37.79	35.82	36.87
Standard Deviations	3.36	3.03	3.18	3.44	3.52
Sample Size	464	135	177	694	655

economic educators hold Ph.D.s in either economics or education. Those with Ph.D.s in education often have substantial coursework in economics and are familiar with the thinking of economists on economic issues.

High school economics teachers were the next closest in their opinions to those of either economists or economic educators. The obvious reason for this affinity is that high school economics teachers have more education in economics than other teachers. Economics teachers are more likely than other teachers to have taken economic courses while attending college, and are also more likely to have participated in inservice courses or workshops in economics after they graduated from college (Walstad, 1992). Their thinking about economic topics, therefore, is more likely to be influenced by economists, and by economic educators who often teach these preservice and inservice economics courses. Economists and economic educators have less influence on other teachers, as all three analyses showed.

Economics teachers, however, had a greater similarity with journalists than they did with economists. The reason may be because coursework or knowledge was not the only factor influencing the thinking of high school economics teachers. Some studies have estimated that it may take as many as five or more economics courses before teachers show a meaningful level of economic understanding, and thus begin to think like economists (Bach and Saunders, 1965). Most economics teachers have not taken five or more courses, or developed an economist's framework for thinking about economic issues. Economic knowledge also depreciates after the courses are completed, and there is evidence that most economics teachers completed their last economics course over eight years ago (Walstad and Watts, 1985). Given these conditions, current thinking about economic topics is likely to be shaped by the information and "analysis" provided by the news media.

The other high school social studies teachers were the group who differed most from economists or economic educators in their views on economic propositions. The primary reason is probably that they had the least economics coursework of any group. In fact, one study of college transcripts found that prospective social studies teachers had taken only one economics course, on average (Galambos, Cornett, and Spitler, 1985). This lack of formal instruction in economics means that their opinions about economic topics were more likely to be shaped by public opinion or the media than by education in economics.

Journalists were somewhat inclined to think the same as economists or economic educators, but not as much as economics teachers. Again, the differences probably arose because of less education or training in economics for this group. Most journalists major in journalism or other fields, and take few economics courses. What journalists learn about economics often comes from on-the-job training in writing about economic events and issues, and from reading what other journalists write about these issues.

IV. CONCLUSION

The review of past survey studies showed evidence of a general consensus among economists in their views on many economic topics. The consensus was not universal; it varied by topics and by country-origin of the economists. The strongest degree of consensus was found in the U.S. and Canada, less consensus was found among economists in Germany, Switzerland, and Great Britain, and even less was found among economists in Austria, France, and Belgium. Nevertheless, there seemed to be greater similarities in the thinking of North American and European economists on economic issues than there were differences.

The thinking of economists on issues where there is consensus *and* dissension is expected to have an influence in the economic education that occurs in a country, in part by influencing economic educators and journalists. How well economic education works and how economically literate a society becomes may depend on the effectiveness of the transmission of the economic thinking to groups such as teachers or journalists. The new survey evidence from the U.S. presented in this chapter suggests that the transmission of economic thinking is less than ideal, and that significant gaps exist in the flow of information *or* the reception of this information across some groups. Economists and economic educators seemed to think alike on economic propositions, and teachers and journalists seemed to think alike. Teachers' and journalists' opinions, however, were not similar to those of economists and economic educators. Although high school economics teachers showed somewhat more affinity for economists' ways of thinking than did other teachers or journalists, even among this key group there was greater concordance with the views of other teachers and journalists than there was with those of economists or economic educators.

NOTES

Syed Murtaza Ali, a graduate student in economics at Nebraska, provided valuable computational assistance with the data analysis for this chapter.

1. For example, in a review of the status of the economics major, Siegfried et al. (1991) state: "A broad consensus exists among economics faculty that enabling students to 'think like an economist' is the overarching goal of economics education." (p. 199)

2. That led one reader of the *Times*, Mr. Peter Sieber, to write a letter to the editor concluding that "the economic effects of economists ... are more likely to be unfavorable than favorable to Britain" (Oct. 25, 1971).

3. Some questions from the Kearl et al. survey that were unique to the U.S. policy experience, or dated, or both – e.g., a question on the Ford administration's fiscal policy – were not included in the European surveys.

4. Presumably the group of teachers whose primary assignment was economics or who taught an Advanced Placement course in economics would be the ones most likely to think like economists. There are, however, other classification schemes that could be used to divide the teacher group. The sensitivity of teacher responses to alternative schemes (e.g., all teachers who have taught an economics course within the last five years) are issues that will be examined in further studies.

5. Several points should be noted about Table 5.1: (a) Economist data are from Alston, Kearl, and Vaughan (1992); (b) Means were calculated by assigning a value of 1 to generally agree, a value of 2 to agree with provisos, and a value of 3 to generally disagree; and, (c) Respondents to the surveys did not complete every item, so the N varies across items and the percentages may not total to 100. The subsequent analysis is based on the responses provided to each proposition and not on a global deletion of those not responding to every item.

6. The chi-square statistics was calculated by the formula:

$$\chi^2 = \sum_{i=1}^{2} \sum_{j=1}^{3} (O_{ij} - E_{ij})^2 / E_{ij}$$

where i = 1, 2 is the index for economists and one of the other four groups and j = 1, 2, 3 is the index for the three responses, with no opinion or no response deleted from the analysis. E_{ij} is the expected number in cell ij and O_{ij} is the observed number in this cell. Because our sampling technique may have generated responses that reflect more than pure simple random sampling error, inferences based on the chi-square distribution may be suspect.

7. Spearman's rho is like a simple correlation coefficient but is designed for use with rank ordered data. Let d_i be the difference between the rank order of the i-th proposition (i = 1, 2 ... 28) by two different groups. Spearman's rho is then defined by:

$$\text{Spearman's rho} = 1 - \frac{6 \Sigma d_i^2}{(28)^3 - 28}$$

If the ordering in two sets of data are identical, then Spearman's rho = +1. If they are perfectly related in an inverse manner, then rho = –1. If there is no concordance, then rho = 0.

8. No statistical test for rank correlation differences among groups was performed because the data were based on average responses of unequal numbers from nonsimple random samples.

REFERENCES

Alston, R. M., Kearl, J. R., & Vaughan, M. B. (1992). Is there a consensus among economists in the 1990's? *American Economic Review, 82*(2), 203-209.

Bach, G. L., & Saunders, P. (1965). Economic education: Aspirations and achievements. *American Economic Review, 55*(3), 329-56.

Block, W., & Walker, M. (1988). Entropy in the Canadian economics profession: Sampling consensus on the major issues. *Canadian Public Policy, 14*(2), 137-150.

Frey, B. S., & Eichenberger, R. (1992). Economics and economists: A European perspective. *American Economic Review, 82*(2), 216-220.

Frey, B. S., Ginsburgh, V., Pestieau, P., Pommerehne, W. W., & Schneider, F. (1983). Consensus, dissension and ideology among economists in various European countries and in the United States. *European Economic Review, 23*, 59-69.

Frey, B. S., Pommerehne, W. W., Schneider, F., & Gilbert, G. (1984). Consensus and dissension among economists: An empirical inquiry. *American Economic Review, 74*(5), 986-994.

Galambos, E., Cornett, C. M., & Spitler, H. D. (1985). *An analysis of transcripts of teachers and arts and science graduates*. Atlanta, GA: Southern Regional Education Board.

Kearl, J. R., Pope, C. L., Whiting, G. C., & Wimmer, L. T. (1979). A confusion of economists? *American Economic Review, 69*(2), 28-37.

Ricketts, M., & Shoesmith, E. (1992). British economic opinion: Positive science or normative judgment? *American Economic Review, 82*(2), 210-215.

Siegfried, J. J., Bartlett, R. L., Hansen, W. L., Kelley, A. C., McCloskey, D. N., & Tietenberg, T. H. (1991). The status and prospects of the economics major. *Journal of Economic Education, 22*(3), 197-224.

Walstad, W. B. (1992). Economics instruction in high schools. *Journal of Economic Literature, 30*(4), 2019-2051.

Walstad, W. B., & Watts, M. (1985). Teaching economics in the schools: A review of survey findings. *Journal of Economic Education, 16*(2), 135-146.

CHAPTER 6

RESEARCH ON HIGH SCHOOL ECONOMICS IN THE UNITED STATES: FURTHER CONSIDERATIONS

William Becker

William Greene

Sherwin Rosen

Over twenty years ago Nobel laureate George Stigler (1970) argued that "economics belongs in everyone's education once we have learned how to teach it." Because the logic of economics is not easy to learn or teach, he concluded that "Economics is not yet ready to be made a part of the basic curriculum of all educated men" (p. 80). Judging from the extent to which economics courses are now offered within the United States and even mandated for high school graduation in some states, the education establishment and state legislators rejected Stigler's conclusion. Ignoring why this change occurred, we address what has been learned about the teaching and learning of economics in high schools. Attention is given both to the ways in which learning has been measured and to research findings. Alternative measures of "value added" and problems of sample selection are also considered. We argue that test scores cannot be interpreted as cardinal measures and that only relative comparisons are possible. We find that standardized test scores show no great difference between one method of instruction or program and another.[1]

I. MEASUREMENT OF KNOWLEDGE

Business, political, and labor leaders have shared the economists' views that the general public does not understand economics, although they have not always agreed on what constitutes an understanding of economics. Soper and Walstad advanced the notion that high school students do not know economics. With the support of the National Council on Economic Education (NCEE, previously the Joint Council on Economic Education, JCEE), Soper and Walstad (1987) developed the *Test of Economic Literacy* (TEL), a nationally normed 46-item multiple choice test.[2] Walstad and Soper (1988) reported that their selected sample of 2,483 students averaged only 20.34 questions correct in a mid-school-year administration of the TEL. At a news conference at the 1988 Allied Social Science Meetings, Walstad labeled shocking the fact that only 41.7 percent of the questions were answered correctly whereas guessing would yield 25 percent correct (11.5 questions), on the average.[3]

But are these results shocking? The standard deviation was 7.45 answers correct, which implies a standard error of 0.15 questions and little likelihood of obtaining these results if students were just guessing. Before concluding that students know economics, however, recognize that the TEL was constructed so that each question tends to identify students who know economics from those who do not. Reliability is built into the test by using questions that differentiate the same students in the same way; students with higher scores on the test should get any question correct with higher probability than those with lower scores. This rule for inclusion makes questions dependent, and the probability of successful guessing on each question is not fixed at 0.25. Whether any percentage correct is higher or lower than what is expected depends on the test construction. Whether 40 percent correct is a failing grade likewise depends on test construction. There is no unique cardinal standard upon which grades can be based.[4]

In addition to sponsoring the development of the TEL, the NCEE directed a survey of high schools in the 1986-87 school year. The resulting data set, known as the National Assessment of Economic Education (NAEE), involves information on 121 classrooms and 3,266 high school students (Baumol and Highsmith, 1988). The NAEE had only one administration of the TEL as a year-end test; the average was 20.7, which is slightly lower than the 22.14 year-end average reported by Walstad and Soper (1988) for their sample of 2,483 students. The NAEE data also provide extensive qualitative information on students, teachers, and schools. Forty-three scholars were introduced to this NAEE data base, the Walstad-Soper TEL data base, and econometric modeling in economic education research (Becker and Walstad, 1987) at Princeton University summer workshops in 1987 and 1988; much of the recent research reported here is the outcome of those workshops.

II. RESEARCH DESIGN, MODELING AND FINDINGS

One might be tempted to subtract the midyear average TEL score from either of the two year-end averages reported above as a measure of what is learned in a half year of high school. This difference ignores numerous covariates that influence economic learning and knowledge of economics.[5] To assess economic learning, researchers have used a "change-score model" in which the posttest minus pretest score is the dependent variable and explanatory variables reflect the effects of individual characteristics (race, sex), human capital (IQ, prior grades, attitudes), utilization rates (study and class time), and technology (alternative teaching methods or equipment). Others use an "attainment model" in which the postmeasure is regressed on the pretest (when it is available) and the other explanatory variables to assess economic knowledge. With these two models researchers have learned the following about efforts to raise high school student learning and knowledge of economics.[6]

Special Projects

Within the United States, projects administered by Junior Achievement, local business organizations, and trade associations are aimed at increasing student understanding of certain aspects of an economic system or of specific institutions within that system (for a listing of organizations and projects see Banaszak, n.d.). Few studies of the outcomes from these projects have been undertaken and none has appeared in the academic, refereed journals typically read by economists. In contrast, as reviewed by Walstad (1992), there is a substantial body of published research on the Developmental Economic Education Program (DEEP). Watts (1991) also discusses the projects that have been conducted as part of DEEP, and Watts (1985) provides analysis of a statewide program.

The DEEP projects share a common goal of raising high school student understanding of basic economics, although no uniform curriculum is dictated. Participating districts are expected to cooperate with a NCEE-affiliated state council or a collegiate center for economic education in two basic functions: conducting inservice programs for teachers (typically consisting of economics and education courses) and building economics into the curriculum through formal economics courses and other courses as well. The NCEE has no direct control over what is done under the umbrella of DEEP; it provides stimulus, materials, expertise, and leadership by example.

The many studies of DEEP show that high school students do learn economics in various types of courses and that teacher inservice programs are beneficial to student learning. Rhine (1989), however, reports the curious results that DEEP is effective in states that mandate course work in economics, but it has a negative influence on student performance in states without a mandate. Rhine's results may be due to sample selection and variable definition problems, however. Whether a school district is or is not in DEEP may be of little importance compared to how successful it is in getting students and teachers into the study of economics (Becker and Walstad, 1990). Peterson's (1989) NAEE study supports this conclusion.[7] It appears that it is the two basic functional parts of DEEP (teacher training and curriculum change) that are important and not the imprimatur.

Student Ability

Research confirms that the higher a student's aptitude or intelligence, the greater the learning in economics. The pretest score is typically the single most important variable in explaining attainment. It also influences change scores, although the bias caused by correlation between the error and a pretest regressor in these specifications has been relatively ignored by researchers.[8]

Student attitudes toward economics are thought to affect the learning of economics. Early work at the elementary grade levels suggests that the direction of causality is from learning of economics to positive student attitudes towards economics and not the reverse (as reviewed by Walstad, in Becker and Walstad 1987). This direction of causality is supported by Beron's (1990) NAEE results that student performance influences student interest more than wanting to take more courses affects performance. These results may be sensitive to model specification, since they are based on attitude attainment and not changes in attitude. They suggest, however, that if students are to learn economics, we should first figure out how to teach it; they will then develop an appreciation for the subject.

Teacher Ability

There is a positive relationship between teacher knowledge of economics and learning of economics by students in their classroom (Weaver, Deaton and Reach, 1987). Similarly, teacher attitudes toward economics may influence student attitudes toward economics (Schober, 1984; Marlin, 1991). Buckles, Strom and Walstad (1984) report that high school teachers do not want inservice programs on economics content as much as inservice programs that present teaching materials. Teachers may be able to learn economics if it is taught through materials that teachers could use in their high school classroom (Thorton and Vredeveld, 1977).

Bosshardt and Watts (1990) report that teacher training in economics and the quality of the students are important factors in student learning of economics. In both fixed- and random-effects models, they found student learning to be associated with instructors. In the fixed-effects model, for example, 32 of the 0-1 covariates included to represent the 94 instructors were significant. Lopus (1990) reports that student knowledge of economics in the NAEE data is significantly related to expenditures for teachers with advanced degrees, smaller class sizes, and economic education consultants for teachers; student knowledge is not related to teacher experience. Becker and Walstad (1990) and Walstad and Van Scyoc (1990) found that teacher coursework was significantly and positively related to student achievement, thus confirming earlier findings. Lynch (1990), however, notes that the first few courses in economics that a teacher takes may contribute little to the teacher's high school students' learning unless those students are being taught in an economics course (as opposed to a history or social studies course). Using a nonlinear regression specification, Lynch found that the overall influence of economics courses taken by teachers was positive only after teachers had completed at least four courses in economics.

Grimes and Register (1990) report that in the NAEE data, high school students in unionized schools score higher on the TEL than students in nonunion districts. They suggest that while their results are consistent with those of Eberts and Stone (1987), where a positive effect of unions on learning in elementary schools was found, a unique and compelling rationale is lacking.[9] One can speculate, however, that the perception of union benefits attracts the better teachers.

Clearly there is more to learn about the role of teachers in economic education. Next to student ability, teacher ability may be the most important variable in the learning equation. Although the argument is made that teacher preparation in economics is inadequate, no one has answered the relevant question: "relative to what?" Are social studies teachers less prepared to teach economics than all the other subjects they teach? Are social studies teachers less prepared to teach economics than mathematics teachers are prepared to teach trigonometry, calculus or statistics? Competence in teaching as in any other occupation is a relative measure and not an absolute.

Course Work

Within the United States, 15 states mandate a separate one-semester course in economics for high school graduation; one requires a course for college-bound students, four more states require that a course be offered as an elective (Highsmith, 1989). It simply is assumed that any course work in "economics" increases economic literacy, regardless of the content of the courses or the training of the teachers. In the case of mandated courses, however, Marlin (1990) calls this assumption into question.

There is no uniformity in the content of high school economics courses or the economics that is taught as a part of social studies, history, and other more general courses. The AEA Committee on Economic Education and NCEE, however, have devoted significant resources to establishing guidelines. In the late 1950s these organizations cooperated in the formation of the National Task Force that addressed what constituted good high school instruction in economics. Saunders, Bach, Calderwood and Hansen (1984) outlined the content for precollege economic education, which provided the basis of the TEL. Their framework was hotly debated at a MIT conference, the proceedings of which appeared in the Spring 1987 issue of *The Journal of Economic Education.*

Although the question of what economic concepts are to be taught at the high school level is not settled, students can learn economics in high school economics courses, as well as in social studies, history, and business courses, if the teacher is trained in economics. Chizmar et al. (1985) reported that learning in economics improves students' skills in other social studies. Different sets of prepackaged classroom materials have been shown to work in these varied settings (Chizmar and Halinski, 1983; and Martin and Bender, 1985). Dawson (1982), for example, reports particularly favorable results when economics is "infused" into an American history course. Walstad and Watts (1985), however, question how many students are exposed to any significant economics instruction through infusion. In consumer courses, learning of economics might even be negative according to Walstad and Soper (1988). Peterson (1989) reports that in the NAEE data better students avoid economics courses. He is dubious of conclusions from studies of learning in various types of courses when such selection is not modeled.

Technology

Computers are the latest in a long string of technologies that have been touted as potential replacements for classroom teachers and for producing a major change in education as we know it today. In the 1950s and 1960s television, programmed learning, and flash cards were considered revolutionary. In the 1970s, television and the show-and-tell approach of Sesame Street were pushed as the wave of the future. Games and simulations also caught on. Now we hear that interactive computing and interactive television are the future of education.

To date, there is little research that shows any one of these existing technologies superior to another, or indeed that anything is superior to the classroom teacher. Hansen, Kelley and Weisbrod (1970) hypothesized that finding no significant average differences ignores distributional effects. No researcher has followed up on the notion of matching teaching techniques to individual high school student attributes and benefits from learning economics. This may be because court decisions and social and political pressures within the United States make homogeneous ability grouping, tracking, and other forms of curricular selectivity difficult in high schools. These issues, however, need to be addressed by researchers.

Physical capital may be a poor substitute for human capital in precollege teaching. Rosen (1987) argues that in the economics of education industry, the student-teacher ratio becomes the most important constraint. Teaching and learning require a two-way communication that becomes increasingly unidirectional as the scale of the media is enlarged. Thirty years ago, the AEA-CEE and NCEE cooperated in the development of a national television course, *The American Economy*. Although this series had over a million viewers daily and was shown to be effective as a teaching tool (Saunders, 1964; and Bach and Saunders, 1965), it did not give rise to additional programming and did not revolutionize the teaching of economics. If such mass media teaching is desired by students and society, after thirty years why hasn't it made the small classroom obsolete? Why do parents continue to lobby for smaller classes and not for more TV courses?

The conclusion that no superior technology has emerged does not imply that none could be used. Alternative technologies can complement the classroom teacher and allow for more individualized instruction. Just as *The American Economy* television series was shown to be instructive, more recent TV series such as the NCEE's *Give and Take, Economics U$A*, and *Understanding Taxes* can be used to teach secondary students (Chizmar et al., 1985). The question is at what cost? Computers can complement classroom instruction (Lewis et al., 1985), but is it worth the cost to have each student sitting at a terminal? Furthermore, microcomputers may have made obsolete all previous evaluations of the role of mainframe computers in education. There is no research to date that shows any great breakthrough in the educational process. Taking a cue from Stigler, Rosen (1987) claims that there has not been a major innovation in education since the invention of the printing press, which made inexpensive textbook publication possible.

Studies have attempted to determine the extent to which textbook quality is related to student achievement in economics. Miller (1988), for example, assigned numerical ratings to textbooks for coverage of specific concepts in the *Framework* of Saunders et al. (1984). This measure of coverage revealed many acceptable high school economics textbooks. Miller also found that student test scores on the TEL tend to be related to textbook coverage but his study design was not sufficient to control for other explanations of this correlation.

Sex and Race

Conventional wisdom holds that males have a relative advantage in numerical skills while females excel in verbal skills. This belief has given rise to an extensive literature on gender differences in learning economics.

Siegfried's (1979) summary of earlier work suggests that high school males know more economics than females, as measured by multiple-choice tests. Watts

(1987) shows that males have higher levels of economic understanding as early as grade five. Males and females tend to learn the same amount during high school and college, so the gap that materializes before high school never closes during the schooling experience. The recent work of Lumsden and Scott (1987) suggests that this gap may increase in the college economics course.

Although studies show a statistically significant gap in male and female learning of high school economics, the difference is typically small in magnitude – on the order of a couple of multiple choice questions, when background variables are controlled. In an exception to this finding, Heath (1989) reports that male students outperformed women by 10 TEL points in economics courses after controlling for the fact that women do not elect to take economics classes. The work of Peterson (1989) suggests, however, that Heath's results may be sensitive to the peculiar way in which those who did not take economics had their TEL scores censored.[10] Using the same data, Evans (1992) found no interaction between the gender of teacher and student and concluded that devoting scarce resources to recruit women selectively into education to provide role models for young women may be an inefficient use of those resources.

Regardless of the magnitude of the difference, the work of Ferber, Birnbaum and Green (1983) and Lumsden and Scott (1987) suggests that observed gender differences may be the product of the multiple choice instrument. Women tend to do better than men on essay exams. Lumsden and Scott state: "One cannot avoid the uneasy feeling that the now generally accepted 'truth' of female inferiority [in the learning of economics] is based on ad hoc rationalizations" (p. 366).

As with gender, the effect of race on student learning of economics is not great. In Buckles and Freeman (1984), for example, whites show a slight but insignificant advantage in learning economics in seven of the ten pre-college grades considered. In their national study, Walstad and Soper (1989) found that blacks score little more than one question lower than whites on the TEL, with statistical significance depending on the model specification. Peterson (1992) found no significant difference between blacks and whites electing to study economics and no significant difference in their terminal knowledge of economics. Unlike his finding of a role model effect for women, however, Evans (1992) found a relationship between the race of the teacher and that of the student for African-Americans, which was especially strong for students whose mothers did not graduate from college. Evans concluded that spending resources to attract racial minorities into teaching thus may be socially beneficial.

Age and Time Usage

Older students know more economics and are able to learn more abstract concepts than younger students. Buckles and Freeman (1984) and Watts (1987 and earlier articles) demonstrated, however, that students younger than 18 years of age can learn economics.

Although there are no studies that explicitly measure time on task at the precollege level, the study by Jackstadt and Gootaert (1980) suggests that working 20 hours or more per week substantially reduces knowledge and learning of economics. Supposedly, students who spend so much time working cannot devote sufficient time to schoolwork. Females, however, appear to be less adversely affected by part-time employment, for some unknown reason. Lillydahl (1990) found that modest levels of employment during high school may not interfere with student academic performance but that students who work in excess of 20 hours per week are absent more often from school, spend less time on homework, and have lower academic performance scores. These findings stand in contrast to some of the general education research that shows high school grade point averages unaffected by part-time employment (Green and Jaquess, 1987). The influence of time usage on student learning is not yet settled.

Lasting Effects

High school courses in economics do raise the economic understanding of students, at least in pre-post testing. Still, the lasting effect of high school courses in economics has been debated for years (Siegfried and Fels, 1979). The early work of Saunders (1970) suggests that students who had an economics course in high school enter their first course in college economics with a greater understanding, yet upon completion of that course they knew little if any more than those who never took a high school course. Myatt and Waddell (1990) report similar results, except the decay in learning does not show up until the student reaches the intermediate courses.[11] The reason for the decay in learning is not clear, but one can speculate that students with high school economics spend less time on college economics to achieve a target grade and spend more time in other activities. The empirical results of Brasfield, Harrison and McCoy (1993), however, show a high school economics course to positively influence students' grades in college introductory macro- and microeconomics.

The new Advanced Placement Program in Economics, developed by the College Board and the Educational Testing Service and being promoted by the NCEE, enables high school students to earn college credit for economics learned in high school (Buckles and Morton, 1988). Whether or not this Advanced Placement Program will yield positive effects on student learning of economics as they move through college remains to be seen. Past experience with high school economics courses may not have been overly encouraging but we might be wise to look at the results of other disciplines that have had more experience with advance placement courses before drawing a conclusion.

III. TEST SCORE CHANGES AS VALUE ADDED

As with education generally, most research in economic education has been based on test scores. The differences in these test scores are used as the "value added" by the treatment. The market for new high school graduates does not place a value on student learning; it values the final level of accomplishment. Employers buy terminal high school aptitudes and skills, not a change in test scores. What the student knew four years ago in the first semester of the freshman year is irrelevant to the employer, except insofar as it affects the rate of learning. Knowing the difference between test scores is of little help to a student or society without knowing the economic value of this difference.

Changes in test scores may have administrative value to a principal or classroom teacher, but that may have little relationship to the economic concept of value. Just as water has a high "value in use" but a low "value in exchange," some basic skills, such as an ability to reconcile a checkbook, may have high value in use but low value in exchange. Other skills may have a high value at one point in time and little value at another; for example, the ability to manipulate a slide rule fell in value with the availability of the cheap hand calculator and portable computer. Although some skills may be viewed as essential for education, their market value is determined by demand and supply. The normative beliefs of a principal, school board, chamber of commerce, state legislature, or school faculty about the importance of intellectual skills is elusive without reference to what employers are paying for the bundle of skills embodied in the high school graduate, and what skills they desire from the graduate. (The satisfaction derived from learning and its change score measurement is ignored here for brevity, but is modeled in Becker, 1982.)

The distinction between the value of specific forms of knowledge and student test scores is not appreciated by all economists and even less by many educators. For example, Blinder (1991) argues:

> I have no doubt that the market pays for total, not incremental, ability. But, if Y measures economic knowledge, and K and L are the factor inputs ..., then
>
> $$Y_2 = F(K,L) + Y_1,$$
>
> where Y_1 is knowledge after high school and Y_2 is knowledge after college. Scholars interested in college education must still study the production function $F(K,L)$ even if they ultimately care only about Y_2. (p. 252)

Aside from the academic questions related to the assumed functional form [e.g., does $F(K,L) + Y_1 = F(K,L,Y_1)$?] and its estimation (as discussed in endnotes 6 and 8), the relevant practical question in an exchange economy is what are the values of the Ys relative to other goods and services?[12] The importance of considering market valued measures of schooling is evident from the work of Card and Krueger (1990) and Eric Hanushek (1986, 1989). Card and Krueger analyzed the earnings of a large sample of male workers in the United States in 1979 and the characteristics of the public school each attended in the 1920s, 1930s and 1940s. Their work and that of Angrist and Krueger (1991) suggests that class size, teacher's pay, the length of school term and mandatory attendance positively influence the financial returns from education. In his review of 147 studies, however, Hanushek (1986) found that the teacher/student ratio, teacher pay and other expenditure variables are unrelated to student performance on multiple choice tests.

Hansen, Kelley, and Weisbrod (1970) called attention to the problem of valuing individual student learning and its implications for curriculum reform but few have followed their lead. As they state, who receives the benefits of instruction and how they weight those benefits will affect the valuation. Putting a monetary value on the benefits of one course in economics may be difficult if not impossible but researchers can explore the effect of instruction in economics on the decisions of unequally endowed students to go to college, to select different majors, or to pursue other benefits that are known to have economic value. The studies by Beron (1990), on student knowledge and the desire to take additional courses, and Vredeveld and Jeong (1990), on student-teacher goal agreement, are good beginnings in seeking answers to questions about the alternative ways in which students and teachers value economic education. Surely there are many other ways in which knowledge of economics might influence the decision-making processes and be related to observable market outcomes.

IV. PROBLEMS OF DATA LOSS

In addition to the problem of valuing changes in scores, there is a practical problem of measuring change: students drop out or are forced out between the pre and the posttest, and the process that determines who is out is likely related to the process that determines scores. For example, teachers who observe that their average class score was low on the pretest may not administer the posttest, or students with low scores might be encouraged not to take the posttest. As demonstrated by Becker and Walstad (1990), this data loss may bias estimators in attainment and change score models.[13]

Missing observations on key variables can also devastate a large data set. In the Walstad and Soper (1988) TEL data, 18 percent of the 3,031 matched pre-post scores were discarded because of missing data on other variables; in Walstad and Soper (1989), the matched pre-post sample had grown to 3,427 but the usable sample had shrunk to 1,630 records. In the NAEE data, questionnaire data are missing on a third of the teachers and usable samples of only several hundred observations are not unusual. The reasons for and consequences of such large data loss need to be addressed.

Other problems resulting from self-selection into a sample were identified 30 years ago by Saunders (1964), in what we believe is the first multiple regression analysis of an educational output, although they have been largely ignored since. A particularly troubling problem may be a school district's willingness to get involved in programs like DEEP and a student's desire to take economics courses, as recognized by Peterson (1989). An analysis similar to that in Murnane, Newstead, and Olsen's (1985) study of the relative quality of public versus Catholic schools may be useful in the analysis of the effect of one type of special program or project versus another.

In the absence of randomized experiments, one can always find selection problems at some point in the sampling process. Heckman and Hotz (1989) provide specification tests for selecting among alternative nonexperimental estimators. In considering selectivity problems, however, researchers should not lose sight of the relevant population to which generalizations are to be made. For instance, why should we care if we cannot teach a subject to the uninterested and unwilling? We are always going to be teaching to selected individuals, so why shouldn't our experiments reflect the actual conditions under which we work? Why worry about what will never apply? There are many situations in education for which potential selection problems can be raised but for which there are no practical consequences.

V. CONCLUSION

What we know about the effectiveness of high school courses, materials, and organizations aimed at advancing an understanding of economics is empirical. Learning that is registered for one treatment versus another is measured on an ordinal scale. At best relative comparisons are possible; absolute scores have little meaning.

Typically standardized test scores have not shown any great difference between one method of instruction or program versus another. This may simply reflect a shortcoming of these instruments, however. Consideration of alternatives to the standard paper and pencil test instruments for assessing the value of economic education efforts is needed. A better conceptual basis also is needed to integrate the why, how, and what teachers teach with what motivates students to learn. With alternative measures of success and a better conceptual base we might be able to give new answers to Stigler's old question: "Why should people be economically literate?"

NOTES

We benefitted from the reviews of Dawson (1977), Wentworth, Hansen and Hawke (1977), Siegfried and Fels (1979), Becker (1983a, 1983b, 1983c), Becker and Walstad (1987), Hallows and Becker (forthcoming), Highsmith and Baumol (1989), Siegfried and Walstad (1989), Watts (1990), Walstad (1992), and the annotated bibliography provided by the National Center for Research in Economic Education, University of Nebraska. Comments were provided on earlier versions by S. Becker, G. Dawson, R. Fels, K. Goldberg, P. Grimes, W. L. Hansen, R. Highsmith, P. Kennedy, T. Kniesner, J. Lopus, N. Peterson, J. Manahan, P. Saunders, J. Siegfried, W. Walstad, and M. Watts.

1. This review is an updated version of our earlier reviews that appeared in *The American Economic Review* (1990) and *Journal of Economic Education* (1990). With few exceptions, it is limited to the literature written for economists.

2. Soper and Walstad (1983, 1988) also developed the *Survey on Economic Attitudes* (SEA) as a two part, 28 item measure of attitudes toward economics as a subject and attitudes toward economic issues. The initial draft of Nelson and Sheffrin (1991) critical comments about the TEL provides insights into their confusion about the manner in which the *Test of Economic Literacy* and the *Survey of Economic Attitudes* were prepared and administered. Their own hypothesis test of whether high school classes are advancing the ideology of the TEL designers showed (p. 161) no statistical significant difference in scores from pre-test to post-test on "ideological questions" versus "definitional questions." Their test statistic was based on the 1620 students for whom they had pre- and post-test data. With this large of sample size standard errors are small so it is impressive that no statistical difference was found, although Nelson and Sheffrin try to conclude otherwise. Walstad (1991) points out other flaws in Nelson and Sheffrin's critique of the TEL.

3. The importance of economic education at the high school level may be seen in the fact that Walstad's comments appeared in all the major newspapers and weeklies. In *Vital Speeches of the Day* (March 25, 1989), for example, he wrote:

> "So typical high school students score only 15 percentage points above a chance score on this test. Clearly 40 percent correct represents a failing grade under even the most liberal grading standards. This level of economic knowledge among most high school students is shocking!"

4. According to Walstad (1990) almost any norm-referenced test can be interpreted as criterion-referenced by analyzing the level of performance or achievement the scores indicate. For example, a threshold score can be specified for the Graduate Record Exam as the minimum knowledge level for admission to a graduate school. Walstad seems to interpret this score as a single judgment about what constitutes an acceptable level of performance. But Walstad overlooks that this threshold is set, at least in part, by the number of students needed to fill classrooms; it may have little to do with a test taker's absolute competence. It is simply the score that puts x number of students above it, where x is the number of students of interest to the screening agent. The significance of testing for relative ranking (norm-referenced) versus competency (criterion-referenced) is considered further in Becker and Rosen (1992).

5. Economic education researchers have considered randomized experiments, but typically they have not been able to influence the administrative assignment or student

selection. Researchers tend to use self-selected or quasi-experimental designs in which assignment of students to control and experimental groups is nonrandom. Students either choose to be in a course or are assigned to fulfill graduation and schedule requirements.

6. Many of the results regarding student learning and knowledge of high school economics parallel the research findings for college students in the principles course. Siegfried and Fels (1979), in their review of the college studies, consider the many variants of the two basic models identified here:

> "(1) absolute achievement – the post-test score; (2) absolute improvement – the difference between the post-test and the pre-test score; (3) percentage improvement – absolute improvement divided by the pre-test score; and (4) gap closing measure – absolute improvement divided by the potential gain in score (which is the difference between the perfect score and the pre-test score). The absolute achievement score reflects the level of understanding at a point in time. It is a stock measure. The absolute improvement score measures the increment of learning during a course. An alternative is to use the post-test achievement score and control for initial economic understanding by including the pre-test score as an independent variable in the regression analysis." (p. 929)

Hanushek (1986, p. 1156-1157) considered a "level" form, in which the post-test is the dependent variable, and a "value-added" form, in which the dependent variable is the post-test minus pre-test. He states that in the value added form it is preferable to include the initial achievement measure as one of the inputs instead of using the difference as the dependent variable. As discussed in footnote 8, regressing the post-test on the pre-test and other covariates is not an equivalent alternative to using the difference between the post and pre-tests as the dependent variable. Both models suffer from statistical problems that have been relatively ignored.

7. Diamond and Medewitz (1990) use the nonlinear programming method Data Envelopment Analysis (DEA) to show that in the NAEE data participation in DEEP increases the efficiency of some classes and decreases the efficiency of other classes but overall the influence of DEEP is not favorable. Unfortunately the statistical properties of DEA are not well developed.

8. There are studies that show a negative relationship between a pretest and learning, where learning is defined by the difference between the post and pretest. Inherent in the model

$$\text{post} - \text{pre} = f(\text{pre}, \dots)$$

is a regression to the mean problem, however. The post - pre learning measure is bounded; it cannot exceed the posttest score, when the pretest is zero, and is conceptually troubling when the pretest is greater than the post test. As the change score approaches the extremes, the error is truncated, a mean of zero is not possible, and least squares estimators are biased. Simultaneity is introduced because the pretest score enters on the left and right hand side of the equation. As demonstrated by Becker and Salemi (1977), when learning is modeled and estimated correctly these problems can be overcome and learning can be related positively to the pretest, as one would expect. These problems cannot be overcome, however, by simply regressing the posttest on the pretest in a model of the type

$$\text{post} = h(\text{pre}, \dots)$$

This attainment model still has the regression to the mean problem as long as the test's ceiling and floor are reachable, although the estimated pretest coefficient typically will be positive. Any measurement error in the pretest, however, will result in correlation with the error term and the least squares estimators will be biased. To see this let "true" represent the unobservable true pre knowledge that is measured with error V. In a linear relationship, with variables measured as deviations from their means, and only one fixed slope parameter, α, to be estimated, we then have

$$\text{pre} = \alpha\text{true} + V$$

Let exp = 1, for a student in the experimental group, and 0, for a student in the control group. Ignoring all other covariates, a linear learning equation h ( ) is ideally written

$$\text{post} = \rho\text{true} + \omega\text{exp} + U$$

where $E(V) = E(U) = 0$, and $E(U\text{true}) = E(U\text{exp}) = E(V\text{true}) = 0$.

Because true pre knowledge is unobservable, however, the attainment equation actually estimated is

$$\text{post} = \beta\text{pre} + \omega\text{exp} + \varepsilon$$

For those in the control group (i.e., exp = 0),

$$E(\text{post}\,|\,\text{pre}) = \beta\text{pre} + E(e) = \beta\text{pre} - [\beta E(V\,|\,\text{pre})],\ \text{where } \beta = \rho/\alpha\,.$$

But since pre = αtrue + V, V and pre are dependent and $E(V\,|\,\text{pre})$ cannot equal zero. Thus, $E(\text{post}\,|\,\text{pre})$ cannot equal βpre, for those in the control group, and similarly $E(\text{post}\,|\,\text{pre}) \neq \beta\text{pre} + \omega$, for those in the experimental. Becker and Morey (1980) provide a simple framework that shows how the pretest may be correlated with the error term ε because the tests are administered in sequential time periods. Rogosa and Willett (1985) also consider individual student differences in measuring change over time. More complex panal data procedures could be addressed in the measurement of change. Salemi and Tauchen (1987) raise other issues in the specification of learning equations.

9. George Vredeveld, a reviewer of the Grimes and Register paper, raised an issue regarding the lack of control for geographical regions that tend to be related to union activity and high school student learning of economics.

10. Heath reports that from the initial sample of 3266 students, she could use only 610 records. Of these 610 students, those who did not elect to take an economics course had their actual TEL test score coded as zero. Tom Kniesner, a discussant of her paper, pointed out that the inclusion of this hypothetical score in the regression may have been the source of the high gender effect.

11. [*Ed. note*: Also see Chapter 9 for more discussion.]

12. Blinder (1992) applauded Albert Shanker for his proposal to conduct a nationwide contest in which the rewards are assigned "not by educational attainment at the end but by improvement over the period." According to Blinder, teachers' union leader Shanker is a good intuitive economist because "success is judged by performance ... That is how manufacturers are judged in a market economy. We examine the car, not the factory." But consumers do not examine the car to see if it has gotten better over a three year period; consumers examine the price and the car's characteristics relative to other cars in the market at the time of purchase. Similarly, those interested in an equity position within the company do not examine the car to see if it has gotten better; investors examine the expected return on equity, which may have little to do with winning a contest based on nonmarket values. The Wallace Co., a Houston, Texas oil-supply company, won the prestigious U.S. Commerce Department's Malcolm Baldrige National Quality Award in 1990; this distinction did not prevent Wallace from filing for Chapter 11 bankruptcy protection less than two years later. Similarly, for a school to win a national award for its test score improvements over a three year period may say nothing about the

marketability of its students' skills or parents' willingness to pay to have students attend that school.

13. Becker and Walstad (1990) take the learning model of Walstad and Soper (1988) as given and hypothesize that teachers determine whether to administer the posttest on the basis of the average pretest scores of the class and other student characteristics that are also in the Walstad-Soper model. To assess whether the average pretest as well as other measures of peer grouping should be in the learning equation is yet to be determined. Murnane, Newstead, and Olsen's (1985) residual analysis for selecting among alternative estimators may be helpful in such an analysis.

REFERENCES

Angrist, J., & Krueger, A. (1991). Does compulsory school attendance affect schooling and earnings? (Working Paper No. 3572). Cambridge, MA: National Bureau of Economic Research, Inc.

Bach, G. L., & Saunders, P. (1965). Economic education: Aspirations and achievements. *American Economic Review, 55*(3), 329-356.

Banaszak, R. (no date). *Directory of organizations providing business and economic education.* San Francisco: Foundation for Teaching Economics.

Baumol, W., & Highsmith, R. (1988). Variables affecting success in economic education: Preliminary findings from a new data base. *American Economic Review, 78*(2), 257-262.

Becker, W. (1982). The educational process and student achievement given uncertainty in measurement. *American Economic Review, 72*(1), 229-236.

Becker, W. (1983a). Economic education research: Part III, statistical estimation methods. *Journal of Economic Education, 14*(3), 4-15.

Becker, W. (1983b). Economic education research: Part II, new directions in theoretical model building. *Journal of Economic Education, 14*(2), 4-10.

Becker, W. (1983c). Economic education research: Part I, issues and questions. *Journal of Economic Education, 14*(1), 10-17.

Becker, W., Greene, W., & Rosen, S. (1990). Research on high school economic education. *The American Economic Review, 80*(2), 14-22.

Becker, W., Greene, W., & Rosen, S. (1990). Research on high school economic education. *Journal of Economic Education, 21*(3), 231-245.

Becker, W., & Morey, M. (1980). Pooled cross-sectional and time-series evaluation: Source, result and correction of serially correlated errors. *American Economic Review, 70*(2), 35-40.

Becker, W., & Rosen, S. (1992). The learning effect of assessment and evaluation in high school. *Economics of Education Review, 11*(2), 23-45.

Becker, W., & Salemi, M. (1977). The learning and cost effectiveness of AVT supplemented instruction: Specification of learning models. *Journal of Economic Education, 8*(2), 77-92.

Becker, W., & Walstad, W. (Eds.). (1987). *Econometric modeling in economic education research.* Boston: Kluwer-Nijhoff.

Becker, W., & Walstad, W. (1990). Data loss from pretest to posttest as a sample selection problem. *Review of Economics and Statistics, 72*(1), 184-188.

Beron, K. (1990). Joint determination of current classroom performance and additional economics classes: A binary/continuous model. *Journal of Economic Education, 21*(3), 255-264.

Blinder, A. (1991). Research in economic education and the teaching of economics. *Journal of Economic Education, 22*(3), 251-254.

Blinder, A. (1992). Adam Smith meet Albert Shanker. *Business Week* (December 14), 20.

Bosshardt, W., & Watts, M. (1990). Instructor effects and their determinants in precollege economic education. *Journal of Economic Education, 21*(3), 265-276.

Brasfield, D., Harrison, D., & McCoy, J. (1993). The impact of high school economics on college principles. *Journal of Economic Education, 24*(2), 99-111.

Buckles, S., & Freeman, V. (1984). A longitudinal analysis of a developmental economics education program. *Journal of Economic Education, 15*(1), 5-10.

Buckles, S., & Morton, J. (1988). The effects of advance placement on college introductory economics courses. *American Economic Review, 78*(2), 263-268.

Buckles, S., Strom, R., & Walstad, W. (1984). An evaluation of a state consumer and economic education program: Implications for effective program delivery. *Journal of Economic Education, 15*(2), 101-110.

Card, D., & Krueger, A. (1990). Does school quality matter? Returns to education and the characteristics of public schools in the United States. National Bureau of Economic Research, Inc. (Working Paper No. 3358).

Chizmar, J., & Halinski, R. (1983). Performance in the basic economics test (BET) and "Trade-offs." *Journal of Economic Education, 14*(1), 18-29.

Chizmar, J., McCarney, B., Halinski, R., & Racich, M. (1985). "Give and take," economics achievement, and basic skills development. *Journal of Economic Education, 16*(2), 99-110.

Dawson, G. (1977). Research in economic education at the precollege level. In D. Wentworth, W. L. Hansen, & S. Hawke (Eds.), *Perspectives on economic education* (pp. 85-103). New York: Joint Council on Economic Education.

Dawson, G. (1982). A note on the teaching of economics through American history. *Journal of Economic Education, 13*(1), 65-68.

Diamond, A. M., Jr., & Medewitz, J. N. (1990). Use of data envelopment analysis in an evaluation of the efficiency of the DEEP program for economic education. *Journal of Economic Education, 21*(3), 337-354.

Eberts, R., & Stone, J. (1987). Teacher unions and the productivity of public schools. *Industrial and Labor Relations Review, 40*(3), 354-363.

Evans, M. (1992). An estimation of race and gender role model effect in teaching high school. *Journal of Economic Education, 23*(3), 209-217.

Ferber, M., Birnbaum, B., & Green, C. (1983). Gender differences in economic knowledge: A reevaluation of the evidence. *Journal of Economic Education, 14*(2), 24-37.

Green, G., & Jaquess, S. (1987). The effect of part-time employment on academic achievement. *Journal of Educational Research, 80*(6), 325-329.

Grimes, P., & Register, C. (1990). Teachers' unions and student achievement in high school economics. *Journal of Economic Education, 21*(3), 297-306.

Hallows, K., & Becker, W. (forthcoming). What works and what doesn't: A practitioner's guide to research findings in economic education. *International Journal of Social Education.*

Hansen, W. L., Kelley, A., & Weisbrod, B. (1970). Economic efficiency and the distribution of benefits from college instruction. *American Economic Review, 60*(2), 364-369.

Hanushek, E. A. (1986). The economics of schooling. *Journal of Economic Literature, 24*(3), 1141-1177.

Hanushek, E. A. (1989). The impact of differential expenditures on school performance. *Educational Researcher, 18*(5), 45-51, 62.

Heath, J. (1989). An econometric model of the role of gender in economic education. *American Economic Review, 79*(2), 226-230.

Heckman, J., & Hotz, V. J. (1989). Choosing among alternative nonexperimental methods for estimating the impact of social programs: The case of manpower training. *Journal of the American Statistical Association, 84*(408), 862-874.

Highsmith, R. (1989). *A survey of state mandates for economics instruction.* New York: Joint Council on Economic Education.

Highsmith, R., & Baumol, W. (1989). *Education in economics: Evidence on determinants of effectiveness.* Mimeo.

Jackstadt, S., & Gootaert, C. (1980). Gender, gender stereotyping, and socioeconomic background as determinants of economic knowledge and learning. *Journal of Economic Education, 12*(1), 34-40.

Lewis, D., Dalgaard, B., & Boyer, C. (1985). Cost-effectiveness of computer assisted economics instruction. *American Economic Review, 75*(2), 91-96.

Lillydahl, J. (1990). Academic achievement and part-time employment of high school students. *Journal of Economic Education, 21*(3), 307-316.

Lopus, J. (1990). Do additional expenditures increase achievement in the high school economics class? *Journal of Economic Education, 21*(3), 277-286.

Lumsden, K., & Scott, A. (1987). The economics student reexamined: Male-female differences in comprehension. *Journal of Economic Education, 18*(4), 365-375.

Lynch, G. (1990). The effect of teacher coursework on student learning: Evidence from the TEL. *Journal of Economic Education, 21*(3), 287-296.

Marlin, J. (1991). State mandated economic education, teacher attitudes, and student learning. *Journal of Economic Education, 22*(1), 5-14.

Martin, D., & Bender, D. (1985). "Trade-offs," field dependence/ independence, and sex-based economics comprehension differences. *Journal of Economic Education, 16*(1), 62-70.

Miller, S. (1988). Student test scores and textbook deficiencies: Is there a relationship? *Journal of Private Enterprise, 4*(1), 85-96.

Murnane, R., Newstead, S., & Olsen, R. (1985). Comparing public and private schools: The puzzling role of selectivity bias. *Journal of Business & Economic Statistics, 3*(1), 369-377.

Myatt, A., & Waddell, C. (1990). An approach to testing the effectiveness of the teaching and learning of economics at high school. *Journal of Economic Education, 21*(3), 355-363.

Nelson, J., & Sheffrin, S. (1991). Economic literacy or economic ideology. *Journal of Economic Perspectives, 5*(3), 157-165.

Peterson, N. (1989). Self-selection in the NAEE database. Presented at the Western Economic Association meeting, Lake Tahoe, Nevada.

Peterson, N. (1992). The high school economics course and its impact on economic knowledge. *Journal of Economic Education, 23*(1), 5-16.

Rhine, S. (1989). The effect of state mandates on student performance. *American Economic Review Proceedings, 79*(2), 231-235.

Rogosa, D. R., & Willett, J. B. (1985). Understanding correlates of change by modeling individual differences in growth. *Psychometrika, 50*(2), 203-228.

Rosen, S. (1987). Some economics of teaching. *Journal of Labor Economics, 5*(4), 561-575.

Salemi, M. K., & Tauchen, G. E. (1987). Simultaneous nonlinear learning models. In W. Becker & W. Walstad (Eds.), *Econometric modeling in economic education research* (pp. 207-223). Boston: Kluwer-Nijhoff.

Saunders, P. (1964). The effectiveness of 'The American Economy' in teaching secondary school teachers. *American Economic Review, 54*(3), 396-400.

Saunders, P. (1970). Does high school economics have a lasting impact? *Journal of Economic Education, 2*(1), 39-55.

Saunders, P., Bach, G. L., Calderwood, J. D., & Hansen, W. L. (1984). *A Framework for Teaching the Basic Concepts*. New York: Joint Council on Economic Education.

Schober, H. (1984). The effects of inservice training on participating teachers and students in their economics classes. *Journal of Economic Education, 18*(3), 282-296.

Siegfried, J. (1979). Male-female differences in economic education: A survey. *Journal of Economic Education, 10*(2), 1-11.

Siegfried, J., & Fels, R. (1979). Research on teaching college economics: A survey. *Journal of Economic Literature, 17*(3), 923-969.

Siegfried, J., & Walstad, W. (1990). Research on teaching college economics. In P. Saunders & W. Walstad (Eds.), *The principles of economics course: A handbook for instructors* (pp. 270-296). New York: McGraw-Hill.

Soper, J., & Walstad, W. (1983). On measuring economic attitudes. *Journal of Economic Education, 14*(4), 4-17.

Soper, J., & Walstad, W. (1987). *The test of economic literacy: Examiner's manual* (2nd ed.). New York: Joint Council on Economic Education.

Soper, J., & Walstad, W. (1988). What is high school economics? Posttest knowledge, attitudes, and course content. *Journal of Economic Education, 19*(1), 37-51.

Stigler, G. (1970). The case, if any, for economic education. *Journal of Economic Education, 1*(1), 77-84.

Thorton, D., & Vredeveld, G. (1977). In-service education and its effect on secondary students: A new approach. *Journal of Economic Education, 8*(1), 93-99.

Vredeveld, G. M., & Jeong, J-H. (1990). Market efficiency and student-teacher goal agreement in the high school economics course: A simultaneous choice modeling approach. *Journal of Economic Education, 21*(3), 317-335.

Walstad, W. (March 25, 1989). Economic literacy in the schools. *Vital Speeches of the Day, 55*(11), 327-328.

Walstad, W. (1991). A flawed ideological critique. *Journal of Economic Perspectives, 5*(3), 167-173.

Walstad, W. (1992). Economics instruction in high school. *Journal of Economic Literature, 30*(4), 2019-2051.

Walstad, W., & Soper, J. (1988). A report card on the economic literacy of U.S. high school students. *American Economic Review, 79*(2), 251-256.

Walstad, W., & Soper, J. (1989). What is high school economics? Factors contributing to student achievement and attitudes. *Journal of Economic Education, 20*(1), 23-38.

Walstad, W., & Van Scyoc, L. (1990). The effect of textbooks on economic understanding and attitudes in high school economics courses. *Journal of Research and Development in Education, 24*(1), 46-54.

Walstad, W., & Watts, M. (1985). Teaching economics in the schools: A review of survey findings. *Journal of Economic Education, 16*(2), 135-146.

Watts, M. (1985). A statewide assessment of precollege economic understanding and DEEP. *Journal of Economic Education, 16*(3), 225-237. [Errata. (1985). *Journal of Economic Education, 16*(4), 286.]

Watts, M. (1987). Student gender and school district differences affecting the stock and flow of economic knowledge. *Review of Economics & Statistics, 69*(3), 561-566.

Watts, M. (1991). Research on DEEP: The first 25 years. In W. Walstad & J. Soper (Eds.), *Effective economic education* (pp. 81-98). Washington, DC: National Education Association and Joint Council on Economic Education.

Weaver, A., Deaton, W., & Reach, S. (1987). The effect of economic education summer institutes for teachers on the achievement of their students. *Journal of Educational Research, 80*(5), 296-299.

Wentworth, D., Hansen, W. L., & Hawke, S. (Eds.). (1977). *Perspectives on economic education.* New York: Joint Council on Economic Education.

CHAPTER 7

AN ASSESSMENT OF ECONOMICS INSTRUCTION IN AMERICAN HIGH SCHOOLS

William B. Walstad

Prior to 1960 serious problems confronted economics instruction in American high schools. A major concern was the limited amount of economics taught because few high school students ever took a separate course in economics, or received economics instruction in the context of other social studies courses. Compounding that problem was the way that economics was taught. Instruction in separate economics courses was descriptive, dry, and rarely included economic analysis. Coverage in textbooks and other instructional materials lacked economic analysis, and many organizations were inundating the schools with pamphlets and other materials, some of which were simply propaganda. Many high school teachers were inadequately prepared to teach economics or deal with slanted materials, so teachers' value judgments often substituted for analysis in classroom discussions of economic problems or issues. Finally, economists and educational organizations showed little interest in, and provided no guidance for, the teaching of economics below the college level.

To address these problems, the American Economic Association (AEA) and the Committee on Economic Development (CED) established the National Task Force on Economic Education in 1960. A report was issued a year later that offered recommendations for improving economic education in high schools and at lower grades (Bach et al., 1961). The twelve recommendations, which are listed in Table 7.1, served as a blueprint for sweeping changes in economics instruction in high schools in the United States for over three decades.

Table 7.1: Recommendations of the 1961 National Task Force on Economic Education

Increase Instruction

1. We recommend that more time be devoted in high school curricula to the development of economic understanding.
2. We recommend that wherever feasible students take a high school course in economics or its equivalent under another title (such as Problems of American Democracy); and that in all high schools of substantial size there be at least an elective senior-year course in economics.
3. We recommend that courses in problems of American democracy (now taken by perhaps half of all high school students) devote a substantial portion of their time to development of economic understanding of the kind outlined.
4. We recommend that more economic analysis be included in history courses.
5. We recommend that all business education curricula include a required course in economics.
6. We recommend that economic understanding be emphasized at several other points in the entire school curriculum.

Content Revision

7. We recommend central emphasis on the rational way of thinking presented in Chapter II should be a prime objective of the teaching of economics.
8. We recommend that examination of controversial issues should be included, where appropriate, in teaching economics.

Teacher Education

9. To improve the ability of teachers, we recommend several steps.
    a. We recommend that teacher certification requirements in all states require a minimum of one full year (6 unit) course in college economics for all social studies and business education teachers.
    b. We recommend that school boards and administrators consider these certification standards as minimum requirements, and they take steps to enforce higher standards wherever feasible.
    c. To help present teachers improve their economic competence, we recommend increased use of summer workshops, teacher participation in a nationwide television economics course planned for 1962-63, and return to college for additional work in economics.

Table 7.1: Recommendations of the 1961 National Task Force on Economic Education Continued

d. We recommend that colleges preparing teachers improve the economics courses offered for this purpose, and establish other opportunities for high school teachers to increase their economic understanding.

Materials

10. We emphasize the need for more effective high school teaching materials and recommend that steps be taken by private publishers, foundations, and others to increase the supply of such materials.

Involvement of Others

11. We recommend that professional economists play a more active part in helping to raise the level of economics in the schools.
12. We urge widespread public support, both private and governmental, for the improvement of economics in the schools.

Source: Bach et al., 1961, pp. 64-77.

This chapter assesses whether any substantial gains have occurred in the teaching and learning of economics in American high schools since the early 1960s.[1] The answer is in some ways simple, and in others, complex: simple because the overall improvement in economic education in high schools has been substantial; complex because it requires assessing how much progress has been made in such areas as course enrollments, achievement outcomes, coverage and emphasis in economic content, teacher preparation, educational materials, and, support from economists and organizations.

The breadth of the assessment forces some constraints on what can and should be covered in this chapter. First, a detailed analysis of research methods is omitted to avoid duplication because there are other writings on research questions, theoretical models, and econometric problems (Becker and Walstad, 1987). Second, this chapter offers a broader and more historical perspective than found in the review of research models and major empirical findings in Chapter 6. Third, the primary focus is on economic education in senior high schools. Some findings on economic education in lower grades and other topics are described at times, as they relate to the high school results, but they receive minor attention because they are addressed in other publications (Walstad and Soper, 1991).

The assessment is divided into seven sections and follows the order of the recommendations in the National Task Force report. The first section describes course enrollment trends in economics and other subjects, looks at the influence of state mandates and testing, and explains what efforts have been made to integrate economics into the school curriculum. The second section briefly reviews the empirical research on coursework and economics achievement. The third section describes the economics content recommended for high school students and discusses the controversies over the content guidelines. Section four turns to teacher education and examines its influence on student performance. Changes in instructional materials are identified in section five. The sixth section discusses the role of economists and organizations in expanding and strengthening economic education. The concluding seventh section describes the current concerns about economics instruction in American high schools.

I. ECONOMICS IN THE HIGH SCHOOL CURRICULUM

More teaching of economics in the schools was called for in the first six recommendations of the National Task Force (Table 7.1, #1-6). Increases in instruction can be achieved by having students take a separate economics course, by including more economics in related high school courses, and by infusing the teaching of economics in other subjects in the kindergarten through twelfth grade curriculum. Data and studies show that there is more widespread inclusion of economics in the school curriculum than in past years, but the penetration is still limited.

Economics and Other Courses

As shown in Table 7.2, enrollments in economics courses in public and private high schools increased significantly over the years. In 1961, only about 16 percent of public and private secondary students in grades 9 to 12 took an economics course. By 1982, about 22 percent of high school graduates completed an economics course. The percentage doubled to 44 percent by 1990. The dramatic increase from 1982 to 1990 probably reflects the implementation of state mandates for economics coursework during the 1980s, which will be discussed later.

Traditionally, economics courses are taught in the social studies curriculum in high school. A typical sequence in the social studies would have students take a year of civics in ninth grade, a year of world history or world studies in tenth grade, and a year of United States history in eleventh grade. In the twelfth grade, students would have the option of taking two semester-length courses from a set of courses that would include economics, United States government, psychology, sociology or social problems, and other course titles that vary from year to year (Jenness, 1990, p. 20). There are, of course, deviations from this norm because some school districts offer economics in grades nine, ten or eleven, and because in recent years more states and school districts have made

Table 7.2: Enrollment in Economics and Other Courses (as a percentage of all high school graduates)

	Selected Years					
Courses	1961	1973	1977	1982	1987	1990
Economics	16%	20%	22%	22%	29%	44%
Psychology	8	22	22	24	27	25
Sociology	18	32	24	19	17	19
Government	44	45	46	46	48	59
Problems of Democracy	21	11	7	3	5	3
Government & Economics	---	---	---	3	9	10
Consumer Courses	4	14	---	15	14	14
Consumer Economics	2	6	---	6	6	6
Consumer Education	2	8	---	9	8	8
General Business	24	20	---	18	17	16

Source: Walstad, 1992, p. 2023, and National Center for Education Statistics (1993).

economics a required course for students. The placement of economics in the twelfth grade, however, has a long tradition in the social studies curriculum.

The middle part of Table 7.2 offers a perspective on enrollment trends for economics compared with other subjects that are usually taught as social studies electives in high school. The percentage of high school graduates taking an economics course increased substantially, but so did the percentage taking a psychology course until 1987, and then enrollments fell. Interest in sociology also rose and fell over the years. The fraction of high school graduates completing courses in United States government is much larger than for economics because government is often a required course. Its enrollment has shown the same large increase from 1987 to 1990 as economics.

The National Task Force saw "no practical alternative" to a semester or full-year course in economics for achieving the level of economic understanding it had outlined (p. 66). The enrollment data suggest that more students today are meeting that objective, with the percentage of high school graduates who took the course almost tripling since 1961. Table 7.2 also shows that many high school graduates (56 percent in 1990) received no formal instruction in economics in a separate course, and therefore learned economics in other ways, if at all.

Government and Economics Courses

In the 1960s, a "Problems of American Democracy" course was taken by many high school students. This course was considered by the National Task Force to be a possible equivalent to a separate economics course, especially if more economics was included in the "problems" course (Table 7.1, #2 and #3). As shown in Table 7.2, the percentage of high school graduates taking a problems course has fallen over the years, from about 20 percent to only about 3 percent by 1990. That change occurred with the addition of other political science or government courses to the social studies curriculum, which substituted for the problems or issues course.

During the 1980s, a "government and economics" course emerged that has some potential to fulfill the expectations of the National Task Force. The percentage of students who completed this course rose from three percent in 1982 to ten percent in 1990. What is not clear from the data in Table 7.1, is whether a government and economics course lasts for a year or a semester. A semester course may be more appealing to social studies educators because it allows students to take other elective or required social studies courses in another semester. In that case, however, a semester course in government and economics would not be equivalent to a semester course in economics.

Consumer Economics Courses

Other alternatives to a separate course in economics for many noncollege-bound students, and also for some college-bound students, are elective or required courses in "consumer economics" or "consumer education" (Brenneke, 1981). These course are taught in different areas of the high school curriculum – social studies, home economics, or business education – with course placement depending on the school district or state guidelines.

In the early 1960s, consumer economics and consumer education courses were taken by only about 4 percent of high school graduates. Enrollments grew during the 1960s and early 1970s with the increase in interest in consumer topics and issues. The 1982, 1987, and 1990 data indicate that enrollment remained relatively steady with about six percent of graduates completing consumer economics courses and another eight or nine percent taking consumer education courses. The question many economists have raised about these consumer courses, more often than they do about courses in government and economics, is how much economics is learned. Finding on this issue are discussed in the third section.

General Business Courses

The National Task Force called for a required course in economics in the business education curriculum (Table 7.1, #5) that might serve the needs of students who were taking a business or vocational program of studies and who were not likely to attend college. This required course never became part of the business education curriculum, and perhaps the closest substitutes are courses in "general business." Textbooks for these courses cover some basic economics, especially microeconomic concepts, with application to practical business issues and problems (Brown and Clow, 1987).

The titles of general business courses vary and include: (1) introduction to business; (2) cooperative business education; (3) business and office education; (4) entrepreneurship; and (5) business and management. Enrollments in general business courses stood at about 24 percent of high school graduates in 1961. The data in Table 7.2 indicate that enrollments in these courses have declined, but they were taken by about 16 percent of high school graduates in 1990.

State Mandates

As shown in Table 7.3, a significant change affecting enrollments and the status of economics during the 1980s was the rise in the number of states that require some type of course in economics for high school graduation. In 1982, seven states, which accounted for 11 percent of public high school graduates, had a mandated economics course. By 1987, mandates were in effect in thirteen states, covering about 26 percent of high school graduates. Adoption of mandates in California and New York in late 1980s meant that by 1990 about 45 percent of students graduating from public high schools took some form of a required course in economics.

Most mandated courses would be considered similar to a traditional economics course, but there are differences among the courses because some states have adopted a special emphasis in their legislation. The most popular emphasis, found in the legislation for seven states, is for an economics course that features the characteristics and preaches the benefits of the "free enterprise system" (Arizona, Florida, Georgia, Idaho, Louisiana, Tennessee, and Texas). Coverage of "consumer education" topics is stressed in the legislation in four state requirements (Florida, Idaho, Oregon, and Tennessee). One mandate combines the teaching of economics with civics or government (North Carolina). In New

Table 7.3: Public High School Graduates in States Affected by Mandates for Economics-related Courses for Graduation: 1982, 1987, and 1990 (in thousands)

Category	1982	1987	1990
States	AL, AZ, GA LA, OR, SC TN	Plus: FL, ID NH, NC TX, WV	Plus: CA, IN NY
Number of Mandate States	7	13	16
Public H. S. Grads in Mandate States	297	641	1,114
All Public H. S. Grads	2,705	2,433	2,491
Percentage of Public H. S. Grads in Mandate States	11%	26%	45%

Source: Walstad, 1992, p. 2025.

Hampshire, the mandate calls for a course in "basic business and economic education."[2]

Infusion

The National Task Force recommended that more economic analysis be taught in United States and world history courses (Table 7.1, #4). The task force members also wanted more economics included throughout the school curriculum – in both elementary and secondary grades – and believed that some economics could be taught in courses such as geography, civics, or mathematics. The suggestions, combined with attempts to include more economics in problems courses and in the business education curriculum, became the basis for an "infusion" model of curriculum change.

The great appeal of the infusion approach is that it gives teachers and school administrators the flexibility to tailor economics instruction to fit the constraints of a school's curriculum. Many constraints currently make it impossible or impractical for many students to take a separate course or unit on economics, especially in lower grades. Another benefit of the infusion approach is that students receive instruction on basic economics that prepares them for a culminating, "capstone" course on economics in high school. Infusion also has value in making economics an integral part of the education of all students, and not simply a subject that is taught exclusively in a separate course for college-bound students. In principle, at least, that's the way infusion is supposed to work.

The infusion strategy has been widely adopted by schools, as indicated by the results of a national survey in which teachers listed over thirty different classes in which they taught economics (Yankelovich, Skelly, and White, 1981). One significant reason for this development is that state legislation has encouraged the teaching of economics in various sub-4Xjects in elementary and secondary grades. By 1989, 19 states mandated the infusion of economics, sometimes beginning as early as kindergarten (Highsmith, 1989). Although these states account for about 51 percent of graduates from public high schools, it certainly should not be assumed that all students in these states receive a similar type or a high quality of instruction in economics. The infusion legislation differs substantially by state, implementation often depends on the interest of individual school districts, and the quality of instruction varies by teacher.

Testing Students

In recent years, required testing of students is one action that has been taken to improve economics instruction. Required testing of economics is called for in the legislation of at least six states, usually as part of a broader assessment of social studies subjects (Highsmith, 1989). This required testing probably affects 10 percent of high school students.

There are also voluntary tests in economics that students can take, some offered by states and others offered by nonprofit organizations. For example, the Advanced Placement (AP) examinations in economics were developed by the College Entrance Examination Board (CEEB) in 1989 for high ability, college-bound students who want to receive credit from colleges for completing the equivalent of a one semester course in microeconomics, in macroeconomics, or both courses. AP economics students attend a semester or a year-long course in high school that covers the content typical for most introductory college economics courses.

The number of candidates taking an AP exam in economics increased substantially from 1989 to 1991, from about 3,000 per exam in 1989 to about 5,000 per exam in 1991, probably because more teachers and schools established AP-courses, and because more students knew about the courses. Even in 1991, however, only about two percent of high school graduates took an AP exam in economics, and of this group, only about 60 percent received college credit, assuming a score of three or better (qualified to extremely well qualified) was set as the cutoff by the university which accepted this credit (CEEB, 1992).

The development of the AP economics exam and the testing of economics in statewide testing programs are positive indicators of the perceived value of economics for students. Less progress has been made, however, with having economics tested at the federal level. The problem is that economics is viewed as a minor subject in the education of students compared with other social studies subjects such as history or geography. The National Assessment of Educational Progress (NAEP) is widely considered to be the "nation's report card." NAEP has conducted assessments of history, geography, and civics, but economics is yet to be tested. Although economics is being considered for NAEP testing in 1998, the probability of that occurring is far from certain.

II. RESEARCH ON COURSE INSTRUCTION

Extensive research has been conducted on the effectiveness of economics instruction in different types of courses. This research has evolved with the development of instruments for measuring achievement. The basic findings suggest that not all courses are equally effective in promoting student learning of economics.

The TEL and Courses

Research in economic education has been advanced by the creation of a battery of standardized achievement tests in economics. The first national test for measuring the economic knowledge of high school students was the *Test of Economic Understanding*. By the mid-1970s, concerns about the age of the norms and the content validity of the TEU led to a substantive revision that resulted in the first edition of the *Test of Economic Literacy* (TEL). The TEL itself was revised in 1986 (Soper and Walstad, 1987).

The TEL is a valid and reliable test that has the capacity to distinguish high school students with more knowledge from students with less knowledge. On form A of the TEL, students with economics instruction had a mean score of 23 points and students without economics instruction had a mean score of 18 points. Although this score differences appears to be small, it is not uncommon for standardized tests in economics to show this size difference. The reasons are many and are often related to the test construction and measurement (Millman and Greene, 1989). First, limits to the number of questions that can be reasonably completed by students in a fixed time period limit the range of scores. Second, concerns about making a test too difficult for students and demands to balance content coverage restrict score differences. Third, the opportunity for guessing on questions with a high probability of success reduces the spread between scores of different student groups. Fourth, the sample of students with instruction and the sample of students without instruction usually have similar characteristics, and therefore when the classroom time is limited, there may not be much difference in test scores. Finally, the lack of incentive to take the test because it may not count for a grade may limit changes from a pretest at the beginning of a course to a posttest at the end of a course. These and other influences tend to decrease the magnitude of score differences on standardized achievement tests in economics such as the TEL.

Several national studies have used the TEL to examine the contribution of an economics course to economic understanding relative to other courses. In one such study, students were enrolled either in an economics course, a consumer economics course, or a social studies course, such as United States history or government, in which the teacher either included or did not include economics. The regression results showed that students who took an economics course scored 3.8 TEL points higher, and that students who took a social studies course that included economics scored about 1 point higher, when compared to students enrolled in a social studies course where the teacher did not include economics, but there was no significant contribution to economics learning for students in a consumer economics course.[3]

Overall, the research evidence on economics instruction in several types of courses confirms the value of a formal course in economics as a means for improving economic understanding. Other content may be taught in consumer economics courses, but little knowledge of basic economics seems to be transmitted to students. Some courses in the social studies, such as United States history or government, may contribute to economics achievement, but the size of that contribution is limited and probably depends to a large degree on whether a teacher makes a conscious effort to include economics in a course. Social studies courses simply have the potential to lay the groundwork for economics learning in a separate course in economics.

Problems with Infusion and Economics Courses

The coursework findings highlight the need for a more realistic view of the infusion approach to economics instruction. Infusion has great intuitive appeal and is portrayed to school administrators as a relatively inexpensive way of teaching economics. There are obstacles, however, that prevent the realization of any substantial educational benefits, and eliminate the potential effectiveness of the approach. These barriers to economics learning in other high school courses, and even at lower grades, include: (1) deficiencies in the economics preparation of teachers for whom economics is not likely to be a major responsibility or interest; (2) the poor quality of the coverage of economics in textbooks in non-economics subjects; (3) the lack of supplementary materials for those subjects; (4) inadequate discussion in state or school district curriculum guides on how to include economics in different courses or grades, and, (5) limited classroom time for instruction. The obstacles, either separately or in combination, reduce the contribution from infusion to the development of economic understanding (Walstad and Watts, 1985).[4]

There also needs to be more realism about what can be achieved in a high school course in economics alone. The TEL data show that there was a significant gain in economic knowledge from taking an economics course; yet, at the end of the course students could correctly answer only about half the test questions. This low level of performance can be attributed to many factors, some associated with teacher and course characteristics, others related to social and educational problems plaguing high schools and students, and still others connected to measurement issues. The most important reason is the small amount of instructional time actually devoted to economics throughout the school curriculum. Major school subjects, such as math or history, are taught to all students over many years in concentrated units and courses that begin in the early grades. By contrast, intensive development of economic understanding depends almost exclusively on a one-semester course that is typically taught in the last year of high school and that is taken only by a minority of students.[5]

III. CONTENT IN ECONOMICS COURSES

High school instructors who teach economics must answer two major questions: what economics content should be taught, and how should economics be taught. To help teachers with these important decisions, some economists have prepared content guides that identify key economic concepts and methods for teaching economics in the classroom. The development of these guides has not been without controversy.

Economic Concepts and Approach

The primary mission of the National Task Force was to "describe the minimum understanding of economics essential for good citizenship and attainable by high school students, with the goal of providing helpful guidelines for high school teachers, administrators, and school boards" (p. 4). For that reason, two major recommendations (Table 7.1, #7 and #8) and about two-thirds of the report were devoted to the ideal approach and content for teaching economics in high school. The report emphasized an analytical and more objective approach to teaching economics. This approach involved the use of a basic problem solving model where students define an economic problem, identify and weigh goals and objectives, specify the alternative solutions, and analyze the consequences of choosing an alternative. Ideally, teachers would also cover some 45 economic concepts and institutions that were viewed as essential for the economic understanding of high school graduates.

The National Task Force document essentially served as the major content statement for what should be taught in the schools until it was replaced by the *Framework for Teaching Economics: Basic Concepts* (Hansen et al., 1977). The publication of the *Framework* was a significant improvement over the ambitious National Task Force outline because it reorganized and reduced the economic content to a shorter list of essential concepts and emphasized the relationships among economic concepts and topics. The new guide continued to stress the use of an analytical and rational approach to the teaching of economic issues and problems in the classroom, as did the National Task Force report before it. The *Framework* was revised in 1984 to incorporate further content changes, but the key elements of economic understanding were retained (Saunders et al., 1984).[6]

The *Framework* significantly influenced economics instruction and the economics curriculum in American schools. The effects can be found in curriculum guides and in teaching materials produced by school districts, state departments of education, and other organizations (Symmes, 1991). *Framework* concepts are covered in many high school textbooks (Miller, 1988), and textbook publishers given emphasis to the *Framework* in promoting texts. The widespread acceptance and use of the *Framework* indicate that it represents the *current* consensus among many economists and economic educators on guidelines for what economics should be taught and, in general, how economics should be taught in the schools (Buckles, 1991).

Criticisms

Three general criticisms have been leveled against content guides in economics. The first concerns whether economists should make recommendations about economic content for the school curriculum. George Stigler (1963) lamented the professional sponsorship of the National Task Force report because preferential status was given to the views of some economists that would have a profound influence on the views of noneconomists. Stigler recognized that high school economics was in a poor state at the time, but he opposed a monopoly of opinions about the content of high school economics that he felt characterized the report, even if the National Task Force consisted of economists who "are representative of the central range of professional opinion" (p. 654).

A second criticism involves the feasibility of proposed guidelines. Stigler found the contents in the National Task Force report to be similar to a table of contents for a college principles textbook and he wondered how the high school course could ever be successful in teaching this extensive content given the maturity of students and the lack of economics preparation among teachers. Problems with the transfer of ideas from the report to the classroom was also a complaint made by Wagner (1963). He found the content discussion and recommendations to be too broad to guide school programs, and argued that school administrators and teachers would need more help to make economics an essential part of the school curriculum.

The feasibility and usefulness issues raised by Stigler and Wagner were addressed to some extent in the two editions of the *Framework*, and also in instructional materials developed for teachers and students by other economists and educators (Symmes, 1991). The pedagogical work is by no means complete. An extension of the *Framework* is *Economics: What and When*, a "scope-and-sequence" document that describes the economic concepts from the *Framework* in short statements and in student language to make it easier for educators to use (Gilliard et al., 1988). The guide also recommends the grade levels at which the basic economic concepts and generalizations should be introduced and how understanding of economics should progress as students move through the school curriculum. Initial support for the recommendations was provided in a survey study by Watts (1987a), but further work is necessary to establish the effectiveness of propositions for coverage and grade placement of economic concepts.

The third and major criticism focuses on acceptance of the economic content. Reaching a consensus among the economists serving on a committee producing a guide is only the first small step in the on-going debate over the economic content. Once published and circulated, a guide is open to scrutiny by the public. The news media or special interest groups may hold different views about the accuracy or emphasis in economic content, and in the extreme, may want economics taught in a way that may border on preaching or indoctrination. The *Wall Street Journal*, for example, criticized the National Task Force report for problems in content emphasis in four lengthy editorials in 1961 and 1962.[7]

Content guides are subject to further scrutiny from other economists, who may object to the recommendations for what should be taught in the schools. Paul Samuelson (1987) commented on his early involvement in the work of the National Task Force and the difficulty of maintaining a consensus about what should be taught in high school at a 1986 MIT conference:

> About three decades ago, economics made a comeback in the high schools. And, for better or worse, I don't think you're going to be able to put the genie back into the bottle. Around 1960, Lee Bach dragged me, kicking and screaming, into curricular committees trying to decide what should be taught in the new renaissance. Each morning, the rock has to be rolled up the hill again, and here you all are struggling with the perpetual problem of curricular coverage. (p. 107)

At this conference, several prominent economists, often selected for their unique views on economics, offered critiques of each major section of the *Framework*. These criticisms usually arose from larger concerns about the discipline of economics.

The content of the *Framework* represents mainstream economics, albeit in a limited and condensed form. To the extent that there are perceived omissions and limitations in mainstream economics, they will be reflected in the *Framework*. In reply to the critics, Baumol (1988) stated that "there is absolutely nothing wrong with the current state of economics and that, besides, the discipline's fundamental problems are being remedied as quickly as can reasonably be expected" (p. 323). In his view, the alternative paradigms presented at the conference were largely unworkable as the basis for structuring the content of pre-college economics. If this conclusion is accepted, it implies that changes in future editions of the *Framework*, and in the content of most American high school courses in economics, will most likely result from major shifts in mainstream thinking about economics.

IV. TEACHER PREPARATION

Two basic approaches are available for improving the economic understanding of teachers. The first involves reaching students who are preparing to become teachers and getting them to take more economics in their "preservice" training. The other approach stresses improved teacher education in economics through "inservice" courses and workshops for teachers who already are licensed and currently teaching in the schools. Research shows that teacher preparation in economics is essential for student learning of the subject, but preservice and inservice coursework in economics is often limited.

Teacher Coursework

In response to the need to improve the level of economic understanding among teachers, the National Task Force called for states to require a minimum of two semester courses in economics for all prospective social studies and business education teachers (Table 7.1, #9a and #9b). Even higher standards were proposed by a 1985 committee studying teacher education in economics (Hermanowicz et al., 1985). This committee recommended that all future teachers be required to take *one* basic course in economics, or preferably the principles sequence in economics. All prospective teachers of social studies, business education, and home economics courses should be required to take at least *three* semester courses in economics, including the principles sequence and an advanced course. Teachers who specialize in teaching economics in secondary schools should complete the equivalent of a field of concentration in economics consisting of at least *six* semester courses. Teachers of advanced placement or honors courses in economics should complete at least *ten* courses, or the equivalent of a major in economics.

Current state standards for the initial licensure or certification of secondary social studies teachers – those most likely to teach economics – do not fulfill even the minimal recommendations of the National Task Force. Of the 51 certification agencies, only 11 had a specific semester credit-hour requirement in economics in 1988-1989 (Dumas, Weible, and Evans, 1990). The average requirement in these eleven states was 4.8 credits, which represented about 11.5 percent of the minimum 42 credit hours in history and the social sciences required for social studies certification in most states.

Weakness in economics preparation is also found in studies of economics courses taken by employed teachers, but many teachers have taken more economics courses than would be expected based on state certification requirements. One significant reason has been the growth of inservice programs, which has become crucial for correcting some deficiencies in teacher knowledge from preservice education. The inservice activity includes courses and workshops that are offered by many colleges and universities and nonprofit organizations. The largest national effort is conducted through the collegiate network of the National Council on Economic Education. About 120,000 elementary and secondary teachers, roughly five percent of the nation's teachers, annually participate in its programs.

Research on Teacher Education

An important research question is whether the number of courses taken by a teacher makes a contribution to student understanding of economics. This question has been investigated in national TEL studies using different model specifications or estimation techniques, and the results consistently show that teacher coursework in economics significantly contributes to student learning of economics. Compared with courses, findings on the influence of other teacher variables on student economics achievement generally shows insignificant or inconsistent effects in regression studies, although the number of studies may be too limited to draw a firm conclusion about any factor. Among the factors that have been studied include noncredit workshops, the number of years since a teacher's last economics course, the number of years of full-time teaching experience (which may be measuring about the same factor as the number of years since the last economics course), the percentage of the teacher's load that is economics, and teacher attitudes about economics.[8]

If coursework in economics is the only reliable or well-documented way for teachers to improve student learning of economics, it may be worthwhile to find new ways to increase the number of teachers who take economics. This objective can be achieved for future teachers by increasing economics requirements for teacher certification, and by increasing the number of current teachers who take inservice courses. It is difficult, however, to attract teachers to inservice credit courses in economics. A national survey found that only about a quarter of teachers were interested taking credit courses in economics; unfortunately, over half were interested in less effective, noncredit workshops (Yankelovich, Skelly and White, 1981).

V. MATERIALS AND METHODS

Increasing enrollments in economics courses and the inclusion of economics throughout the school curriculum gave publishers, foundations, and other organizations the necessary incentives to produce a variety of instructional materials to meet the growing needs of the market. Indeed, the preparation of new curriculum materials and the use of different teaching strategies are dominant themes in economic education work over the past three decades. These developments have stimulated research on how effective the materials and strategies were with students.

Economics Textbooks

The National Task Force concern over materials (Table 7.1, #10) arose in part from an analysis of 24 textbooks for high school courses in economics and other subjects conducted by a special textbook committee of the American Economic Association in 1959-1960 (AEA, 1963). The report concluded that there were major deficiencies in social studies textbooks that included problems with omission of subject matter, imbalance in content presentation, limited analysis of economic issues, and many factual errors.

A decade later, a rating analysis of 12 high school economics textbooks based on similar evaluation methods and criteria as the AEA study found a substantial improvement in the quality of textbooks (Townshend-Zellner, 1970). The inadequate textbooks were usually first published before 1961, while the adequate textbooks were first published after 1966. The improvement in the latter group was attributed to two factors. First, the content and structure of newer college textbooks, especially in the area of macroeconomics, served as models for the preparation of high school texts. The second, and more critical factor, was author and publisher use of the National Task Force report as a guide to content and inclusion of more economic analysis in textbooks.

That influence is still evident in the content coverage of most high school economics textbooks in the 1980s as measured against the *Framework*, the direct descendant of the National Task Force report. One 1980s study of 11 high schools economics textbooks used the *Framework* as a guideline to assess content coverage and accuracy and gave the textbooks very positive ratings (Miller, 1988). Textbooks also received good ratings on other criteria – physical characteristics, organization, features, instructional activities, and supplementary materials. In addition, high school textbooks now differ significantly in terms of reading or ability level, which is an advantage because it allows the teacher to select a textbook that more closely matches the needs of different types of students taking high school economics.

Despite these positive developments, two basic criticisms of textbooks remain. First, dissatisfaction with a mainstream approach to economics sometimes produces charges that the textbooks are "ideologically biased" or that they promote "indoctrination" (Romanish, 1983; Helburn, 1986).[9] Helburn, for example, views the influence of the *Framework* on the content and structure of economics textbooks as evidence of rigidity: "overwhelmingly, the books provide a consensual lens and an officially defined interpretation of reality – entirely with the accepted neoclassical tradition.... There is no multiplicity of perspectives" (p. 28). Second, general problems in high school textbooks are associated with economics textbooks. These problems include superficial discussion of too many topics, and biased or inadequate coverage of issues related to women, blacks, and Hispanics (e.g., Hahn and Blankenship, 1983).

Although content evaluations of textbooks are common, only recently has the effectiveness of high school economics textbooks been subject to any empirical research. A regression study of economics textbooks generally found negative effects on economics achievement for high school students using business-oriented books, free enterprise texts, and, books written for college undergraduates (Walstad and Van Scyoc, 1990). The effects of textbooks deserves further study because of the dominant influence of textbooks in social studies instruction and in education in general relative to other educational materials or technology.

Social Studies Textbooks

The treatment of economics in high school textbooks for history, government, geography, and sociology that were published the 1969-1972 period were evaluated by two textbook committees (O'Neill, 1973; Weidenaar et al., 1973). Both committees found some increased coverage of economics in the textbooks from earlier editions, but continuing problems included a lack of economic analysis, the absence of economic content in many topics, factual errors and the misapplication of economic ideas, and nonsystematic organization of content.

More recent studies of social studies textbooks have reached similar negative conclusions about the quality of the economics content (Main, 1978; Miller and Rose, 1983). The most serious problem was the absence of economic analysis and *ad hoc* explanations given in texts for many economic events and issues. Numerous examples were found where textbooks developed misconceptions about how a market economy operates and about the role of government in an economy.

Textbooks for United States history, world history, American government, or other social studies subjects provide little assistance for improving students' understanding of economics. There are no convincing reasons or more recent studies to suggest that this textbook situation has changed much in the past decade, although the topic merits further study. The poor quality of economics content in social studies textbooks places greater demands on a teacher that might seek to infuse economics into another subject. The teacher must be more knowledgeable and highly skilled to correct many of the misconceptions presented in the textbooks. These textbook problems provide a partial explanation for why teaching economics in the context of other social studies courses is so difficult, and why it often appears to make an insignificant contribution to student learning in the research studies at the high school level.

Other Materials

The major change in the approach to supplementary materials from the early 1960s was a shift in emphasis from having economists and educators screen educational materials for teachers to having them produce ones that provided specific examples for teachers of how economic concepts can be taught. Published research on the effectiveness of supplementary print lessons or instructional units, however, whether produced by nonprofit organizations or by commercial publishers, is virtually non-existent. The reasons have to do with problems associated with conducting such a study. Even more so than with textbook studies, it is difficult to separate the effects of the supplementary print materials from the teacher and other influences on students.

By contrast, evaluation of the effects of educational programs that use technological media has been given more extensive study over the years. This interest probably arises because of the size of the resources devoted to a media project, wider usage by teachers, and the greater opportunity for researchers to identify the program effects. Research studies typically have shown positive effects from viewing the programs on achievement in economics and other outcomes, such as problem solving skills (Bach and Saunders, 1965; Chizmar et al., 1985). A newer technological application is the use of microcomputer or multimedia programs for teaching economics. Many programs are now available, but research on their effectiveness is only beginning to receive serious study. This newer technology may prove difficult to assess because the scale of the instructional intervention is typically smaller than with a television series, which makes it harder to isolate hardware or software effects.

More supplementary materials are available now in a variety of formats than in years past, but continuing demands from teachers suggest that more high quality materials need to be produced. A survey of high school teachers reported that the three major barriers to teaching economics were: (1) lack of student interest; (2) limited preparation time for teaching; (3) lack of supplementary materials (Soper and Walstad, 1988). The three perceived barriers can be lowered simultaneously when good print, video, or multimedia materials are made available to teachers because they directly aid in stimulating student interest, and help reduce preparation time for teachers. Teachers with a limited background in the subject especially require materials that are relatively self-contained and easy to use with students, which is one of the major reasons that video series have proven to be especially popular and effective. These series, however, are the most expensive type of supplementary materials to develop, and they often outlive their usefulness before a new series or an update is produced.

VI. ECONOMISTS AND ORGANIZATIONS

Effective economic education requires the involvement of economists. This participation was considered such a vital part of economists' work that the National Task Force made it a recommendation (Table 7.1, #11). The evidence indicates that there has been growing participation of economists in economic education work, largely through the Committee on Economic Education of the American Economic Association (AEA) and the National Council on Economic Education.

AEA Committee on Economic Education

The history of professional interest in economic education in the United States is a long one that begins with the founding of the AEA in 1885 and continues to the present (Hinshaw and Siegfried, 1991). Most of the pre-college activity by the AEA was conducted either through its Committee on Economic Education, or indirectly through its influence on the National Task Force.

The flurry of professional activity by the AEA and the active involvement of prominent economists in pre-college economic education from 1959 to 1963 has never been matched in later periods. The work of the AEA Committee on Economic Education from 1964-1986 shifted from the pre-college level and focused primarily on college instruction. The reasons for the shift were understandable given the previous emphasis on the pre-college level. The change also was the result of the specialization that occurred in the delivery of economists' services to the schools as National Council affiliated with the AEA and assumed more responsibility for pre-college economic education after the mid-1960s. Nevertheless, there remains the persistent criticism that individual economists and the economics profession should be doing more to improve economics instruction in the schools.

National Council on Economic Education

The National Council (formerly the Joint Council) was established in 1949 by the CED as a non-profit and non-partisan educational organization to promote economic education in the nation's schools. To achieve its goal, the National Council created a decentralized network to involve many college and university economists in work with the schools. The network structure is a confederation of 50 state councils and 275 college and university centers that are affiliated with the National Council. The state councils operate in a similar way to the National Council, as separate nonprofit and nonpartisan organizations that raise funds and manage programs in economic education in a state. The funding supports educational activities that are conducted by the centers, especially credit courses in economics for teachers, and also the development of instructional materials. The directors of the centers and councils are typically professional economists or educators who serve on the faculty at the associated college or university.

A major project of the National Council and its network was the Developmental Economic Education Program (DEEP), begun in 1964 in response to the National Task Force report. DEEP was a *flexible* approach to curriculum reform in which state councils and local centers worked in partnership with school districts to achieve the integration of economics instruction throughout the school curriculum. Research on the effectiveness of DEEP was conducted continuously since the program's inception. One comprehensive review concluded that DEEP is a "promising and potentially powerful process" to improve the economics curriculum when there is: (1) a commitment to economics instruction by school administrators; (2) good teacher training in economics; (3) quality instructional materials; and, (4) sufficient time in the school day for teaching economics (Watts, 1991). In 1992, the DEEP title was replaced with "EconomicsAmerica" to describe this flexible approach to curriculum reform.

Other Organizations

Interest in economic education is shown by other organizations, but none of these organizations has as comprehensive program for the schools, or receive the support from as many economists in academia and other fields as the National Council. In most cases, the organizations simply produce materials designed to supplement instruction on a particular topic, but make no specific demands for the use of those materials in the classroom (Federal Reserve System, 1992).

In a few cases, organizations have developed and sponsored curriculum projects in economics for the schools. For example, Junior Achievement (JA) developed a business-oriented course called Applied Economics that is widely used in high schools. The appeal of this course stems from three major factors. First, schools save money because student textbooks and a microcomputer are provided essentially at no cost. Second, the program emphasizes an "applied" approach to economics that features a student company simulation and weekly classroom presentations by a local business executive. Third, salary incentives for local JA directors are often based on how many students are enrolled in JA programs. Published research on the effects of Applied Economics in referred, scholarly journals is lacking despite its influence on economics curricula of schools and the potential for advocacy of business views.

VII. CONCLUSION

The available evidence shows substantial improvement in the conditions of pre-college economic education in the United States since 1961:

- More high school students are taking an economics course.
- More schools are teaching economics in related courses and throughout the school curriculum.
- State and national testing programs are devoting more attention to testing economics knowledge and understanding.
- The teaching of economics and economics textbooks are more analytical and less descriptive.
- Economics instruction often covers basic economic concepts that has broad support among economists.
- Teachers are showing greater preparation in economics by taking credit courses and by attending non-credit programs.
- An array of quality textbooks and supplementary materials have been produced by commercial and non-profit publishers.
- A national network of college and university economists and educators has been established to provide teacher education in economics and curriculum development assistance to the schools.
- Research studies have provided new insights into how to increase student understanding of economics.

These developments and related activity illustrate the visible progress which has been made.

Further effort will be required to fulfill the recommendations of the National Task Force. The most critical gap is in the number of students who take economics in high school. Transcript data indicate that about 44 percent of high school graduates took a well-defined high school course in economics in 1990. An analysis of state mandate legislation suggests that about 45 percent of high school graduates were affected by required economics courses, although the quality and focus of the economics in mandated courses vary. By either count, economics is not yet a *universal* subject in the education of American high school students.

Future trends for enrollments in economics courses are uncertain, but are most likely to remain constant or to decrease. No new state requirements for economics instruction have been passed or are being proposed that would boost enrollments. Pressure for more required classroom time for such subjects as history and geography is being exerted by professional groups, and these subjects are given more emphasis than economics in calls for national education reforms. Other social studies subjects also compete with economics for space in the school curriculum and for the attention of students when economics is offered on an elective basis. If enrollments in a separate economics course should decline, then more reliance is placed on the "infusion" approach as the only viable option for teaching economics in the nation's schools. Research findings raise doubts about the effectiveness of the infusion strategy in practice, which appears to work well only under the best of conditions: when there are good instructional materials, teachers trained in economics, and adequate classroom time for teaching economic content.

Another major concern is with teacher education in economics in colleges and universities. Studies show that an increase in the number of college credit-hours in economics taken by teachers has a significant positive effect on student achievement in economics. Greater economic understanding also makes it easier for teachers to infuse economics in instruction in other subjects. Prospective social studies teachers, however, take little economics in their undergraduate training, and therefore most have a poor understanding of the subject, even though they can be certified to teach high school economics. This situation is unlikely to change as long as economics is viewed as a minor high school subject. New social studies teachers take most of their coursework in history, largely because that is the subject they are most likely to teach when they begin their career. When more high schools begin requiring students to take economics, then more teachers will have an incentive to prepare for that teaching responsibility by taking more college courses in economics. Although in-service education in economics for current teachers has been used successfully to overcome past deficiencies in economics coursework, it does not reach all teachers and may be insufficient to correct many problems.

Research on economic education in high schools deserves more attention, as has been suggested throughout this chapter. There are at least five topics for study that focus on different aspects of instruction: (1) more states are mandating economics courses for high school graduation; yet little is known about the influence of mandates on economics achievement or other variables; (2) infusion, which in many schools is the only way economics is taught, needs to be given more scrutiny in both longitudinal and cross-sectional studies to assess the full value of this approach; (3) the introduction of advanced placement and other programs sponsored by outside organizations has unknown effects on students and the curriculum; (4) teacher characteristics, besides the amount of economics coursework, are worthy of more investigation to discover whether other teacher qualities influence the economics learning of students; and, (5) textbooks, or new materials and educational technology, should be evaluated for their contribution to economic understanding. The number of potential areas for research is extensive because only in the 1980s has economic education in American high schools received much empirical study. This research work would also benefit from the development of alternative measures of student outcomes.

A call for public support for economic education was the final recommendation of the National Task Force. The record since the early 1960s shows that many economists, educators, and organizations helped get more economics instruction included in the high school curriculum. That support is still needed because economics is not a universal subject in student's education in the U.S. and there are continual pressures to make room in the curriculum for subjects other than economics.

NOTES

1. This chapter is a revision and update of Walstad (1992).

2. The data in Tables 7.2 and Table 7.3 both show that the percentage of students receiving economics instruction increased in recent years, but there are differences in calculations that explain the differences in the estimates. The data in Table 7.2 shows the percentage of all high school graduates that take a separate economics course, either as an elective, as a school district requirement, or as a state requirement, when the course title on the transcript can be classified as economics. Data in Table 7.3 shows only the percentage of public high school graduates that took some type of economics course to meet a state requirement, but it does not include students taking economics as an elective or as a school district requirement. The content and focus, however, of these mandate courses can vary from "pure" economics to consumer economics to business, and therefore some state mandated courses are not be classified as economics courses under a transcript definition. Data in Table 7.2 probably offers the most realistic and precise estimate of the percentage of American high school graduates who have taken an economics course.

3. For details of this study, see Walstad and Soper, 1988. For examples of other studies, see Rhine (1989) or Becker and Walstad (1990).

4. Research on infusion is still incomplete. Cross-sectional studies of economics achievement in high school courses may be ill-suited for measuring the full value of infusion, especially its effects on economic knowledge gained in lower grades. Longitudinal studies may hold more promise in these cases (Buckles and Freeman, 1984).

5. For a discussion of whether this level of performance should be considered as failing, see Chapter 6 and Walstad (1990). For research on the lasting effects of a high school economics course, see Chapters 6 and 9.

6. A history of pre-college economic education as reflected in the *Framework* is discussed by Sumansky (1986). In 1993, the second edition of the *Framework* underwent a minor revision to reflect a name change from the Joint Council to the National Council on Economic Education and the adoption of an EconomicsAmerica theme. Also see Chapter 2.

7. One editorial, "Statism for Sophomores," accused the report of being insufficiently critical of Communist economies, apologetic of private enterprise, and concluded that the report is a "plea for preserving the sort of instruction that is calculated to rear a generation deeply distrustful of economic freedom" (WSJ, 1961, p. 18).

8. Different studies showing the positive effects of teacher coursework include: Walstad and Soper, 1988; Becker and Walstad, 1989; Lynch, 1990; and Bosshardt and Watts, 1990. For research studies on other teacher factors, see Walstad (1992).

9. For a response to the charge of ideological bias, see Walstad and Watts (1984) or Watts (1987b).

REFERENCES

American Economic Association (AEA), Committee on Economic Education, Special Textbook Study Committee. (1963). Economics in the schools. *American Economic Review, 53*(1), Part 2.

Bach, G. L., Bellack, A. A., Chandler, L. V., Frankel, M. L., Gordon, R. A., Lewis, B. W., Samuelson, P. A., & Bond, F. A. (1961). *Economic education in the schools.* New York: Committee on Economic Development.

Bach, G. L., & Saunders, P. (1965). Economic education: Aspirations and achievements. *American Economic Review, 55*(3), 329-356.

Baumol, W. (1988). Economic education and the critics of mainstream economics. *Journal of Economic Education, 19*(4), 323-330.

Becker, W. E., & Walstad, W. B. (Eds.). (1987). *Econometric modelling in economic education research.* Boston: Kluwer-Nijhoff.

Becker, W. E., & Walstad, W. B. (1990). Data loss from pretest to posttest as a sample selection problem. *Review of Economics and Statistics, 72*(1), 184-188.

Bosshardt, W., & Watts, M. (1990). Instructor effects and their determinants in precollege economic education. *Journal of Economic Education, 21*(3), 265-276.

Brenneke, J. S. (Ed.). (1981). *Consumer and economic education in the public schools.* New York: Joint Council on Economic Education.

Brown, B. J., & Clow, J. E. (1987). *Our business and economic world.* Boston: Houghton Mifflin.

Buckles, S. (1991). Guidelines for economic content in school programs. In W. B. Walstad & J. C. Soper (Eds.)., *Effective economic education in the schools* (pp. 24-34). Washington, DC: National Education Association and Joint Council on Economic Education.

Buckles, S., & Freeman, V. (1984). A longitudinal analysis of a developmental economics education program. *Journal of Economic Education, 15*(1), 5-10.

Chizmar, J. F., McCarney, B. J., Halinski, R. S., & Racich, M. J. (1985). 'Give and take,' economics achievement, and basic skills development. *Journal of Economic Education, 16*(2), 99-110.

College Entrance Examination Board (CEEB). (1992). *Advanced placement course description: Economics - May 1993, May 1994.* New York: CEEB.

Dumas, W., Weible, T., & Evans, S. (1990). State standards for the licensure of secondary social studies teachers. *Theory and research in social education, 18*(1), 27-36.

Federal Reserve System. (1992). *Public information materials, 1992-1993.* New York: Federal Reserve Bank of New York.

Gilliard, J. V., Caldwell, J., Dalgaard, B. R., Reinke, R. W., & Watts, M. (1988). *Economics: What and when: Scope and sequence guidelines, K-12.* New York: Joint Council on Economic Education.

Hahn, C. L., & Blankenship, G. (1983). Women and economics textbooks. *Theory and Research in Social Education, 11*(3), 67-76.

Hansen, W. L., Bach, G. L., Calderwood, J. D., & Saunders, P. (1977). *A framework for teaching Economics: Basic concepts.* New York: Joint Council on Economic Education.

Helburn, S. W. (1986). Economics and economics education: The selective use of discipline structures in the economics curricula. In S. Hodkinson & D. J. Whitehead (Eds.), *Economics education: Research and development issues* (pp. 6-32). London: Longman.

Hermanowicz, H. J., et al. (1985). *Economic education for future elementary and secondary teachers: Basic recommendations.* New York: Joint Council on Economic Education.

Highsmith, R. J. (1989). *A survey of state mandates for economics instruction, 1987-88.* New York: Joint Council on Economic Education.

Hinshaw, E. C., & Siegfried, J. J. (1991). The role of the American Economic Association in economic education: A brief history. *Journal of Economic Education, 22*(4), 373-381.

Jenness, D. (1990). *Making sense of the social studies.* New York: MacMillian.

Lynch, G. J. (1990). The effects of teacher course work on student learning: Evidence from the TEL. *Journal of Economic Education, 21*(3), 287-296.

Main, R. S. (1978). The treatment of economic issues in high school government, sociology, U.S. history, and world history texts. *Journal of Economic Education, 9*(2), 115-118.

Miller, S. L. (1988). *Economic education for citizenship.* Bloomington, IN: Social Studies Development Center, Indiana University.

Miller, S. L., & Rose, S. A. (1983). The great depression: A textbook case of problems with American history textbooks. *Theory and Research in Social Education, 11*(1), 25-39.

Millman, J., & Greene, J. (1989). The specification and development of tests of achievement and ability. In R. L. Linn (Ed.), *Educational measurement* (3rd ed.) (pp. 335-366). New York: American Council on Education and MacMillan Publishing.

National Assessment of Educational Progress (NAEP). (1989). The future role of NAEP as the nation's report card (November 29). (Staff paper). Washington, DC: NAEP Governing Board.

National Center for Education Statistics (NCES). (1992). *Digest of Education Statistics, 1992*. Washington, DC: U.S. Government Printing Office.

O'Neill, J. (1973). *An evaluation of the economics and the teaching strategies in 11th and 12th grade U.S. and world history textbooks*. New York: Joint Council on Economic Education.

Romanish, B. A. (1983). Modern secondary economics textbooks and ideological bias. *Theory and Research in Social Education, 11*(1), 1-24.

Samuelson, P. (1987). How economics has changed. *Journal of Economic Education, 18*(2), 107-110.

Saunders, P., Bach, G. L., Calderwood, J. D., & Hansen, W. L., with Stein, H. (1984). *A framework for teaching the basic concepts* (2nd ed.). New York: Joint Council on Economic Education.

Soper, J. C., & Walstad, W. B. (1987). *The test of economic literacy: Examiner's manual* (2nd ed.). New York: Joint Council on Economic Education.

Soper, J. C., & Walstad, W. B. (1988). The reality of high school economics: The teacher's perspective. *Journal of Private Enterprise, 4*(3), 85-96.

Stigler, G. J. (1963). Elementary economic education. *American Economic Review, 53*(2), 653-659.

Sumansky, J. M. (1986). The evolution of economic education thought as revealed through a history of the *Master curriculum guide in economics: Framework for teaching the basic concepts*, Revised 1984. In S. Hodkinson & D. J. Whitehead (Eds.), *Economics education: Research and development issues* (pp. 48-63). London: Longman.

Symmes, S. S. (1991). DEEP: A process for curriculum renewal. In W. B. Walstad & J. C. Soper (Eds.), *Effective economic education in the schools* (pp. 49-69). Washington, DC: National Education Association and Joint Council on Economic Education.

Townshend-Zellner, N. (1970). A new look at high school economics texts. *Journal of Economic Education, 2*(1), 63-68.

Wagner, L. (1963). Task force to classroom. *American Economic Review, 53*(2), 660-673.

Wall Street Journal. (1961). Statism for sophomores. *Wall Street Journal* (December 6), 18.

Walstad, W. B. (1990). Research on high school economics: Comment. *Journal of Economic Education, 21*(3), 248-253.

Walstad, W. B. (1992). Economics instruction in high schools. *Journal of Economic Literature, 30*(4), 2019-2051.

Walstad, W. B., & Soper, J. C. (1988). A report card on the economic literacy of U.S. high school students. *American Economic Review, 78*(2), 251-256.

Walstad, W. B., & Soper, J. C. (1989). What is high school economics? Factors contributing to student achievement and attitudes. *Journal of Economic Education, 20*(1), 23-38.

Walstad, W. B., & Soper, J. C. (Eds.). (1991). *Effective economic education in the schools*. Washington, DC: National Education Association and Joint Council on Economic Education.

Walstad, W. B., & Van Scyoc, L. (1990). The effect of textbooks on economic understanding and attitudes in high school economics courses. *Journal of Research and Development in Education, 24*(1), 46-54.

Walstad, W. B., & Watts, M. (1984). A response to Romanish: Ideological bias in secondary economics textbooks. *Theory and Research in Social Education, 11*(4), 25-35.

Walstad, W. B., & Watts, M. (1985). Teaching economics in the schools: A review of survey findings. *Journal of Economic Education, 16*(2), 135-146.

Watts, M. (1987a). Survey data on precollege scope-and-sequence issues. *Journal of Economic Education, 18*(1), 71-91.

Watts, M. (1987b). Ideology, textbooks, and the teaching of economics. *Theory Into Practice, 26*(3), 190-197.

Watts, M. (1991). Research on DEEP: The first 25 years. In W. B. Walstad and J. C. Soper (Eds.), *Effective economic education in the schools* (pp. 81-98). Washington, DC: National Education Association and Joint Council on Economic Education.

Weidenaar, D. J., Harrington, P. V., Horton, R. V., & Shermis, S. S. (1973). *An evaluation of the economics and teaching strategies in social studies textbooks, high school (grades 10-12)*. New York: Joint Council on Economic Education.

Yankelovich, Skelly, & White, Inc. (1981). *National survey of economic education 1981*. New York: Playback Associates.

CHAPTER 8

ECONOMIC UNDERSTANDING IN THE UNITED KINGDOM

David J. Whitehead

Economics was introduced into the school curriculum in the 1950s, and by the next decade was growing fast in popularity, especially in the final two years of schooling prior to university entrance. Since that time, it has been normal for potential university students to study only three subjects between the ages of 16 and 18, to a greater depth than elsewhere in the world. Consequently, the school economics curriculum resembled a slightly diluted first year university course, and only recently have real attempts been made to render the syllabus more appropriate for the majority of students who do not proceed to further study of the subject in higher education. Though economics became increasingly popular in the 1960s, it was not until 1972 that it became possible to train as an economics teacher, when the Department of Economic Education was established at the London University Institute of Education.

This overview of the development of economic education in the United Kingdom summarizes a plethora of articles and wide-ranging analysis. An eclectic synopsis of the debate about the justification for including economics in the curriculum is complemented by a brief analysis of the sometimes tendentious arguments used by economists. Next follows a descriptive section on how the economics curriculum is delivered in British schools. After an exposition of what is taught in economics syllabuses, there follows a resume of how it is taught, and what resources are available to teachers. Final sections focus on how teachers of economics and cognate subjects are trained, and on the nature of assessment of economic understanding.

I. WHY TEACH ECONOMICS?

What are the views of academic economists concerning the teaching of their subject in schools? When economics was first introduced into the school curriculum in the U.K. in the 1950s, it encountered resistance from some professional economists, amongst whom the most distinguished was Lord Robbins. He took the view that scarce school time should be allocated in more valuable ways, and that in any case, economics was too difficult a subject for school students. Any superficial understanding they gained at school would have to be "untaught" when they got to university. This view is now only held by a few die-hards, and most instructors on introductory university courses are no longer surprised by how well students who have already taken economics at school have been taught.

Economists justify the inclusion of their subject in the school curriculum on several grounds. The first may be characterized as the "good citizen" argument (Whitehead, 1977, pp. 45-67). If citizens are to play an effective part in decision making in their society, they need to be able to understand the issues which rival political parties debate. Lawton would argue that education may be seen as a set of rights, and that if economic education is excluded from the curriculum, then we are denying young people the right to understand and make informed judgments about this field of human experience (Lawton, 1981, pp. 55-56).

Secondly, economists argue that students should be exposed to economics because it is a unique social science. Educational philosophers like Hirst argue that there are discrete forms of knowledge, each of which require the development of creative imagination, judgment, critical thinking, communication skills and so forth, in unique ways (Hirst, 1974, pp. 30-53). Each form has its own particular concepts, a distinctive logical structure arising from a unique conceptual framework within which experience can be understood, its own tests against experience in accordance with particular criteria which are peculiar to that form, and its own distinctive methodology. It could be argued that the social sciences constitute one discrete form of knowledge, and that economics should be taught as an exemplar within this area.

Additionally, economics enables students to see how models are built in social sciences, how theories are derived and tested, and provides them with an example of a school subject that is not just a set of self-evident truths to be learned. It is a living, controversial subject. Students are often unfamiliar with such characteristics, and find it difficult to come to terms with them. This reinforces the importance of teaching such a subject.

Related to this is the question of values. The ability to distinguish between facts and values is important in all the social sciences, and the study of economics provides a medium for such discrimination to be practiced (Whitehead, 1985, pp. 72-92).

It is also maintained that economics is a discipline which imparts useful intellectual training. Students studying economics should develop a capacity for reasoning and for logical expression of ideas based on a study of the relevant data.

Finally, economics and cognate subjects are thought to be of vocational value. Economics is seen as self-evidently useful for students going into business. This will of course only be the case if syllabuses reflect the kinds of skills and knowledge which business enterprises require. However, it is preferable to consider economics as an element of a liberal education, not because it is useful, but because it is an important and distinctive mode of understanding. It should be defended against the encroachment of a short-sighted vocationalism, which is incorrectly considered more appropriate for the development of entrepreneurial dynamism. In fact, a liberal education makes it easier to deal with present problems, because it encourages the imagination to look beyond them.

Liberally educated people are able to take the long view, so they may be more flexible and inventive: qualities we are seeking to develop in our fledgling entrepreneurs, in order to obtain a "grosser national product." Students should be empowered to make their own judgments about their economic system, based upon sound political and economic literacy, some knowledge of the world of work, and a clear understanding and articulation of their own viewpoint resulting from the liberal aspects of their education.

II. THE ECONOMICS CURRICULUM IN BRITISH SCHOOLS

Economics has been taught to 16- to 18-year-old students for the last thirty years, and it is now the third most popular subject studied at this level, after English and mathematics. The Advanced Level examination is taken by all students who seek to proceed to higher education studies. In order to gain entry to university, it is necessary typically to gain sufficiently high grades in three subjects. For example, economics students at school may also be studying history and geography. If they wish to read economics at university, they may need to obtain the grades B, B and C in the three subjects to satisfy the entry requirements of their first choice university. Each of the three subjects studied occupies about five hours of timetabled lessons each week, over the two year period of grades 12 and 13. The curriculum studied by such Advanced Level students is explained in the next section.

In 1991, there were 43,160 entries for economics at Advanced Level. This compared with, for example, 49,126 entries for English literature, 41,744 for history, and 73,472 for mathematics. In the last two years, there has been a slight decline in the number of economics students, which has been compensated by a very fast growth in the number of students choosing business studies. The two subjects are seen as complementary rather than competitive, and their growth has generally been at the expense of other subjects and among students who now stay on for grades 12 and 13 at school who previously would have left at the age of 16. Both subjects taken together represent the most popular option among 16- to 18-year-olds still at school. Approximately 25 percent of the school population in grades 12 through 13 are studying economics and/or business education.

It is also possible for students to take an Advanced Supplementary Level examination in economics, which represents about a half of the full Advanced Level syllabus, taught over two years. Entries for this examination totalled 1,306 in 1991.

Economics is not included as a discrete subject in the National Curriculum (which covers grades 1 through 11), but it features as an optional subject in grades 10 and 11. Students aged 16 take the General Certificate of Secondary Education, which is assessed by individual subject examinations. So a typical student might take eight subjects, the required statutory minimum of English, mathematics, technology, science, geography or history, art or music, and a modern language, and an optional subject, of which economics might be one.

In 1992, almost 20,000 students took GCSE economics. In addition, over 97,000 took GCSE business studies. Taking into account other related syllabuses, there were about 177,000 entries for economics and similar subjects in 1992, which constituted approximately 28 percent of the year 11 school population taking GCSE examinations that year. On the whole, the growth of business studies has been at the expense of other optional subjects rather than being chosen instead of economics. The GCSE economics course is typically taught over two years with four or five lessons per week. Because neither economics nor business education are required by the National Curriculum, it is likely that some decline in the number of students studying these subjects will take place in the future. This is despite the fact that their popularity amongst students is high and increasing.

Students also all have an entitlement to aspects of economics and business education within the National Curriculum, taught either through the subject technology or as a cross-curricular theme called "economic and industrial understanding." The intention of this requirement is that teachers of other subjects should introduce the economic and business elements, dimensions or perspectives of their subjects where appropriate. Exposure to these contributions could be in grades 7 through 11. However, skepticism prevails about the value of such options as a means of furthering economic education, similar to that voiced in the U.S. (Walstad, 1992, pp. 2019-2051, Walstad and Soper, 1989, pp. 35-36). There, economics is often taught through the infusion approach. This makes life simpler for timetable compilers, who have to juggle with one less variable when devising the school curriculum. While providing a taste for prospective serious students of the subject, it also ensures that economics features (if only slightly) as an integral part of the education of all students.

However, research findings highlight the need for a more realistic view of the infusion approach to teaching economics. Teachers of other subjects may lack the knowledge to infuse relevant economic concepts, or be disinclined to do so. Resources to aid teachers to incorporate economics into other subjects may be inadequate. Little knowledge is gained when students learn economics through social studies or consumer economics courses. Overall, evidence on the infusion/single subject approaches to economics instruction confirms the value of a formal course in economics as a means of improving economic understanding.

III. WHAT ECONOMICS IS TAUGHT IN THE U.K.?

The economics curriculum for students aged 16 to 18 conforms closely to the principles of economics course. (See Appendix 8.1 for an example of a typical syllabus.) Syllabuses are set by examination boards for Advanced Level students, who take the examination at the end of their school career, around the age of 18.

What are the main changes affecting these syllabuses? First, the main problem with the curriculum for 16- to 18-year-olds is that syllabuses have become overloaded. When syllabus committees meet to decide on changes, it is much easier to reach agreement on which new topic to include than it is on what to omit. Thus syllabuses always get longer, and teachers can only just cover all the topics in the time available. A major disadvantage resulting from this situation is that students have insufficient practice at reinforcing their understanding of the fundamental concepts, by the use of case studies or other applied material, because of the need to "get through the syllabus." So they end up with a smattering of knowledge of a very wide range of theories, concepts and issues, but with only a superficial appreciation of all of them.

The main changes that have been advocated concern the inclusion of topics such as the economics of developing countries and the European Community, and the radical reappraisal of the value of teaching some of the neoclassical theory of the firm to this age group. Some European countries, such as France and Denmark, already devote much more space to the problems of the Third World in their school economics textbooks than does the U.K.

Other proposed changes include a reduced emphasis on the theory of marginal productivity, national income accounting, the components of aggregate demand and the minutiae of the monetary system. It is also suggested that there should be more discussion of market failure, welfare issues, and current policy issues.

One new course places the emphasis upon investigation and presentation (the Ridgeway Project). Students have to undertake an industry study, and examine a real problem currently facing a local firm. Students must analyze the problem, using the skills and concepts of the economist, and must suggest coherent solutions, using their communication skills. They need to convince their teacher that they have simulated the role of an economic consultant in their handling of the assignment.

Another new course adopts a Core/Modules approach, and embraces both economics and business studies (the Wessex Scheme). In the first year, students investigate the unique approaches of both subjects. In the second year, they proceed to specialize on one or other of the subjects. The common core consists of four elements: Foundation; Income, Wealth and Expenditure; People, Markets and Power; and Change – the impact of change on business and the economy. The elective modules include: a new business proposal; multi-national companies; the economic/business system of another country; cost/benefit analysis; law and the environment; development economics; accounting for business; and a local industrial study. The modules are taught by means of supported self-study packages with a strong emphasis on investigation and presentation (Whitehead and Dyer, 1991).

More radical teachers argue that economics does not help us to understand, let alone solve, major current problems. The restriction of syllabuses to the neo-classical paradigm deprives students of alternative insights, which would better help them understand societal problems. Such dissenters argue that it is important for students to know that there is disagreement about the causes of persistent economic problems, and that much economic theory is highly controversial. These criticisms seem to have been rather muted since the collapse of Marxist regimes in Eastern Europe!

In the future, all syllabuses for 16- to 18-year-olds will have to incorporate core skills. These are: to develop communication, problem solving and personal skills and, in appropriate subjects: numeracy, IT skills and a foreign language. It is likely that economics will provide an appropriate vehicle for the conveying of all these skills.

Students between the ages of 14 and 16 study for the General Certificate of Secondary Education. The optional subject economics has syllabuses set by examination boards, for which schools enter their candidates. These syllabuses have been undergoing radical reappraisal in recent years. The main changes have been to encourage a more activity-based approach, and to incorporate work on assignments or coursework into the final examination. Teachers have become more concerned to impart higher order skills, such as the application of their understanding to interpret and analyze data, and the ability to distinguish between facts and values. Students are also taught to evaluate evidence before reaching a conclusion.

A final syllabus innovation is the International Baccalaureate (Bates, 1989). Today, about 500 schools offer the IB. Its economics curriculum has already gone some way to meet the criticisms of the content of economics courses mentioned earlier. Microeconomic theory is reduced to its basics, and topics such as development issues and comparative economics are stressed. More emphasis is placed on the international economy and the problems of less developed countries. Treatment of capitalism is not confined to conventional models of the sole trader, partnerships and limited companies, but also ranges over peasant co-operatives, communal farms, parastatal organizations and foreign-owned multinationals.

IV. HOW IS ECONOMICS TAUGHT?

It would be wrong to give the impression that pedagogic practices in the U.K. are wildly at variance with those practiced in the rest of Western Europe, or indeed in the rest of the world. Probably the majority of classroom time is still used for conventional teaching and note taking, but it would be true to say that several teaching innovations have been taken up quite avidly by teachers of economics in the U.K. The first of several less didactic techniques introduced was the use of case studies. These are now widely employed, either in the form of lengthy business school cases, or as short excerpts of stimulus material which can be used to illustrate a principle or provide an application of a piece of analysis. Examiners cast a long shadow, and such techniques were included by teachers with rather more alacrity when they became part of the examination.

The same is not yet true of role plays and simulations, though teachers have been quite keen to use such activities occasionally, especially now that many more are readily available from publishers. There are collections of assignments, role play exercises and simulations, often published in ringbinder format for ease of photocopying. The collection *Trade-Offs: Simulations and Role Plays for Economics* (Whitehead, 1988) is an example of this new breed of publication. The latest handbook, *New Developments in Economics and Business Education*, provides an annotated list of some 85 role plays and simulations, together with the sources from which they may be obtained, for use in teaching economics at all levels (Whitehead and Dyer, 1991).

In the 1970s, several television series were produced, both by the BBC and the independent companies, aimed at students of economics. Current affairs programs are also videotaped and used in the classroom. These have continued to proliferate in the '80s and '90s, and teachers have at their disposal a panoply of well produced audio-visual material. However, the teacher is now even more indispensable, in interpreting the analysis put forward by the program presenters. Television was once thought likely to become the panacea for a range of educational ills; we now know that this was optimistic. It plays its part more humbly, but still has an important role.

So does that great hope of the 1980s: computer aided learning. The first generation of teaching programs were for use on mainframe computers, and they were never used widely. The second generation of software was produced for microcomputers, but much of it was pedestrian and had few advantages over conventional exposition. The third generation is much more sophisticated, and makes better use of the computer's processing facilities.

Computer aided instruction appears to have a comparative advantage in two main spheres: simulations and data bases. Some of the latest programs have certainly capitalized on these strengths, in particular, *Eureco/Secos* (Statistics, 1992)[1] and *Running the British Economy* (Longman, 1992).[2]

Secos is a package which includes all the main data analysis functions. It is simple for either teachers or students to create their own data sets, for example on local or regional trends. Data are stored in tables which are accessible through a simple tree structure. All the tables may be modified, and calculations are performed on lines, columns or whole tables. The program includes: sort, time lag, indices, growth rate, proportions, averages, correlation, standard deviation and line of best fit. *Eureco* runs under *Secos*. It is a data base made available by Eurostat, and contains statistics for all 12 EC countries, plus the U.S. and Japan, on population, employment, national accounts, principal aggregates, money and finance, foreign trade by zone and product, balance of payments, energy and public finance.

Running the British Economy is by far the most frequently used of all simulations. It requires students to run the economy (which is not necessarily that of the U.K.) for up to ten years, deciding annually on government expenditure, tax rates and the money supply. The simulation has a "practice" and "real" version, the latter incorporating exogenous shocks which disrupt players' strategies. The government has a welfare function, and the object is to maximize the welfare points gained over the ten years.

The latest version has many new features, which mirror the preoccupations of economic policy-makers: supply side effects, the problem of uncontrollable imports, the importance of capital flows, and the exchange rate. Alternative welfare functions may be chosen, depending on the criteria the teacher wishes to invoke. Many schools take part in an annual nationwide competition, entering teams of students to see who is most successful in running this model economy.

Software programs are also available which are virtually a self-teaching module, in that they incorporate a programmed learning approach, together with self-assessment questions. The latest *Handbook for Economics Teachers* provides a consumers' guide to the best available software, so that teachers' exiguous budgets are optimally allocated.

The principal resource used by teachers and students is still the textbook. It is increasingly difficult for teachers to choose what to use from the wealth of exciting resources on offer, always assuming that they have a budget which enables them to make the choices they want! Textbooks are now full of attractive design features, and the layout includes diagrams, graphs, figures, tables, photographs, cartoons and other stimulating material. Many textbooks also include exercises, assignments or other work for students to do. Alternatively, they are accompanied by a workbook which includes such matter, and are regularly updated.

There are several series of topic books, which cover a subject such as money and banking in more depth than a conventional textbook, and are usually more up-to-date. Books of case studies, data response and multiple choice questions abound. Also, magazines are published for students of economics, which keep them informed of current developments, and which often include articles by Chief Examiners suggesting how to respond to past questions set in the examination. This is obviously also of great value to teachers, who obtain a more accurate idea of what examiners are looking for.

Since 1979, three *Handbooks* have been written by practicing economics teachers. They are full of innovative ideas about stimulating ways of teaching particular topics to different age groups, and have fostered the growth of more heuristic methods in economic education (Whitehead, 1986).

Enterprising teachers also take their students on visits or field trips, for example, to the City of London or to industrial areas such as the North East of England. They also ask visiting speakers to address their students, for example, bankers, industrialists, trade union officials or stockbrokers.

Increasingly, conferences are organized for students. Some are one day courses, where students are exposed to some of the leading figures in their field, and are provided with authoritative statements of current thinking on particular areas of the syllabus. Other courses last for up to a week, often during vacation time, and provide either a refresher or a revision course for students who want to get into top gear just before the examination.

Committed teachers belong to the Economics and Business Education Association, which comprises some 3000 teachers of these subjects (Economics Association).[3] A quarterly journal keeps them up to date with the latest developments in their field, and provides reviews of books and other resources. Annual conferences and local branch activities provide opportunities for teachers to discuss issues of common concern, and share their professional expertise.

Further professional support is provided by links with other European countries. In 1976, the first in a series of biennial conferences was held at Antwerp University. Regular conferences were subsequently held in Dublin, Milan, Göttingen, Manchester, Lyon, Aarhus, The Hague and Königswinter.

Many publications of proceedings have resulted, for example, on *Economics Education in Europe: 1992 and the Developing World*, on *Computers and Economics Education in Europe*, and on *Economics Teacher Training in EEC Countries* (*Economia*, 1993).[4]

In 1990, at the conference at The Hague, it was decided to set up the Association of European Economics Education. The AEEE publishes a journal: *Economia*, which focusses on issues of concern to teachers of economics throughout Europe, including Eastern Europe. Members of the AEEE are interested in the teaching of economics, whether at elementary, secondary or college level. They work in schools, colleges, polytechnics and universities, professional institutions and in educational administration.

V. HOW ARE TEACHERS TRAINED TO TEACH THESE SUBJECTS?

There are approximately 9,000 schoolteachers of economics in the U.K. Typically, they teach 35 lessons per week out of a 40 lesson timetable. Most of their teaching is to the 16-18 age group, with some classes of 13- to 16-year-olds. Most economics teachers have majored in economics at university, and have a teaching diploma (Postgraduate Certificate of Education). Currently no nationally agreed curriculum for teacher training in economics exists, though the government has recently introduced a requirement that beginning teachers should have a range of competencies as a result of their training.

Seneca wrote "Homines dum docent discunt" (even while they teach, men learn). Teacher training programs are informed by that thought. In other words, the aim is to put student teachers into the position where they are simulating the role of a teacher trainer. They need to role play the supervisor, and imagine what advice they would give if they saw someone else performing as they were.

Trainee teachers often aver that they never really fully understood their subject until they taught it. If this is true, then if they want their students to learn the subject, they too should be put in a position where they have to teach it. This obviously has implications for teaching and learning strategies in the classroom. Novitiates are asked to take on the role of their professors so that they may develop powers of self-criticism rather than rely on external prompting for advice on how to change their behavior.

Normally, student teachers have studied for a degree in economics or a cognate subject. Applicants for training courses are accepted if they are enthusiastic about their subject, intelligent, sensitive and open, and have good organizing capacity. Teacher training courses last for one academic year. Students spend some 16 weeks on teaching practice during the year. The curriculum and methods (pedagogy) course takes place when they are pursuing their educational studies at college, and typically comprises the following elements. They gain some understanding of how students learn, the relative efficacy of alternative teaching/learning strategies, how practice derives from educational theory, and how critical insights may be used creatively for professional self-development.

The environment and learning activities at college simulate those which are recommended for school classrooms. Teacher trainers' philosophy is encapsulated in Isaac Stern's dictum: a good teacher is someone who shows you how to learn.

By the end of their course, students are able to devise case studies, run role play exercises and simulations, and manipulate audio-visual resources. They know how to brainstorm. They have reviewed most of the available resources, and are competent to prescribe the most suitable texts for particular groups of students. They know about programmed learning, computer software, and alternative assessment strategies. They have considered the appropriateness of taking classes to neighboring factories, offices, shops and other organizations, preceded by audiotape-recorded or video-taped interviews with management or shop floor personnel. They keep abreast of their subject by regular perusal of their professional journal *Economics*, and by attending in-service courses run by the Economics and Business Education Association, by University Departments of Education or by their local school district.

VI. ASSESSMENT IN ECONOMIC EDUCATION

Almost all public examinations in Britain are set, marked and moderated by examination boards: independent agencies operating in an oligopolistic market. Examiners who grade scripts are appointed by the boards, and are completely independent of the schools. Samples of scripts are second marked by the Chief Examiner for the subject, and all the work is externally moderated by a distinguished outsider. Thus high standards are assured and maintained.

In 1992, of the 19,787 candidates aged 16 who took the GCSE Economics examination, the percentage grade distribution was:

A	B	C	D	E	F	G
12	19	24	18	13	8	4

The results in 1992 for the 40,222 Advanced Level Economics candidates were as follows (percentages):

A	B	C	D	E	N	Unclassified
12	15	15	16	16	11	14

Syllabuses exhibit some degree of product differentiation, both in terms of content and modes of examination, and schools may choose the examination board for whose examinations they wish to enter their students. Teachers have always attempted to do the best for their students by trying to guess what the examiners would ask. Twenty-five years ago, the only method used was the essay examination, and it became quite easy for an experienced teacher to predict likely questions. So one way of viewing recent developments in examination techniques is as an attempt to prevent teachers from helping their students by accurately predicting the questions. The various modes which have been introduced include the multiple choice test, data response items, short answer questions, case studies, project and field work, and oral assessment.

Another reason for including a variety of modes in the examination battery is to obtain a more well rounded picture of the attributes of examinees. For example, they may be fluent essay writers, but cannot mask their ignorance of some basic concepts when answering multiple choice questions. With data response questions, often an excerpt is taken from a newspaper report, and students have to divine the scope for applying their armory of economic principles when the economics extract is disguised in normal English, rather than in patently economics jargon.

Lack of space precludes discussion of the merits and demerits of all the different modes of assessment employed in the U.K. (Walstad, 1991, pp. 61-70). The main advantage of the more recently introduced methods is that they affect learning activities. Instead of an unbroken torrent of words from the teacher, often dictated from his notes to those of the student without passing through the minds of either, teachers are now prepared to examine cases during lessons, are willing to ask their students to discuss data response questions in small groups, and encourage them to explore their economic environment in order to investigate a problem for some course work or a project. They also attempt to develop students' skills in expressing themselves coherently on economics issues, when they are assessed orally in the examination.

Regardless of the validity of the particular method of examination, it is likely that the feedback effect on classroom activities has been beneficial, taking a broader view of the goals of education.

There is now a range of standardized objective tests in Economics, which have been published in the U.S. These tests are available for primary students through to university majors, but the most frequently employed test is that for 17- or 18-year-olds, who have reached university matriculation stage.

In 1989, the *Test of Economic Literacy* (TEL) (Whitehead and Halil, 1989, 1990, 1991) was modified for use in the U.K., and norming data were obtained for it. (The *Test of Economic Knowledge*, for grade 8/9 students, was standardized for the U.K. in 1993). One hundred sixty-two schools collaborated in the standardization exercise. To facilitate international comparisons, attempts were made to match the American sample as closely as possible. For example, students of the same age were chosen to participate in the trials. Also, the sample was divided into groups "with" and "without" Economics. The U.S. sample was divided into male and female respondents, and it was also possible to categorize the U.K. sample in this way.

However, in several respects the American sample could not be replicated. One problem is that a much higher proportion of American than British students stay on at school beyond the age of 16. On the whole, the attrition of British students post-16 consists of those of average and below-average intelligence. Certainly those who are studying Advanced Level subjects at 11th and 12th grade are considerably above average in intelligence. In contrast, the American school samples contained an ability distribution more closely resembling the normal.

The American tests also asked about students' ethnic and socio-economic background. The former would be an inadmissible question for several school districts in Britain, and the latter was not considered likely to have any valid meaning in the context of quite heterogeneous British schools.

The American study distinguished between four types of course taken by students: economics, consumer economics, social studies, and none of these. In order to establish a clear-cut distinction between those who were studying Economics and those who were not, it was decided to include in the "with Economics" group only those studying 11/12th grade Advanced Level Economics.

The test was considered by some teachers to be rather more elementary than the level expected of 12th grade Economics students in their external examination. Another problem in making international comparisons is that British students of Economics at 18+ are taught to a higher level than probably anywhere else in the world (the top 25 percent of the ability range taught for 3 to 4 hours per week for two years).

The total number of respondents in the U.K. sampling frame for the standardization of TEL Form A compared favorably with the U.S. sample (7,549 compared with 4,235). While 75 percent of U.S. students had studied economics, the standardization of the TEL in the U.K. emphasized the importance of the control group, and so the "with economics" group represented only 57 percent of the total sample.

The U.S. overall mean was reported as 22.06; the corresponding U.K. mean was 30.09. In other words, the U.K. sample scored on average 8 more correct responses than the U.S. sample. The U.S. mean for those "with economics" was 21.26 for Grade 11 and 24.04 for Grade 12. These figures compare with 31.84 for 11th grade British students, and 36.87 for 12th grade British students. So British students performed substantially better at both levels than did American students. As stated above, this may be partly accounted for by the fact that the British sample consisted of high ability students with either one or two years of intensive instruction in the subject. This finding also applied to non-economics students, where the U.S. means were 17.2 and 19.78 for 11th and 12th Grades respectively, while the U.K. samples scored 23.53 and 25.62.

While an 11th Grade "with economics" student in the U.S. who scored 29 was performing at the 82nd percentile there, a British student with the same score was only at the 32nd percentile. Only 29 percent of U.S. 12th Graders with economics scored more than 29, compared with 94 percent of U.K. 12th grade economics students. It is remarkable that 57 percent of U.K. 12th grade non-economics students performed better than the mean for U.S. with-economics students!

These higher ratings were reflected in the facility indices. For the U.K. "with economics" sample, only 4 items had a facility index <0.4 in the 11th grade sub-group, and only 1 item in the 12th grade sub-group (compared with 8 items for the U.S. "with economics" sub-group.)

The published data on the U.K. norming trials enable U.K. economics teachers to compare their own students' responses with the national norms. First, teachers may use the test diagnostically. For example, if students opt for a particular distractor, this indicates to the teacher what kind of misunderstanding is typical. Additionally, teachers may be able to identify pupil difficulties with respect to different areas of the syllabus, such as macroeconomics or microeconomics. To facilitate such analysis of individual pupils' responses, item-based information is provided. A second use of the test is to monitor group progress, both with reference to the improvement in class means over time and compared with national norms. To this end, group normative information is provided.

CONCLUSION

Because economics does not feature as a required subject in the National Curriculum in the United Kingdom, it is likely that its significant position at the post-compulsory level (beyond the age of 16) will gradually be eroded. At the same time, the fast growth of business studies at all levels has forced economists to consider the appropriateness of the economics curriculum, and the most important changes since the 1950s in the content of the pre-university economics curriculum are about to be implemented. At the same time, instruments for assessing economic understanding, originally devised for use in the United States, are now being standardized for use in the U.K. It is to be hoped that research into the effectiveness of alternative strategies for developing economic education will be aided by these tests, that future programs will be informed by a more scientific appraisal of teaching and learning models, and that standards of attainment will thus be enhanced.

NOTES

1. Statistics for Education (Secos/Eureco, 1992), 5 Bridge St., Bishop's Stortford, CM23 2JU, U.K. (tel: 0279 652183).
2. Longman Logotron, Dales Brewery, Gwydir St., Cambridge CB1 2LJ, U.K.
3. Economics Association, 1a Keymer Road, West Sussex BN6 8AD, U.K.

4. *Economica*, published by The Association of European Economics Education, lists details of these publications. The Secretary-General of the AEEE is Steve Hurd, Staffordshire University Business School, Stoke-on-Trent, ST4 2DF, U.K.

REFERENCES

Bates, N. J. W. (1989). International Baccalaureate Economics. *Economics, 25*(4), 169-171.

Hirst, P. (1974). Liberal education and the nature of knowledge. *Knowledge and the curriculum* (pp. 30-53). London: Routledge and Kegan Paul.

Lawton, D. (1981). Foundations for the social sciences. In H. D. Mehlinger (Ed.), *UNESCO handbook for the teaching of social sciences* (pp. 55-56). London: Croom Helm.

Walstad, W. B. (1991). Assessment of economic understanding. In D. J. Whitehead & D. H. Dyer (Eds.), *New developments in economics and business education: A handbook for teachers* (pp. 61-70). London: Kogan Page.

Walstad, W. B. (1992). Economics instruction in high schools. *Journal of Economic Literature, 30*(4), 2019-2051.

Walstad, W. B., & Soper, J. C. (1989). What is high school economics? Factors contributing to student achievement and attitudes. *Journal of Economic Education, 20*(1), 23-38.

Whitehead, D. J. (1977). Should economics be taught to all secondary pupils? In T. K. Robinson & R. Wilson (Eds.), *Extending economics within the curriculum* (pp. 45-67). London: Routledge and Kegan Paul.

Whitehead, D. J. (1985). Values in economics teaching. In G. B. J. Atkinson (Ed.), *Teaching economics* (pp. 72-92). London: Heinemann Educational.

Whitehead, D. J. (Ed.). (1986). *Economics education: A second handbook for economics teachers*. London: Heinemann Educational.

Whitehead, D. J. (Ed.). (1988). *Trade-offs: Simulations and role plays for economics*. London: Longman.

Whitehead, D. J., & Dyer, D. H. (Eds.). (1991). *New developments in economics and business education: A handbook for teachers*. London: Kogan Page.

Whitehead, D. J., & Halil, T. (1989). *The test of economic literacy: Standardization in the U.K.* (Economics education paper no. 15). London: Department of Economics, Geography and Business Education, Institute of Education, University of London.

Whitehead, D. J., & Halil, T. (1990). Economic literacy in the U.K. and the USA: An empirical analysis. *Economics, 26*(1), 33-38.

Whitehead, D. J., & Halil, T. (1991). Economic literacy in the United Kingdom and the USA: A comparative study. *Journal of Economic Education, 22*(2), 101-110.

Appendix 8.1: University of London GCE Examination 1993/4 Advanced Level Economics Syllabus (normally two years study to aged 18)

Aims

The aim of the syllabus is to introduce the candidate to some of the main principles of economic theory and their applicability to economic and social problems.
The examination consists of 3 papers: essay type questions (40 percent of marks); data response questions (30%); and multiple choice questions (30%).

The Syllabus

Section A

1. The Economic Problem
   Unlimited wants and limited means of satisfying these wants. Scarcity and choice; opportunity cost. An understanding of the production possibility curve. Factors of production: land, labor (including the role of the entrepreneur) and capital. An understanding of the economic features of these factors: efficiency, mobility and supply. Alternative ways of trying to solve the economic problem: free market, mixed and planned economies. The relative advantages and disadvantages of each system.

2. Production
   Meaning of the term "production." Primary, secondary and tertiary industries. Changes in the size and composition of the population and in its occupational and geographical distribution. An analysis of the concept of the division of labor in terms of comparative advantage as applied to individuals, firms, regions and countries; advantages and disadvantages.

3. Demand
   Definition. Derivation of an individual's demand curve (marginal utility); consumer surplus. Market demand curves. Conditions of demand; distinction between a shift of and a movement along the demand curve. Complements and substitutes. Determinants and calculation of price, income and cross elasticity of demand.

4. Supply
   Definition. Derivation of a supply curve: conditions of supply: distinction between a shift of and a movement along the supply curve. Joint and competitive supply. Elasticity of supply; determinants and calculation of elasticity of supply; influence of time.

5. The Price Mechanism and the Allocation of Resources
   Interrelationship of supply and demand; equilibrium price and output. Significance of elasticities of demand and supply.

Appendix 8.1: University of London GCE Examination 1993/4 Advanced Level Economics Syllabus (normally two years study to aged 18) Continued

6. Modifications and Failures of the Price Mechanism
Effects of taxes and subsidies; maximum and minimum price controls. Production quotas. Merit goods. Public goods. External costs and benefits.

7. Costs and Revenue of the Firm
The meaning of "cost" (including opportunity cost and normal profit); the derivation of average total, average fixed, average variable and marginal cost. The implications of diminishing returns (law of variable proportions) for costs. The implications of increasing, decreasing and constant returns to scale for costs. Revenue: total, average and marginal. The conditions for profit maximization.

8. Price and Output Determination in Different Market Situations
(i) Perfect competition: assumptions, marginal cost and the supply curve. Equilibrium of the firm and industry in the short and long run.
(ii) Monopoly: definition; sources of monopoly. Equilibrium of the firm. Conditions for profitable discrimination.
(iii) Oligopoly: characteristics, price and non-price competition; economic effects.
(iv) Monopolistic or imperfect competition: assumptions; equilibrium of the firm in the long and short run.
(v) Public sector producers: pricing policies of nationalized industries and public utilities.
(vi) Objectives other than profit maximization; implications for price and output.

9. The structure of industry
Different types of business organization within the public and private sectors; the finance of industry. The Stock Exchange; the capital market. Factors affecting the size of firms; advantages and disadvantages of growth. Methods of growth. Vertical, horizontal and conglomerate growth. External economies and diseconomies of scale. Location of industry: influence of regional policy.

10. Competition Policy
Public policies towards mergers, monopolies and restrictive practices.

11. Incomes: The Theory of Distribution
Different types of income and their sources, the marginal productivity Theory.
(i)Wages: wages as the price of labor; demand and supply conditions in different labor markets; non-competing groups. Differences in wages (a) within an occupation and (b) between occupations. Real and money wages. Trade unions and wages. Government policy towards the labor market.
(ii) Rent: economic rent and transfer earnings; the Ricardian theory of rent; quasi-rent. Site values: e.g., rent in city centers; profits as a rent.
(iii)Interest: interest as a price – time preference; the demand for capital; the marginal efficiency of capital.
(iv)Profit: different measures of profit (e.g., returns on capital employed). Distinction between gross profits and net profits. Risk, uncertainty and profit. Function of profits in a capitalist economy.

Appendix 8.1: University of London GCE Examination 1993/4 Advanced Level Economics Syllabus (normally two years study to aged 18) Continued

Section B

12. National Income Accounting
The definition and measurement of income, expenditure and output; net and gross; national and domestic; market prices and factor cost; real and nominal. Problems of measuring National Income. Difficulties in making comparisons over time and between countries.

13. The Circular Flow of Income
The circular flow of income between households, firms and the government; open and closed economies. Withdrawals from and injections into the circular flow (i.e., saving, taxation and imports; investment, government spending and exports). The concept and importance of aggregate demand. The determinants of aggregate demand: consumption; average and marginal propensity to consume (and save); investment; government expenditure (distinction between final government demand and transfer payments); exports and imports.

14. Determinants of the Level of National Income
Income equals planned expenditure (planned withdrawals equal planned injections). Distinction between full employment and equilibrium levels of National Income. Determinants of the multiplier. Determinants of the accelerator. The multiplier and accelerator and changes in National Income.

15. Government Expenditure and Revenue
The growth and changing pattern of public spending. The main items of government expenditure; central and local; current, capital and transfers. Different forms of taxation; central and local; direct and indirect. The balance between revenue from taxation and government expenditure; budget deficits and surpluses. Fiscal policy (discretionary and automatic).

16. Money and Banking
Functions of money; necessary qualities of money. Current measures of the money supply in the United Kingdom. Functions of a bank; various types of bank. Creation of credit. The structure of bank assets and liabilities. The functions of a central bank; the relationship between the Bank of England, the commercial banks and the discount houses. Interest rates.

17. The Demand for Money
Transactions, precautionary and speculative demands for money. The impact on the demand for money of: the price level; income; the price of other assets; the expected rate of inflation.

18. Monetary Policy
Alternative methods of influencing money supply and interest rates. Effectiveness and limitations of monetary policy; alternative perspectives. Interactions of fiscal and monetary policy.

Appendix 8.1: University of London GCE Examination 1993/4 Advanced Level Economics Syllabus (normally two years study to aged 18) Continued

19. International Trade
    Conditions necessary for international trade including the theory of comparative advantage. (The theory of comparative advantage could be usefully linked with the appropriate part of Section A, 2.) The gains from trade. The limitations on international trade; rationale and methods. The terms of trade.

20. The Balance of Payments
    International payments; visible trade; invisibles; the current account; investment and other capital transactions; the balancing item; total currency flows; official financing. Recent trends in the United Kingdom balance of payments. Determination of exchange rates. Definition and explanation of balance of payments disequilibrium.

21. International Economic Co-operation
    International institutions: The International Monetary Fund; The International Bank for Reconstruction and Development (World Bank); the General Agreement on Tariffs and Trade. Regional economic groupings; free trade areas; customs unions; the European Community.

22. Issues of Economic Policy
    Unemployment: recent trends; different types of unemployment, e.g., cyclical, structural; possible remedies, including regional and training policies.
    Inflation: causes of inflation; effects of inflation; possible remedies including prices and incomes policies.
    Balance of payments: consequences of balance of payments disequilibrium. Methods of correcting balance of payments disequilibrium: devaluation/depreciation of a currency; tariffs, quotas and export subsidies; exchange controls.
    Growth: definition; the determinants; benefits and costs of economic growth.
    Possible conflicts between alternative policy objectives.

CHAPTER 9

THE CANADIAN EXPERIENCE AND THE LASTING IMPACT OF ECONOMIC EDUCATION

Anthony Myatt

Charles Waddell

This chapter has two components. The first part begins with a description of governmental jurisdiction and course offerings in economic education typically found in Canadian high schools. This part continues with a discussion of course content, texts, and teacher preparation; it concludes by providing some indication of student enrollment in high school economics by province.

The second part of the chapter reviews previous work on the lasting effects of economic knowledge learned in high school in North America and the U.K. Recent Canadian findings on this topic are also presented.

I. ECONOMIC EDUCATION IN CANADIAN HIGH SCHOOLS

Canada has ten Provinces and (at this writing) two territories. Under the Canadian Constitution, education is a provincial responsibility. Each province and territory has a Department or Ministry of Education. There is no federal equivalent. They are responsible for setting curricula and texts, developing course content and teaching guides, and evaluation. The two territories follow what is done in an adjoining province – Yukon follows British Columbia, and the North West Territories follows Alberta. It is not known what the new territory of Nunavut will do when it comes into being later in the decade.

Course Offerings

All provinces offer self contained courses in economics. Some offer more than one. Alberta is the only province that uses the "infusion" approach. Economics is specifically integrated into a number of courses in science, mathematics and social studies, in addition to offering three "regular" economics courses: Consumer Economics, Microeconomics and Macroeconomics. In the six provinces that offer only one course, it is at the senior level. Saskatchewan has two courses, the first being a prerequisite for the second. Ontario offers three economics courses – none of these has a prior economics course as a prerequisite, but the Ontario Academic Course requires one advanced-level social science or business studies credit. The Advanced Level economics course would satisfy this. Nova Scotia offers six courses in economics. A lower level course is a prerequisite to taking an upper level one.

Course Contents, Texts, and Teacher Preparation

The aims or objectives of the courses are usually very specific and detailed. Ontario's is the most all encompassing and puts the emphasis on the technical economics aspects:

> Economics plays an integral part in the life of everyone. As producers and consumers we make economic decisions in an environment that is affected by the decisions and actions of a variety of business, labour, government, and other institutions, as well as other nations and world organizations. The aims of all economic courses are to provide students with opportunities to:
>
> 1. develop an understanding of economics terms, principles, and issues;
> 2. understand the roles of major institutions and appreciate their interrelationships;
> 3. develop skills that are relevant to personal economic inquiry, reasoning, analysis, and judgement;
> 4. differentiate between economic analyses and economic decisions, which are based on value judgements;
> 5. interpret economic information presented in charts, graphs, and statistical tables;
> 6. apply economic concepts to personal, local, regional, national, and international issues;
> 7. examine the roles, priorities, and concerns of government, business, and labour in our society;

8. examine the mechanisms, strengths, and shortcomings of the market forces present in our society;
9. examine the influence of international events and foreign economic policies on the Canadian economy.

(Ontario Ministry of Education, 1986)

British Columbia by contrast puts the emphasis on a broader, individual development, approach.

(The course) will provide growth in:

1. the ability to engage in appropriate forms of inquiry (problem solving, decision making, critical thinking, creative thinking);
2. establishing a sound knowledge base in economics;
3. developing a reflective ability to select and apply economic skills and knowledge;
4. understanding and accepting personal and shared attitudes of one's own and different societies;
5. creating a positive self-concept.

(British Columbia Ministry of Education, 1990)

It seems to be generally agreed that the high school student has quite different objectives than the university student for enrolling in an economics course. While it might be argued at both levels that an introductory course can only make better newspaper readers and not train an economist, this is more likely the motivation at the high school level. There are no universities that require the high school course as a prerequisite to their introductory economics course. Saskatchewan is the only province that reported that it administers a province-wide test in economics. Nova Scotia includes an economics component in the Grade 12 Nova Scotia Achievement Tests. The test is compulsory for all students, including those who have not studied economics.

The content of the twenty courses offered by the provinces varies greatly. Table 9.1 is a consolidated list of the topic areas covered, which have been grouped by the authors into five sections. There is obviously considerable overlap among these topics. In addition, British Columbia provides Pacific Rim content as a separate topic in each unit of its course. This content was not detailed in the course description.

Table 9.1: Consolidated List of Topics in Canadian Economics Courses

1. Introduction and terminology
2. Business Organization
3. Labour unions
4. Application of Economic Reasoning
5. Demand, supply and the market
6. Distribution
7. Income Determination and the goal of economic equity
8. The Goal of Economic Efficiency
9. International trade

10. Role of government
11. Public finance
12. Personal Finance and Taxation

13. Focus on the future
14. Resources, personal income and consumption
15. Production and growth
16. Energy
17. Human resources

18. The Canadian Economy
19. The Provincial Economy
20. Measurement and Evaluation of Economic Activity
21. Unemployment, inflation and economic stabilization
22. The Goal of Economic Stability: Fiscal Policy
23. Money and banking
24. The Goal of Economic Stability: Monetary Policy

25. Economic History
26. History of economic ideas
27. Comparative economic systems

There is a wide variety of texts and other reference material listed and approved for classroom use by the various provinces. The most often listed text is *Made in Canada; Economics for Canadians* (Thexton, 1988). A new book, *Economics: A Canadian Perspective* (Thexton, 1992), appears to be a successor volume. The material is reorganized to counter some of the criticisms of the earlier book and it is aimed at the same secondary school audience.

We were unable to find any research on teacher preparation in Canada. Our correspondence with the Provincial Departments of Education indicated that the attitude seems to be that a "teacher is a teacher." A teaching certificate in social studies is all that is required to teach economics. Although school boards probably try to match assignments to teacher training, economics teachers do not require any training in the discipline.

Enrollments

Table 9.2 shows the enrollments in secondary schools in Canada by province and grade level. Quebec's secondary school system ends at grade eleven. Students then go to CEGEP's for two years before entering university or the labour force. These institutions are similar to community colleges but students can complete a purely academic program. On the other hand, Ontario's secondary school system goes to grade thirteen – one year more than all other provinces. This extra year is the equivalent to the first year of a university program and Ontario universities offer a three year bachelor of arts.

Enrollments by course are not published. However, we were able to gather some data on enrollments in high school economics courses through correspondence with the provinces. These incomplete data indicate that only about 5 percent of high school students take an economics course. (This varies from a high of 13.5 percent in Nova Scotia to a low of 3.4 percent in Alberta among the provinces for which we have data.) Thus, only about 3 percent (0.6 x 0.05) of all 15-19 year olds take an economics course.

TABLE 9.2: Secondary School Enrollment, Canada: 1990-91

Province	Number of Secondary Schools	Grade Twelve	Grade Eleven	Grade Ten	Total	% of 15-19 Year Olds Enrolled
Nfld.	142	10,799	9,845	10,795	31,439	63.7
P. E. I.	19	2,003	2,159	1,907	6,069	60.8
N. S.	136	11,806	12,021	13,103	36,930	63.7
N. B.	119	11,355	10,813	11,708	33,876	61.4
Quebec	673	-----	71,962	79,632	151,594	44.5
Ontario	1,067	219,259	142,951	147,647	509,857	70.9
Manitoba	157	17,925	15,770	17,306	51,001	62.0
Sask.	164	14,606	13,892	15,300	43,798	61.9
Alberta	350	37,378	31,467	33,668	102,513	56.7
B. C.	401	37,667	39,430	40,238	117,335	57.9
Yukon	5	251	311	277	839	---
N. W. T.	9	343	434	657	1434	68.4
Canada	3,242	363,392	351,055	372,238	1,086,685	60.2

Source: Statistics Canada, 1990-91, p. 12.

II. THE LASTING EFFECTS OF HIGH SCHOOL ECONOMICS

There is a growing body of evidence that taking an economics course in high school has lasting effects on the level of economics understanding of the individual. Studies that have been done in the United States, Canada and the United Kingdom all indicate lasting effects. We will examine some of these studies in more detail.

Evidence from the U.S.

An early article by Saunders (1970) was one of the first to examine this question. Saunders analyzed data collected at Carnegie-Mellon University from 1964 to 1969. He compared the arithmetic means of six explanatory variables for students (some of whom had taken a high school economics course and some of whom had not) with the mean results on two university economics courses and on a national test of economics understanding. He concluded:

> high school economics courses may have some lasting impact on the time spent on their introductory college course, their interest in economics, their C-841 grade and their performance on nationally standardized economics tests – even after they have completed their required one-semester college economics course. (p. 45)

Apparently, students used their knowledge of the subject acquired in the high school course to "buy" leisure time or more study time for other courses. They could do this and still achieve a significantly better grade on the university economics principles course, on average.

Saunders went on to run regressions on the same data both for the data set as a whole and for each term. The results were mixed and no firm conclusions on the lasting impact of high school economics were claimed. The high school economics course grade was not statistically significant for the sample as a whole and, on a term by term basis, in only one of the eight terms. The regressions for the *Test of Economic Understanding* (TEU) and the *Test of Understanding in College Economics* also produced mixed results. As Saunders stated:

> for large numbers of Carnegie-Mellon University students over several terms, it seems that a separate course in high school economics *does* have a significant lasting impact on TEU scores and Recognition and Understanding questions, but that it *does not* have a significant influence on Simple or Complex Application questions taken after a one semester college course. (p. 51)

An interesting question raised by Saunders is what to do with the student who has had a high school economics course. There are three possible choices: push them straight into the intermediate theory courses, put them in separate sections of the university principles course and put them in with the students who have no background in the discipline. He makes a strong case for not taking the first route. He argues that the university economics principles course should have a strong policy orientation and that these students need the repetition to confirm their understanding.

> Given a choice, I clearly opt for a heavier emphasis on using and applying, and reapplying, and reapplying, a relatively limited set of tools to a variety of policy problems rather than for adding any more tools than the average college graduate is ever likely to use in reading his daily newspaper. (p. 55)

The profession seems to agree with this conclusion since there are very few universities that give any recognition whatever to the high school economics course.

Evidence from the U.K.

Attiyeh and Lumsden (1971) also investigated the question of the lasting effects of high school economics teaching. Using a sample of 4700 students entering the first level university economics course in the academic year 1969-70 they concluded:

> (1) Students who had taken A level economics knew substantially more economics than those who had not. Scholarship level economics and A level economics history also added significantly but by a lesser margin to comprehension of economics. O level economics, however, was not a significant explanatory variable. Of non-economics A level courses, mathematics and general studies did have a significant positive effect, history had no significant effect, and geography had a significant negative effect. (2) On average, having attended a further education center rather than a school added significantly to understanding. (3) Males knew significantly more economics than females, but neither age nor year at university at which economics studies were started was important. The effect of intelligence test scores on understanding of economics, while significant and positive as expected, was not substantial. (p. 82)

In reaching these conclusions the U.K. study used as an instrument a 35 question test designed to find out if the student could take a real life economics situation or problem and determine the economics issues involved and the likely outcome or the appropriate economic policy action. The emphasis was then on applications rather on recall of definitions or theories. Students with A level economics performed substantially better, especially on the macroeconomics questions.

The regression analysis used the score on the above test as the dependent variable and twenty-eight explanatory variables. The latter were grouped into five categories. The first were general: age, sex, intelligence test scores and average mark on A level examinations. The second group contained the student's area of specialization at university. The third was the type of secondary school attended – there were five different types. The fourth category related to A level economics. The fifth category contained other examinations taken.

Although Attiyeh and Lumsden reach the same conclusion as the other studies that the high school economics grade is a contributor to better university economics grades, their regressions may have some technical problems with multicollinearity between some of the variables. For example, they found that the intelligence test score was significant but the average A level grade was not. These two variables probably measure the same thing and one of them should have been dropped from the equation. Similarly, age and years since taking A level economics would be correlated.

> The number of years since the A level economics examination was taken unexpectedly did not have a significant coefficient. This suggests that there was no depreciation over time in the stock of knowledge of economics acquired in studying A level economics. (p. 87)

An alternative interpretation is that this variable is correlated with age and the greater understanding that comes with age offsets the depreciation in the impact of A level economics. Controlling for these problems might have influenced the interpretation of the results and produced different signs and coefficient values for other variables.

It is interesting that the student's opinion of his A level economics teacher had a negative sign and was significant. Could this mean that good students recognize poor teaching and poorer students do not?

Recent Canadian Findings

The effectiveness of the teaching and learning of high school economics in Canada was tested by examining the performance of students from a large high school in the Maritimes, who all took the introductory economics course at the local university (Myatt and Waddell, 1990). A total of 928 students were included, and of these 371 had taken the high school economics course from the same instructor. The sample period was 1976-1984. The assumption that the data all came from the same population was tested using a standard F test. The assumption was not rejected.

The study first attempted to explain the performance of all 928 students in the university economics principles course. The equation used was:

$$PCG = a_o + a_1COMPULS + a_2HOURS + a_3MMATH + a_4DMATH + a_5MENG$$
$$+ a_6AGED + a_7SEX + a_8DHSE + a_9CSIZE + a_{10}1984D + a_{11}DI_1 ...$$
$$... + a_{30}DI_{20} + e_t$$

The dependent variable, PCG, is the percent grade in the university economics principles course. COMPULS is a dummy equal to one if the student is in a degree program in which university economic principles course is required and zero otherwise. HOURS is the number of credit hours in economics taken beyond the introductory level. These two variables together were included to measure the attitude of the student to economics. MMATH is the mark on grade eleven or grade twelve mathematics. DMATH is a dummy equal to one if grade twelve mathematics was taken and zero otherwise. MENG is the grade twelve English mark. Grade twelve English is compulsory for all high school students. AGED is the number years between high school graduation and the university economics principles course. SEX is a dummy equal to one for female students and zero for males. DHSE is the high school economics dummy, one if taken and zero otherwise.

The variables CSIZE, 1984D and DI_i all relate to the characteristics of the university economics principles course. Twenty-one different instructors taught sections of the course over the study period. The DI's are then instructor dummies and attempt to pick up the difference in instructor "human capital" or examination standards. For most of the study period each instructor had complete freedom to design the course and set examinations. There was no common content. All but four of these instructor dummies proved to be insignificant when the regression was run.

In 1984 the Department experimented with an alternative delivery system for the principles course. A "mass lecture with tutorials" system was used. The 1984D variable is a dummy to pick up this change. It is equal to one for 1984 and zero otherwise. CSIZE was a numerical variable equal to the university principles class size at the end of the course. Class size was not a significant determinant of grades.

The study found that English grades were slightly more important than mathematics grades but not significantly so. Grade twelve mathematics contributed three percentage points to the university economics mark over grade eleven mathematics. The gender dummy variable suggests that *ceteris paribus* males performed slightly better than females (though since females significantly outperformed males in high school English, the average female mark exceeds the average male mark). The greater the time lag between high school graduation and the university economics principles course (AGED) the better the student did. The 1984 dummy was significantly negative indicating that the change in format made the course harder for students.

The importance of high school economics was tested in two ways. First, the regression was run using the dummy described above. High school economics was highly significant and on average contributed three and one-half percentage points to the university grade in economics. Second, another regression was run using only those students who had taken the high school economics course. Their grade was substituted for the dummy. This equation had a higher R^2. A significant and important influence was found for the high school economics course. The coefficient was 0.613, and was significant at the one percent level.

The study went on to examine the performance of those students in the data base who took the intermediate micro and macro theory courses. The sample sizes were much smaller: 138 and 93 respectively. The explanatory power of the variables was greatly reduced. To quote the original study:

> Overall, the impression we got from these equations was that not only did the effect of high school economics decay over time, but, more particularly, the explanatory power of all the variables that previously performed well decayed also....This could be because the self-selection process had more time to operate as we moved into the higher echelons, or that, as the student matured, our initial measures of ability and attitude became outdated. (p. 361).

III. CONCLUSION

In the first part of this chapter we have attempted a thumbnail sketch of high school economics in Canada. Every province offers some economics, though there is great variety of topics covered. Economics is not compulsory at high school, and only a minority of students in Canada (5 percent) do enroll. Research on the lasting effects of high school economic education also confirms that high school economics does indeed have an impact on the student. This shows up in higher grades in the university economics principles course as well as on other tests of economic understanding.

REFERENCES

Attiyeh, R., & Lumsden, K. G. (1971). University students' initial understanding of economics: The contribution of the A Level economics course and other factors. *Economica, 38*(149), 81-97.

Canada. (1991). *Elementary/Secondary school enrollment*. Ottawa: Statistics Canada (Catalog no. 81-210).

Myatt, A. E., & Waddell, C. M. (1990). An approach to testing the effectiveness of the teaching and learning of economics in high school. *Journal of Economic Education, 21*(3), 355-363.

Ontario Ministry of Education. (1986). *Curriculum guideline: Business studies - economics*. Province of Ontario.

British Columbia Ministry of Education. (1990). *Economics 12: Curriculum guide (CGO299)*. Province of British Columbia.

Saunders, P. (1970). Does high school economics have a lasting impact? *Journal of Economic Education, 2*(1), 39-52.

Thexton, J. D. (1988). *Made in Canada; Economics for Canadians*. Toronto: Oxford University Press.

Thexton, J. D. (1992). *Economics: A Canadian perspective*. Toronto: Oxford University Press.

CHAPTER 10

ECONOMIC EDUCATION IN JAPANESE SECONDARY SCHOOLS

Lucien Ellington

Tadahisa Uozumi

While there is no self-contained economics course in Japanese high schools, inclusion of economics concepts and generalizations within social studies occurs at both the elementary and secondary levels. What follows are descriptions of the context of economic education in Japan, curriculum and textbooks, teachers and pedagogy, the role of the Japanese Research Council on Economic Education, and the future of economic education. Although emphasis is on senior high school economic education, the ninth grade civics course is also described since, because of recent reforms, most students take only one course in senior high school containing significant economics content.

I. THE CONTEXT OF ECONOMIC EDUCATION IN JAPAN

In 1947 during the Occupation, the American 6-3-3 system was adopted with seventh, eighth, and ninth grades included in the junior high or lower secondary school and tenth, eleventh, and twelfth grades constituting the high school or upper secondary school. While the 6-3-3 system is a foreign import, two components of the Japanese prewar educational system, central control of education and the examination system, are still present today. The Tokyo-based

Japanese ministry of education is responsible for the establishment of a national curriculum for all subjects. Students must pass examinations in order to enter public and private upper secondary schools and universities.

Almost 95 percent of all lower secondary school students graduate from upper secondary schools. Approximately 70 percent of upper secondary students attend academic high schools which feature a college-preparatory curriculum. The remainder of Japan's upper secondary students attend vocational high schools. Almost 40 percent of all Japanese high school students go on to attend junior college or university after graduation.

Economic education in postwar Japan is conducted within the framework of "social studies," another Occupation innovation. Before the war young Japanese learned about the social world through studying subjects such as history, geography, and ethics. American Occupation leaders regarded these disciplines as the primary mediums for the inculcation of militarist values in the young. U.S. style social studies replaced the prewar curriculum. The prewar exclusive emphasis upon history and geography was expanded as economics, sociology, anthropology, and psychology content has also constituted the elementary and secondary social studies curriculum since the Occupation. While the Ministry of Education has revised the social studies curriculum several times since the Occupation period, economics remains an important component of several elementary and secondary social studies courses.

II. ECONOMICS IN SOCIAL STUDIES CURRICULA AND TEXTBOOKS

Elementary Economic Education

Japanese students begin to learn economic content in elementary school. The economic content that youngsters learn at this level theoretically assists them to attain the general objectives of elementary social studies as outlined by the Ministry of Education. These general objectives include a basic understanding of social life and cultivation of fundamental awareness of citizenship, both in a democratic and peaceful nation, and in an international community.

The present national course of study for elementary schools underwent revisions in 1989 that were implemented in 1992. Economics concepts are included in third and fifth grade social studies. Third graders learn of the functions of their city or community business district and study such concepts as consumer, good, and price. Sample economic content taught to fifth graders include the current state of agriculture, fishing and manufacturing in Japan, an introduction to international trade and the concepts of import and export, and an introduction to national transportation and communications. Consumer education receives particular emphasis in both grades with a focus upon the daily economic lives of Japanese. ,Economics is not presented to elementary students as a separate academic discipline. It should be understood that in a sense elementary students indirectly learn economic concepts through focusing upon everyday life of families, communities and the nation.

Economics in Lower Secondary Schools

All Japanese lower secondary school students learn economics in two required courses, geography and civics. Economic content in geography includes resources, manufacturing, Japan's linkages through transportation and foreign trade, and Japan's role in the international division of labor.

Students receive the first systematic introduction to economics as an academic discipline in ninth grade civics, which is partially a rudimentary political economy course. Students study such topics as the structure of the economy, the functions of prices, taxes, trade unions, the societal role of enterprise, employment, consumer protection, resource development, the economic role of national and local governments, comparative economic systems, and foreign trade. In April 1993, the month that marks the beginning of the Japanese school year, revisions in the lower secondary school social studies curricula were implemented that had direct implications for economic education.

In the newly revised course of study for civics, additional emphasis is now placed upon teaching young Japanese adolescents about the internationalization of their nation's economy, the movement toward an information-oriented society, and the increased role of credit cards in Japanese life. The new Ministry-approved textbooks that were first used in 1993 reflected the curriculum revisions. For example, one civics textbook included sections on consumers and credit cards and world economic interdependence. Economics content comprises approximately 30 percent of civics.

Economics In Upper Secondary Schools

In all subjects in Japanese schools, the Ministry of Education Courses of Study constitute the national curriculum. Presently, high schools utilize the 1983 social studies course of study. However, in 1994 a new course of study will take effect through a three stage process. Tenth graders will be subject to the new requirements in 1994, eleventh graders in 1995, and twelfth graders in 1996. First, the economic components in the 1983 course of study are described and afterward a description of the new changes is included.

Under the old guidelines, economic content comprised approximately 30 percent of the contemporary society course which was required of tenth graders. Economic content constituted approximately 50 percent of politics-economics, an upper secondary school elective in the old course of study taken primarily by university-bound students. The economics content in these two courses is depicted in Table 10.1 which is excerpted from the English-language translation of the 1983 Social Studies course of study.

In the recently revised course of study the requirement that all upper secondary school students take contemporary society as tenth graders was eliminated. Instead, all senior high school students must take either contemporary society or politics-economics. Japanese educators expect that contemporary society will be the course for vocational high school students who do not plan to attend university. University-bound students will enroll in politics-economics. The Ministry design of the contemporary society course is such that teachers are not expected to go into great depth about economic content. By contrast, politics-economics teachers are expected to provide a systematic and theoretical classroom treatment of economics.

Before the new curriculum guideline changes a student, usually university-bound and interested in social sciences, could take both contemporary society and politics-economics. Enrollment data for the politics-economics course is unavailable. However, it is possible to estimate the number of students taking politics-economics under the 1983 guidelines by using Ministry of Education textbook sales statistics. Nationwide, in 1992 politics-economics textbook purchases constituted a little over 18 percent of all upper-level social studies textbook sales. Since a student could take politics-economics in either the second or third year of high school, it is likely that slightly under 40 percent of all secondary school graduates took politics-economics when the old guidelines were in effect.

The new situation eliminates the previous student heterogeneity of contemporary society and more distinctly tracks the college and non-college bound into one course or the other. There is little change in the economic content for contemporary society and politics-economics except for more emphasis in both courses on Japan's role in the international economic community and the recent demise of many socialist economies.

Japanese teachers are required to follow the Ministry courses of study and to utilize textbooks which have received approval from the Ministry textbook screening system. There should be high congruence among Japanese secondary teachers as to what economic content is important for students to learn in the classroom. Evidence of this congruence received empirical support in a study in which a random national sample of 88 Japanese civics and contemporary society teachers rated the relative importance of teaching students 22 separate economic concepts (Ellington and Uozumi, 1988). The five ranking categories ranged from very important (5) and important (4) to unimportant (1). The top ten economic concepts by rank order were: supply and demand, inflation/deflation, GNP, role of government, markets and prices, balance of payments, exchange rates, competition/market structure, fiscal policy, unemployment, monetary policy, and productivity.

TABLE 10.1: Present Contemporary Society and Politics-Economy Courses of Study

CONTEMPORARY SOCIETY

- *Economic society and national welfare of the present age*
  - — Development of science and technology, and economic life of the present age (enlargement of production and modern enterprises, price mechanism and role of the government, economic system, etc.)
  - — Characteristics and internationalization of the Japanese economy (trends in the national income, business fluctuations, general trends in the balance of payments, etc.)
  - — Harmonious economic development and realization of welfare (protection of consumers and responsibility of enterprises, respect for human beings and the prevention of pollution, improvement of working conditions and relations, social security and realization of a welfare society, etc.)

POLITICS AND ECONOMY

- *Japanese economy and national welfare*
  - — Characteristics and function of the present economy, changes in economic society, markets and enterprises of the present day, etc.
- *Structures of the national economy and economic growth*
  - — National wealth and national income, stabilization and growth of the economy, roles of the monetary system and finance, etc.
- *International economy and international co-operation*
  - — Trends in the international economy, changes in economic systems, the role of Japan and the direction taking place in the development in the international economy, etc.
- *Present state of the Japanese economy and national welfare*
  - — Industrial structures of Japan and problems of the Japanese economy, basic problems concerning improvements of the people's life and realization of welfare, especially development of science and technology, use of resources and energy, prevention of pollution, improvement of labor relations, protection of consumers, promotion of the social security system, etc.

Except for productivity, over 80 percent of the sample of Japanese teachers assigned 4s or 5s to each of these concepts with 86 percent constituting the mean level of agreement (assigned 4s and 5s) for the ten concepts. By contrast, when a national sample of American high school economics teachers were asked to rank the same 22 concepts by order of classroom importance, the mean level of agreement (assigned 4s and 5s) for the top ten concepts by teachers from that nation was 72 percent.

The economic concepts that were ranked in the top ten by Japanese teachers also suggest specific patterns of economic content emphasis. Balance of payments/exchange rates, fiscal policy, GNP, and unemployment were included in the Japanese teacher list of the ten most important economic concepts but were absent from the American list. Macroeconomics has traditionally received more emphasis in Japan than in the United States, as reflected by Japanese courses of study, textbooks, and teacher responses in the 1988 study.

While Japanese ranked balance of payments/exchange rates 6/22 in importance, American teachers ranked the same concept 22/22, or last in order of importance. This concept had the highest variance in rank of any of the items in the comparative study. The variance suggests that even before the Ministry of Education in the late 1980s placed a stronger emphasis upon internationalization, Japanese teachers paid considerable attention to at least one international economics concept.

A more recent study (1990) suggests that high school contemporary society and politics-economics teachers are particularly interested in teaching students about various aspects of the Japan-U.S. economic relationship. This is significant for two reasons. It is an indicator that high school social studies teachers are responding to government imperatives to internationalize the curriculum. Also, while the uniform national curriculum is certainly a centralizing force, teachers have some freedom to focus upon topics that they consider to be particularly important such as bilateral Japan-U.S. economic relations.

In a national survey of 73 contemporary society and politics-economics teachers, 83 percent reported agreed or strongly agreed upon the importance of teaching about the U.S. economy and U.S.-Japan economic relations. Approximately 60 percent of respondents reported spending two to five hours per academic year teaching about the U.S.-Japan economic relationships while 14 percent of respondents reported spending six to ten hours on the subject. Respondents were asked to indicate from a list of nine possible topics about the U.S. economy and U.S.-Japan relations which topics they covered in the classroom. While 96 percent of the respondents reported teaching about the U.S.-Japan trade imbalance, and 59 percent claimed to teach about free trade and protectionism using U.S. and Japanese examples, all other topics listed failed to be covered by as much as half of the teachers.

Economic Content in Secondary Social Studies Textbooks

Even though there seems to be evidence of variance in coverage of economic content in Japanese secondary classrooms, the textbook is the primary instructional tool. Courses of study, despite some recent liberalization, constitute the curriculum and Ministry officials must approve textbooks. Approved books tend to be detailed reflections of courses of study.

Japanese secondary social studies textbooks are compact and are almost always completely covered by the teacher during the academic year. Despite their size, texts usually contain a high percentage of quantitative content. For example, one 217-page politics-economics textbook was found to contain 93 pages of detailed charts and graphs. The economics sections of civics, contemporary society, and politics-economics textbooks include graphs on rates of individual output over the past 70 years for the five leading world economies, consumer prices, wholesale prices, wage demands, wage settlements, and world imports and exports for leading industrialized countries over the last 20 years.

The question of treatment of controversial political economy issues has been raised in two studies of Japanese high school social studies texts. American reviewers in a joint Japanese-U.S. textbook study (1981) found Japanese economic content to have more ideological diversity than American texts. Japanese authors were more likely to include such topics as unemployment and labor relations than their American counterparts. The economics content in contemporary society textbooks was examined in a 1989 study by the Japan Institute for Social and Economic Affairs (Kezai Koho Center). Reviewers claimed a bias that suggested private enterprise is interested only in profits and that Japanese consumers are too weak to affect actions of the private sector. Center officials filed a request with the Ministry of Education for inclusion of a more objective description of the relative power of companies and consumers in future contemporary society texts.

III. TEACHERS AND TEACHING METHODS

Characteristics of Secondary Social Studies Teachers Responsible for Economics Content

Although specific subject matter-gender statistics are unavailable, the large majority of secondary social studies teachers are male. In 1989 men constituted 85 percent of all upper secondary school teachers and 67 percent of the lower secondary school teaching force. Women most likely represent less than five percent of the secondary school social studies teachers since the majority of women in secondary schools teach home economics and physical education.

Although as university students the majority of Japanese secondary school teachers major in a discipline other than education, prospective teachers' academic fields are much more likely to be history or politics than economics. Johnson and Shima (1986) identified lack of university economics training as a major problem of Japanese teachers. When the authors of this chapter interviewed 15 civics and contemporary society teachers in nine different schools in Aichi Prefecture in 1987, the maximum number of economic courses any teacher had taken in university was four.

There is also a lack of opportunities for practicing teachers to improve their economic understanding through formal study. The long Japanese school year prevents most teachers from participating in workshops or obtaining graduate degrees. However, the nature of the high school teacher's daily schedule does allow some time for study. The relatively light teaching load of Japanese high school teachers – the average is approximately 15 hours a week – affords them some time to read and conduct research in their academic areas of interest. Also, secondary teachers tend to view themselves as subject matter specialists and there is a strong tradition of local subject matter associations. Still, it should be stressed again that the majority of secondary school teachers responsible for courses containing significant amounts of economic content are more likely to be primarily interested in other subjects than economics.

One of the authors found evidence of a somewhat neutral to cold attitude on the part of teachers toward economics in a 1987 survey of secondary social studies teachers in Aichi Prefecture in which 82 responses were obtained. When asked to rate seven possible topical priorities for emphasis in the social studies classroom, respondents ranked economics and consumer education last. Economics ranked behind such topics as global education, history, and human rights education.

Instructional Methods

A national curriculum and university entrance examination system emphasizing student memorization of large amounts of information influences most secondary teachers to rely on textbook-based lectures and to require student acquisition of large amounts of factual information. Observations of teachers in civics and contemporary society classes indicate they tended to cover economics by lecturing, writing statistics on the chalkboard and referring students to the textbooks. Teacher questions to students were confined to the fact and comprehension levels of Bloom's *Taxonomy*. It was extremely rare for students to ask questions of the teacher. The following case study drawn from observation of economics instruction in a civics class in Tsu, Japan, is illustrative of typical instructional style and student-teacher interactions.

Case Study

Civics class, Lower secondary school Tsu, Japan:

> The bell has rung and the 43 ninth graders, the boys in summer uniforms of white shirts and black pants, and the girls in gray skirts and white blouses, rise and bow as the teacher walks in the room. The teacher bows back, everyone is seated, and the lesson begins. The topic is the effect of the recent rise in the yen's value upon the Japanese economy. The teacher asks students to name possible good and bad effects of the yen's rise. The teacher calls upon two students who rise from their seats to give answers. Two other students volunteer answers. Although one or two answers indicate confusion over the economic effects upon Japan of the rising yen, there are also correct answers such as cheaper overseas travel for Japanese and lower profits for Japanese exporters.
>
> The teacher, after taking only a few minutes to ask the question, lists economic effects of the rise of the yen upon the chalkboard. All students in the class appear to be diligently taking notes. Several effects listed are: cheaper prices for Japanese abroad, increased difficulty for Japanese exporters, small Japanese companies going bankrupt, and increased difficulty for Japanese who wish to purchase foreign goods.
>
> The teacher uses the current yen-dollar situation to introduce his lecture on exchange rates. The students follow the teacher with their textbooks and, upon his suggestion, refer to several exchange rate graphs and tables. All textbooks are open on the left side of student desks while notebooks are on the right side of the desk. Other than the opening ten minute dialogue between the teacher and students there are no questions in the remainder of the 50-minute period.

While foreign observers have noted the relatively sophisticated nature of secondary school economics content, American anthropologist Thomas Rohlen's 1983 assertion in reference to Japanese classroom pedagogy that "...efficiency is high and inspiration low," still holds true today.

The Influence of University Entrance Examinations Upon Economic Education

For over a century, university entrance examinations have exercised a strong influence upon Japanese secondary education. Since in contemporary Japan almost 40 percent of all high school students attend university, the influence of the university entrance examination upon secondary education has grown stronger relative to the past. However, unlike other social studies fields, the substantial pressure upon teachers and students caused by impending university examinations is not largely true in the case of economics.

A major component of the present university-entrance system is a common national examination jointly administered by the National Center for University Examinations and local universities. Individual university faculties (departments) often administer a second examination to applicants who score above their established "cut off" point for the common examination. The common examination is an achievement rather than an aptitude test. All 132 public universities, as well as some private institutions, utilize the common examination. Although university faculties have some discretion, most applicants who take the common examination are required to take examinations in four or five subject matter areas (foreign language, Japanese language, mathematics, social studies, and natural science). In 1992, 68 percent of all applicants taking the common entrance examination were tested in social studies.

Within the social studies subject area, applicants may choose to be tested in one of five subfields. In 1993, the high school students who chose the subfields which contain economics content represented under nine percent of all examinees in social studies. This is because most students and teachers believe it is more difficult to achieve a high score in the subfields with economics content (ethics and politics-economics, and contemporary society) than in the history subfields.

The statistics presented in Table 10.2 below certainly seem to support this belief. There is little strong incentive for Japanese high school students to learn a voluminous amount of economics content for university-entrance examinations since most choose not to take the economics-related social studies subfields. It is of interest that this lack of pressure upon most students to learn economics for university examinations does not cause their teachers to be more innovative in the classroom.

Two sample 1993 NCUEE university-entrance questions from the contemporary society and ethics and politics-economics are included in Table 10.3 on the next page.

TABLE 10.2: Number of Students, Percentage, and Results of the 1993 NCUEE Social Studies Examination by Subfield

Subfield	N	%	Score
Ethics and Politics-Economics	31,292	7.2%	62.34
Japanese History	174,385	40.2	73.37
World History	126,217	29.0	65.71
Geography	95,259	21.9	69.47
Contemporary Society	6,593	1.5	62.09

Note: Score is average score, with 100 being a perfect score.

TABLE 10.3: 1993 NCUEE University Entrance Examination Sample Economics Questions

1. Which of the following statements is incorrect as a description related to firms' acquisition of capital funds? Select one from (1) through (4) below. ______

    (1) Capital funds raised through issuance of stock shares do not need to be repaid.
    (2) Corporate bonds represent a way to borrow capital funds through issuance of securities.
    (3) Borrowing from banks is called direct financing.
    (4) Corporate retained earnings constitute part of equity capital.

2. Which of the following statements is incorrect as a description related to "effective demand management policy"? Select one from (1) through (4) below. ______

    (1) Demand backed by ability to buy is called effective demand.
    (2) Keynes contended that the volume of employment is determined by the size of the effective demand.
    (3) Imports by a country constitute an effective demand for its products.
    (4) An increase in effective demand under the condition of full employment will cause inflation.

The Japanese Research Council on Economic Education

The Japanese Research Council on Economic Education was established in 1968 as a non-profit organization and utilized the American National Council on Economic Education as a primary model. The JRCEE's major purpose is to improve economic education in elementary and secondary schools.

Major JRCEE projects include two economic education seminars for teachers, and since 1968, the publication of the monthly *Economic Education*. In 1989 the JRCEE also began publication of *Research on Economic Education* which appears annually. Other JRCEE work includes financial support for a few teachers to participate in a U.S. university summer economic education workshop, and recommendations to the Ministry of Education about curricula, instructional materials and textbooks, and translation of American economic education curriculum materials.

In the one-day fall and two-day summer seminars economists and businessmen lecture on such topics as the future of the Japanese economy and the European Community and the Japanese economy. Some senior high school teachers also give lectures and demonstrations on pedagogy and research in economic education in the seminars. Senior high school teachers are also contributors to JRCEE publications.

While the JRCEE plays a needed role in promoting and improving economic education in Japan, its overall national influence is minor. A valid criticism of the JRCEE is that it is too Tokyo-centered since most staff live in that city and few nationwide programs are offered. Also, the JRCEE membership is small and comprised largely of senior high school teachers. Currently, plans have been formulated for expansion of the organization to include teachers at other grade levels.

IV. THE FUTURE OF ECONOMIC EDUCATION IN JAPAN

By the beginning of the 21st century Japan will probably have a more internationalized economy than at present. Also, in the near future citizens and policymakers must contend with serious problems such as the aging of the Japanese population and changing economic roles of women.

If Japan's future citizenry is to be truly economically literate several changes within economic education seem advisable. These include increasing the university economics training of social studies teachers and changing their somewhat negative attitudes toward economics, expanding the JRCEE's scope and membership, and the encouragement of innovative approaches to teaching economic concepts in the high school classroom.

Japanese already enjoy some of the very highest educational levels in the world and classroom achievement is one reason why the country ranks among the world's strongest economies. A more economically literate future citizenry will serve only to enhance the prospects for continuation of economic success.

NOTES

The authors would like to thank Professor Kiyoshi Kawahito of Middle Tennessee State University for his translation assistance.

REFERENCES

Economic Planning Agency/Government of Japan. (1983). *Outlook and guidelines for the economy and society in the 1980s*. Tokyo: Printing Bureau, Ministry of Finance.

Ellington, J. L. (1992). *Education in the Japanese life-cycle*. Lewiston, New York: The Edwin Mellen Press.

Ellington, J. L., & Uozumi, T. (1988). Economic education in Japanese and American secondary schools. *Theory and Research in Social Education, 16*(2), 103-114.

The Japanese Research Council on Economic Education. (1988). *The history of the Japanese Research Council on Economic Education in 20 years*. Tokyo: Japan Research Council on Economic Education.

Johnson, J. D., & Shima, H. (1986). *Success of economic education in the United States and Japan.* Unpublished manuscript. Eau Claire, WI: Center for Economic Education, University of Wisconsin.

Kato, K. (1983). *Social studies curriculum making in Japan (1): Nationally-described course of study.* Unpublished paper. Kyoto: Joint Conference of Japanese and American Social Studies Education.

Ministry of Education, Science, and Culture: Government of Japan. (1983). *Course of study for elementary schools in Japan, course of study for lower secondary schools in Japan, course of study for upper secondary schools in Japan.* Tokyo: Printing Bureau, Ministry of Finance.

Ministry of Education, Science, and Culture: Government of Japan. (1989). *Education in Japan: A graphic presentation.* Tokyo: Ministry of Education.

Ministry of Education, Science, and Culture: Government of Japan. (1989). *Elementary school teacher's guide: Social studies.* Tokyo: Gakkotosho Company.

Ministry of Education, Science, and Culture: Government of Japan. (1989). *Lower secondary school teacher's guide: Social studies.* Osaka: Isakashosokei Company.

Ministry of Education, Science, and Culture: Government of Japan. (1989). *Upper secondary school teacher's guide: Civics.* Tokyo: Zitsukyoshupan Company.

Ministry of Education, Science, and Culture: Government of Japan. (1992). *Japanese government policies in education, science and culture 1990, Japanese government policies in education, science and culture 1991.* Tokyo: Printing Bureau, Ministry of Finance.

Obunsha. (1992). *The right answers to questions of the university entrance examination.* Tokyo.

The Policy Committee of The Comprehensive Policy Division of the Social Policy Council. (1983). *Internationalization of Japanese life.* Tokyo: Printing Bureau, Ministry of Finance.

Rohlen, T. P. (1983). *Japan's high schools.* Berkeley: University of California.

Uozumi, T. (1983). *Social studies curriculum making in Japan (2): Examples of school curriculum and local curriculum.* Unpublished paper. Tokyo: Joint Conference of Japanese and American Social Studies Education.

Uozumi, T. (1987). A study on economic education in social studies (1): The present situation of American economic education and its implication. *The Bulletin of Aichi University of Education* (Kariya, Japan), *36* (Educational Science), 15-31.

Uozumi, T. (1988). A study on economic education in social studies (2): Problems and reform orientation in Japanese economic education. *The Bulletin of Aichi University of Education* (Kariya, Japan), *37* (Educational Science), 1-13.

Uozumi, T. (1989). The internationalization of Japan and international education: Some research and practices at teachers college. *The Review of Social Sciences* (The Society of Social Sciences of Aichi University of Education, Kariya, Japan), *29*, 183-201.

Uozumi, T. (1991). Senior high school economics teachers' attitude about and treatment of the U.S. *The Review of Social Sciences* (The Society of Social Sciences of Aichi University of Education, Kariya, Japan), *31*, 45-56.

Yamane, E. (1985). Economic education in Japan at the precollege level. *Journal of Economic Education, 16*(4), 273-276.

CHAPTER 11

ECONOMIC LITERACY IN GERMAN-SPEAKING COUNTRIES AND THE UNITED STATES: METHODS AND FIRST RESULTS OF A COMPARATIVE STUDY

Klaus Beck

Volker Krumm

A corollary of the world's emerging global economy, and the ensuing competition for economic markets, is that interdependencies among countries become more necessary and extensive. As a consequence, the economic dimension of life becomes more differentiated for all nations and their citizens, and there are more opportunities for improving quality of life by using the possibilities afforded by a world-wide common market. Yet the key to achieving higher levels of quality of life lies in an understanding of economic facts, and of the interrelationships and effects of co-operating within this complex marketplace. Whether acting for personal benefit or as representatives for a variety of institutions, individuals must posses a knowledge and understanding of underlying economic principles and concepts.

The future of national and international development and economic well-being is dependent on the capability of future generations to manage the increasingly more complex conditions of economic activities. It is, therefore, important to assess the level of economic knowledge, especially of the young people from different nations.

We have representative data from Soper and Walstad (1987) for the United States on the achievement level in economics of high school students at the age of about 17 years. We decided to gather comparable information for the same age group in Austria and Germany. It is now possible to compare our results for Austria and Germany with those reported by Soper and Walstad for the United States to assess the economic knowledge of the student populations of these countries.

Of course, a valid comparison is based upon the assumption that the different instruments used in the different countries for the measurement of economic achievement are equivalent. To achieve this objective, we developed a German version of the *Test of Economic Literacy* (TEL) used by Soper and Walstad for the United States (for details of this procedure see Beck and Krumm 1991).

To have a well-adapted instrument with respect to language, economic terminology, and culture is only one of the conditions necessary for a useful comparison. A second condition concerns the relative opportunities of the students sampled to learn the subject content of that which is being measured, i.e., economic concepts and principles. Differences in scores across sample nationalities may be due in part to the divergent educational systems themselves and to the amount of time allocated to the study of economics in the curriculum. For an international comparison, it is necessary to look at these cross-national differences within a framework of cultural fairness. That is, we have to work out to which extent the different groups of our German-speaking students are expected to succeed in performing a test for the measurement of their relevant capabilities. Furthermore, with regard to measurement methods, especially validity, it would be of interest to know whether a specific instrument used in different cultures captures the expected results, given differences across curricular content for the various types of relevant education.

With respect to methodology, we first outline the most important features of economic education in Austria and Germany in contrast to the United States (Section I). We then look at the validity of the instrument – the German TEL (called *W*irtschaftskundliche *B*ildung-*T*est: WBT) – in terms of teachers' judgments on the 77 different items of the WBT (II). We conclude with the presentation of some empirical results from Austria and Germany as compared with those for the United States (III).

I. ECONOMIC EDUCATION IN AUSTRIA, GERMANY, AND THE UNITED STATES

School System Related Differences

The main difference between the American system, on the one hand, and the Austrian and German systems, on the other, is that students in the United States in the age group of 16 to 17 years (grades 11 and 12) essentially attend one basic type of school type, namely the (senior) high school. There, they usually have a choice among several subjects, one of which is economics. In contrast, in

Austria and Germany, the students of the same age group are distributed among several different types of schools. Only the elementary schools (grades 1 - 4) are of the comprehensive type in both countries.

At the age of 10, and again at the age of 14 (Austria) and 15 (Germany), students in these respective school systems must choose which of (at least) five school types they want to attend. These types are mainly distinguished by the vocational and career prospects they offer to their students (a short description of their main features is listed on Table 11.1). Austrian and German students, therefore, make a choice among different sets of subjects when they choose a particular type of school, and having made the decision, they are (with some minor exceptions) no longer free to choose subjects which are of personal interest for them. The curriculum within a special school type is mandatory (i.e., students will either have to learn economics if they attend a school which offers this subject as one of its special set or they will have no chance to learn economics because the school type they have chosen doesn't offer this course).

Normally in Austria and Germany, the decision of school type is not influenced by the student's interest in special subjects. Rather, students seek the certificates they can attain from their choice of school and the role their choice of education can play in career plans. The choice to attend one type of school and not another implies that a student wants to acquire special skills and academic qualifications suited for his or her individual vocational plans. The result is that, among 16 to 17 year old students, some may receive a more intensive education in economics and also in business affairs if intending to either study these subjects at the university (see Table 11.1, #2), or to enter a business-oriented academy (similar to American undergraduate colleges) with the goal of securing a middle management job (see Table 11.1, #3). A student of this age might, as an alternative, choose an apprenticeship of three years (ground level) in one of approximately 40 different commercial vocational orientations like retail, wholesale, industry, insurance, banking, etc. (Benner, 1992; see Table 11.1, #5). Other students may choose to attend schools of general education where business and economics don't play a major role if any (middle and upper cycle of secondary schools; see Table 11.1, #1, 4). School type 4 (SSG) exists only in Germany. We omit it therefore from empirical comparisons (Section III).

Table 11.1 also provides the approximate percentages of the age group of 17-year-old students attending the different school types. These figures are somewhat rough estimates since it is very difficult to get consistent forms of data due to the organization of the educational systems, but they highlight the importance of the vocational schools in Austria and Germany. There are, of course, also differences between the Austrian and the German school systems. For purposes of the comparison presented in this paper, however, these differences are irrelevant. The more important concern involves the determination of which of the Austrian/German students are most similar to American high school students. Looking only at the formal structure of the various educational

TABLE 11.1: School Types and Percentage Enrollments for Austria and Germany

No.	Type and Description	Percentage of all 17-year-old persons attending: Austria	Germany
1	*General Secondary School (GSS)* Schools of general education (not vocational) which provide the possibility of attending university.	15.3%	27.3%
2	*Senior Vocational School (SVS)* Schools of general and vocational education permitting entrance to university as well as to business (with a degree). The vocational qualification is in Austria higher than in Germany.	3.8	2.0
3	*Intermediate Vocational School (IVS)* School of vocational education providing a middling training for a career in business (no entrance to university).	5.8	10.3
4	*Secondary School [Germany only] (SSG)* School of general education (not vocational) providing a middling degree for entrance to secondary higher education institutions.	----	----
5	*Dual Vocational System (DVS)* School of vocational education for apprentices offering a one-or-two-days training per week ("theoretical background" for the "practical" work in the firm for the rest of the week).	49.4	30.7
5a	*Dual Vocational System/Retail [commercial depts.] (DVS/R)*		
5b	*Dual Vocational System/Industry [commercial depts.] (DVS/I)*		
	Other school types	25.8	29.7
	Sum	100.0	100.0

systems, we might view Austrian and German General Secondary School students as most comparable to American high school students. One must bear in mind, however, that students attending this type of school are representatives of the best overall quality of Austrian/German students. With respect to the general level of intellectual competencies, the Austrian/German students in the Intermediate and the Dual Vocational Schools would be more similar, in effect, to the American high school students on the average, with the difference that the students in the German-speaking sample have already made a decision as to their vocational specialization. A more comparable sub-sample may be selected, however, by focusing on the curricula and length of subject and course instruction for the various groups of Austrian/German students. Nevertheless, it should be kept in mind that these students don't participate in economics courses because of personal interest in this subject but rather due to their choice of career. If a student wants to go into the world of commerce, there is no chance to avoid economics. On the other hand some students, based on their career aspirations may, in the worst case, never receive any economic education.

Time Budget-related Differences

In all three countries, the study of economics is never merely a single course offering (i.e., "economics course"). Instead, many courses may include an economics-related content. In the United States, economic theory and principles may be included in the general subject headings such as "consumer economics," "social studies," "government/world studies," etc. The same is true for Austria and Germany; only the combinations of general subject areas differ slightly (e.g., "history & social studies"). However, there remains one important difference between the United States and Austrian/German samples: in Austria and Germany, the amount of teaching time for every subject and the subject content are fixed according to school type.

Tables 11.2a and 11.2b provide information about the number of hours per week for subjects with some degree of economic content according to school type, subject and grade. At this point it should be noted that Austrian and German schools normally have 40 weeks of instruction per year, and the mandated curricula are valid for one whole year. To approximate the amount of economic education available to Austrian/German students, it would appear that one need only count the number of hours a student is (presumably) instructed in economic topics. This results in a ranking of economic knowledge by the different types of schools' students which, therefore, may be interpreted in terms of an expectation of the outcomes of the testing procedure. As evidenced by Tables 11.2a and 11.2b, it can be expected that Austrian/German students of school type 2 (SVS) would attain the highest scores followed by students of school types 3 (IVS), 5 (DVS), and 1 (GSS).[1] We have to stress that the mere

TABLE 11.2a: Economic Knowledge Related Subjects by Type of School with Hours of Instruction Per Week: AUSTRIA

	1 GSS				2 SVS					3 IVS			5a DVS/R			5b DVS/I		
Subject — Grades:	9	10	11	12	9	10	11	12	13	9	10	11	10	11	12	10	11	12
1. History & Social Studies	2	2	2	2									--	1	1	--	1	1
2. History & Social Studies (Economic History)							2	2	2									
3. Geography & Economics	2	2	2	2									2	--	--	2	--	--
4. Geography & Economics (Economic Geography)					3	2	2	3	3									
5. Accounting & Economics + Mathematics					4 +2	2	3	3	3	4 +2	2	4	2	3	2	2	4	4
6. Business & Management					3	3	3	3	3	3	4	4	2	2	2	2	2	2
7. Special Business & Management (e.g., retail, industry)								3										
8. Economics									2			2						
Sum per grade	4	4	4	4	12	7	10	14	13	9	6	10	6	6	5	6	7	7
Sum total	16				56					25			17			20		
Rank	5				1					2			4			3		

TABLE 11.2b: Economic Knowledge Related Subjects by Type of School with Hours of Instruction Per Week: GERMANY

	1 GSS			2 SVS						3 IVS			4 SSG		5a DVS/R			5b DVS/I		
Subject — Grades:	11	12	13	8	9	10	11	12	13	9	10	11	9	10	10	11	12	10	11	12
1. Social Studies															2	2	1	1	1	1
2. Bookkeeping															2	--	--	2	--	--
3. Economic Maths										2	1	--			1	--	--	1	--	--
4. Accounting (partly with EDP)				--	2	2	3	--	--	4	3 +1	3 +2			--	2	2	--	3	3
5. Business, Economics, and Management	1	1	1	1	4	4	3	6	6				2	1	4	2	2	3	2	1
6. Business & Management										3	3	3								
7. Special Business & Management (e.g., retail, industry, organization)										--	3	3								
8. Economics										--	--	2								
Sum per grade	1	1	1	1	6	6	6	6	6	9	10	11	2	1	9	6	5	7	6	5
Sum total	3			31						30			3		20			18		
Rank	5/6			1						2			5/6		3			4		

quantity of hours of instruction, while a necessary variable, is insufficient in itself as a measure of economic educational opportunity in Austria and Germany. As was mentioned above, there exist differences among school types in the overall ability levels of their respective students. Although in school type 1 (GSS), the number of hours devoted to economics is less than that available in other types, it is possible that the quality of instruction within that time period is both better and more in-depth. A second problem in interpreting, in a cursory manner, these data for the different school types is that students on the lower levels of intelligence are more appropriate for jobs where they have to carry out orders; preparing them for these jobs requires more business-related knowledge than economics-related overview, that is we have to expect that their time at school is mainly used for business education. A careful inspection of the actual curricular content is required to provide a measure of the quality of economic instruction in a given course by school type. Only by looking at school type and subject as well as the length of instruction we can formulate a hypothesis about the outcomes of test administration which in turn, if confirmed, will assure that our instrument is valid.

Curriculum-related Differences

To gain insight into the measurement-related contents of the different curricula, we used the American *Master Curriculum Guide In Economics* (MCG) as a referential framework (Gilliard et al., 1989), which in turn is the basis of the TEL/WBT. In Table 11.3, we have crosstabulated the 22 economics concepts from MCG against the curricula of our different schools, marking in the cells whether or not a MCG-concept is treated. Brackets signify that a concept is not explicitly contained in an Austrian or German syllabus, but is mentioned indirectly or in additional remarks. If, for example, an aim in the German syllabus runs as follows: "Survey of fusion of firms and competition-policy regulations of processes of concentration in a social market economy," we assigned this to MCG-concept 5, "Economic Institutions and Incentives," but within brackets.

The analyses for Austria shows mainly the following:

- All students receive economics lessons at school which should be just as demanding with regard to the aims as lessons on the basis of MCG.
- Until the 8th grade – look at the column "HS" meaning "lower secondary school" – these lessons are nearly identical for all students and comprise in total about three hours per week over three years in a subject called "Geography & Economics."

TABLE 11.3: Analysis of Syllabus Plans of the Different School Types on the Basis of the 22 TEL/MCG-Concepts

		Austria						Germany				
TEL/MCG-Concept	School Type:	HS	GSS	SVS	IVS	DVS/R	DVS/I	GSS	SVS	IVS	DVS/R	DVS/I
1	Scarcity	(x)	x	(x)	(x)	(x)	(x)	x	x		(x)	(x)
2	Opp. cost/trade offs											
3	Productivity	x	x	(x)	(x)	x	x	x	(x)			
4	Economic systems	x	x	x	x				x	x	x	x
5	Econ. inst. & incentives	x	x	x	x				x	(x)	x	x
6	Exchange, money, interdep.	x	(x)	x	(x)			x	x			x
7	Markets & prices	x	x	x	x	x	x	x	x	x	(x)	x
8	Supply & demand	(x)	(x)	x	(x)		(x)	x	x	x	x	x
9	Compet. & market struct.	x	x	(x)	(x)	x	x		x	x	x	x
10	Income distribution	(x)	(x)	x	x			x	x		x	x
11	Market failures			x					x			
12	Role of government	(x)	(x)	x	(x)			x	x	x	x	x
13	Gross national prod.	x	(x)	x	x				x	x		
14	Aggregate supply			(x)	(x)				x		x	x
15	Aggregate demand			(x)	(x)				x		x	x
16	Unemployment	x	(x)	(x)	(x)				x	(x)		
17	Inflation & deflation	x	(x)	x	x				(x)	x		
18	Monetary policy	(x)	(x)	x	(x)				x	x	x	x
19	Fiscal policy	(x)	x	x	(x)				x			
20	Comp. advant./trade barr.	(x)	x	(x)					x			
21	Bal. of payment/exch. rates	(x)	x	x	(x)		(x)		x	x		
22	Int. growth & stability	(x)	x	x	x				x			
Number of Matches with TEL/MCG		(18)	18	21	19	4	6	7	21	11	11	12
Rank (expected in WBT performance)		not appl	3	1	2	5	4	5	1	3/4	3/4	2

- From the 8th school year on, all students receive economic lessons, although in differing class-years, with qualitative and quantitative differences. Mostly the concepts of economics are to be found in two subjects, namely "Geography & Economics" and "Economics" (Tables 11.2a, #3, 8). The other subjects are mainly business and business-related courses.
- Directly or indirectly, roughly the same concepts are to be found in the Austrian economics curricula as in the MCG.
- The Austrian syllabus plans do not allow, as in MCG, the setting of the cognitive level at which the concepts should be taught. The formulation of the aims, however, shows that, when they leave school, Austrian students should have nearly the same knowledge, problem awareness, and faculty of judgment that the MCG demands from American high school students "with economics."

The German version of the TEL, the WBT, seems to be a test which is principally appropriate for the aims of Austrian teaching of economics. It is not unfair to administer it to Austrian students.

The analysis for Germany shows quite different facts:

- Until the 8th grade there is – with some exceptions – no substantial instruction in economics.
- There is only one group, namely school type 2 (SVS), which receives lessons on economics-related objectives nearly to the same extent as the MCG would demand.
- The concepts of economics are in two subject areas, "Economics" and "Social Studies."
- Some German syllabi allow the setting of the aims on a cognitive taxonomy which is slightly different from that in the MCG. It is, therefore, possible to make a more precise prediction on the measurement results we should receive from these students assuming they would have learned all that their teachers offered and that they used no sources of information other than school instruction. This is, of course, a very artificial assumption which we do not pursue at this time.
- Across the different school types, the WBT is more or less difficult depending on the extent to which the MCG-concepts are taught. There is no group which did not receive lessons at least on a substantial part of topics tested with the WBT.

Judging from the number of occurrences of matchings in Table 11.3 between the TEL/MCG-concepts and the syllabus plans of our different schools, it can be seen that the rank order of expected outcomes differs from those in assessing data in Tables 11.2a,b.

II. TEACHERS' JUDGMENTS ON THE WBT-ITEMS

If our analyses of curricula are valid, and if teachers heed the curricular content, we should expect Austrian/German teachers to judge the WBT as a valid instrument for testing the economic knowledge of their students. Therefore, we asked them to answer the following questions: "Please look at the 46 items of the WBT and tell us whether – in your opinion – they are rather good or rather poor indicators for "economic literacy." You may express your judgment on a scale running from 1 (very good indicators) to 5 (very poor indicators)." We omitted the teachers of school type 1 (GSS) because they were not involved in the teaching of economics.

To eliminate any connotative differences among teachers for the concept of "Economic Literacy," as represented by the WBT, we presented different groups of teachers the terms "Basic Economic Education" (wirtschaftliche Grundbildung), "Basic Economic Knowledge" (wirtschaftliches Grundwissen), and "Knowledge about Economy" (Wirtschaftskenntnisse). Moreover, we wanted to know whether teachers from different school types differ in their judgments. Neither school type nor the different terms for the concept produced significant differences within the ratings.

Table 11.4, therefore, shows only the overall means for each item. As one can see, the judgments of teachers are quite good in both Austria and Germany, with a slight tendency in Austria to lower values. In total, only four items fall on the negative side of the scale (with nearly complete agreement between Austria and Germany): A2, A40, B2, B40. After having inspected the curricula, it is easy to discover the reason for these low ratings. All four items make use of the concept of opportunity cost which is not treated in the curricula of the German-speaking countries (see Table 11.3). To date, we have not been able to discover the reason for this omission, but we suspect that this concept appears to curricula developers as overly advanced for students in the secondary level of education.

TABLE 11.4: Ratings of Austrian and German Teachers on WBT Items

	Form A				Form B			
	Austria (N=82)		Germany (N=166)		Austria (N=64)		Germany (N=139)	
Item	Mean	S.D.	Mean	S.D.	Mean	S.D.	Mean	S.D.
1	2.0	.9	2.1	.9	2.3	1.2	2.1	.9
2	3.3	1.3	3.4	1.3	3.4	1.2	3.6	1.2
3	1.8	1.0	2.3	1.0	1.9	.9	2.2	1.1
4	2.0	.9	2.3	1.0	2.3	.9	2.3	1.0
5	3.0	1.2	3.3	1.3	2.5	1.2	2.9	1.2
6	1.8	.9	2.0	.9	1.7	.9	1.9	.8
7	1.5	.7	1.9	.9	1.5	.8	1.9	.9
8	1.8	.9	2.3	1.0	2.2	1.1	2.5	1.1

TABLE 11.4: Ratings of Austrian and German Teachers on WBT Items Continued

	Form A				Form B			
	Austria		Germany		Austria		Germany	
Item	Mean	S.D.	Mean	S.D.	Mean	S.D.	Mean	S.D.
9	1.8	.8	2.0	.9	1.7	.9	2.0	1.0
10	2.5	1.1	2.9	1.2	1.9	.9	2.3	1.0
11	2.2	1.0	2.2	.9	2.1	.9	2.3	1.0
12	1.7	.9	2.2	1.1	2.2	1.0	2.6	1.0
13	1.5	.8	1.8	.9	1.5	.7	1.9	.8
14	2.0	.8	2.2	1.0	1.8	.9	2.3	1.0
15	2.3	1.1	2.4	1.0	2.3	1.1	2.5	1.1
16	2.0	.9	2.0	.9	1.7	.9	2.1	.9
17	2.6	1.2	2.5	1.1	2.3	1.1	2.6	1.2
18	1.8	.9	1.9	.9	2.1	1.0	2.1	.9
19	1.9	.8	2.1	.9	1.9	.9	2.1	.8
20	2.4	1.1	2.8	1.2	2.1	.9	2.2	.9
21	1.8	.7	2.4	1.0	1.6	.8	2.1	.9
22	2.7	1.3	2.8	1.2	1.8	1.0	2.6	1.1
23	2.2	1.1	2.6	1.0	2.5	1.3	2.8	1.1
24	2.2	1.0	2.5	1.1	1.8	1.0	2.4	1.1
25	2.4	1.0	2.7	1.1	1.9	1.0	2.4	1.1
26	1.8	1.0	2.1	1.0	1.4	.6	2.2	1.0
27	1.9	.9	2.3	1.0	2.1	1.0	2.3	1.0
28	2.1	1.1	2.4	1.1	2.0	.9	2.5	1.1
29	2.5	1.2	2.7	1.2	2.3	1.2	2.8	1.0
30	1.9	1.1	2.3	1.0	1.8	.9	2.1	.8
31	1.9	1.1	2.3	1.1	1.6	.9	2.1	1.0
32	1.9	1.0	2.5	1.1	1.6	.9	2.2	1.0
33	2.1	.9	2.5	1.0	1.5	.7	2.1	.9
34	1.8	.9	2.4	1.0	1.7	.6	2.3	.9
35	2.1	1.1	2.5	1.2	1.8	.9	2.3	1.1
36	1.8	1.1	2.2	1.0	1.8	.8	2.4	.9
37	1.9	1.0	2.2	1.0	1.6	.9	2.1	1.0
38	2.0	.9	2.4	1.1	1.9	.9	2.5	1.0
39	2.1	1.0	2.4	.9	2.1	1.0	2.5	1.0
40	2.7	1.2	3.4	1.2	2.9	1.3	3.6	1.2
41	2.1	1.1	2.6	1.0	2.1	.9	2.7	1.0
42	1.7	.8	2.3	1.0	2.1	.8	2.7	1.0
43	2.1	1.0	2.6	1.0	2.0	.8	2.8	1.0
44	2.3	1.0	2.5	1.1	2.0	1.2	2.2	1.0
45	1.7	.9	2.1	1.0	1.6	.6	2.1	.9
46	2.0	1.0	2.5	1.0	1.9	.9	2.5	1.0
Avg.	2.0	.5	2.3	.3	2.0	.4	2.3	.4

Note: 1 = very good; 3 = mean; 5 = very bad

All in all, the teachers judge the items of the WBT as "good" indicators for "economic literacy." Their ratings are, on the average, a little better than those of the university professors we surveyed similarly in our pilot study (form A: mean 3.15, standard deviation .70; form B: mean 3.3, standard deviation .77; see Beck and Krumm, 1991, p. 20). Supposing that teachers' ratings are more curriculum oriented (or curriculum affected), whereas professors' ratings are more related to the "structure of the discipline," we can look at both sets of survey results as rather strong arguments for the content validity of the WBT. In summary, the teachers' ratings support the results of our curriculum analyses that the use of the WBT is a valid instrument for measuring the economic literacy of students in Austria and Germany.

III. EMPIRICAL RESULTS AND COMPARISONS

Formal Aspects

A first glance at the most important statistics, reported in Table 11.5, shows that Form A and B are roughly equivalent for Austria and Germany. There are no greater differences between our countries in all figures reported. Compared to the TEL we have to state that the values for Cronbach's alpha (the internal consistency), and for the average item-total correlations (the average discrimination coefficients – see Table 11.6) are a bit worse. We suppose that the reason for this lies in the greater heterogeneity of the curricula to which our students are exposed. Depending on the school type visited they are taught in different

TABLE 11.5: Comparative Aggregate Statistics for TEL and WBT

	Form A			Form B		
	TEL	WBT		TEL	WBT	
Country	U.S.	AU	GER	U.S.	AU	GER
Sample size	4,235	1,664	4,612	3,970	1,690	4,537
Alpha	.87	.82	.83	.88	.83	.82
Mean	22.06	22.48	22.06	22.13	23.25	23.19
S.D.	8.33	7.23	7.28	8.68	7.32	7.28
S.E.M.	3.06	3.08	3.04	3.04	3.03	3.06
Average Item-To-Total Correlation	.32	.29	.30	.34	.28	.29

Source: Soper and Walstad, 1987, p. 12, 15, for U.S. TEL data.

sectors of economics with different weights and under different aspects (e.g., a more practical one in school types 3 and 5, or a more theoretical one in school types 1 and 2). This results in more "low" discriminating items (see Table 11.6) in the WBT (10 for forms A and 11 for form B) than in the TEL (7 for form A and 3 for form B). Nevertheless, looking at the absolute height of both groups of coefficients their values seem to be just acceptable.

TABLE 11.6: Item Discrimination and Percent Correct on WBT/TEL

Item	Form A						Form B					
	Austria (N=1,664)		Germany (N=4,612)		U.S. (N=4,235)		Austria (N=1,690)		Germany (N=4,537)		U.S. (N=3,970)	
1	.15	65%	.17	66%	.19	88%	.14	34%	.02	39%	.31	65%
2	.26	31	.22	33	.37	53	.18	32	.10	37	.27	53
3	.16	14	.16	19	.36	47	.19	20	.24	24	.42	54
4	.21	29	.16	30	.26	44	.25	69	.29	65	.26	53
5	.18	24	.24	26	.32	35	.26	31	.23	31	.37	30
6	.34	50	.36	46	.31	49	.34	50	.35	44	.33	48
7	.32	85	.40	79	.47	68	.34	84	.40	79	.44	71
8	.31	73	.35	73	.26	64	.32	68	.28	68	.37	67
9	.36	76	.41	69	.40	44	.36	72	.44	68	.45	50
10	.23	35	.34	32	.42	44	.15	71	.16	71	.27	65
11	.41	74	.42	65	.27	41	.38	67	.36	74	.38	67
12	.21	68	.20	71	.43	68	.19	42	.32	15	.26	29
13	.30	64	.25	64	.40	57	.32	68	.30	66	.41	58
14	.21	38	.25	38	.37	61	.34	52	.36	51	.34	45
15	.26	48	.31	50	.38	60	.37	78	.39	75	.44	75
16	.33	43	.39	39	.43	59	.27	69	.34	72	.42	61
17	.23	45	.24	47	.33	38	.26	48	.23	46	.39	46
18	.41	79	.47	74	.44	75	.26	82	.25	80	.27	62
19	.40	64	.46	54	.44	68	.39	59	.44	52	.43	69
20	.30	37	.34	38	.30	35	.28	44	.37	45	.19	24
21	.33	51	.33	54	.29	61	.28	52	.28	55	.29	60
22	.14	17	.06	17	.10	32	.28	57	.25	54	.34	50
23	.25	31	.22	24	.26	38	.22	40	.21	40	.19	43
24	.25	60	.28	54	.45	60	.30	40	.13	35	.32	46
25	.01	6	.02	6	.21	29	.00	21	.16	31	.36	37
26	.34	50	.30	47	.44	47	.28	51	.24	48	.43	51
27	.29	49	.27	48	.35	41	.37	72	.39	64	.34	56
28	.23	43	.27	46	.29	45	.14	29	.07	29	.34	38
29	.40	57	.42	53	.38	38	.44	64	.42	58	.36	36
30	.36	62	.35	17	.39	60	.39	53	.41	47	.49	65
31	.27	36	.27	34	.31	40	.35	62	.29	63	.36	59
32	.12	47	.22	53	.08	19	.35	33	.38	29	.37	33
33	.04	29	.02	31	.13	35	.33	72	.39	66	.40	34
34	.29	38	.37	39	.46	41	.36	40	.35	39	.46	43

TABLE 11.6: Item Discrimination and Percent Correct on WBT/TEL Continued

Item	Form A						Form B					
	Austria (N=1,664)		Germany (N=4,612)		U.S. (N=4,235)		Austria (N=1,690)		Germany (N=4,537)		U.S. (N=3,970)	
35	.08	32	.07	35	.14	33	.14	29	.07	30	.22	32
36	.40	77	.49	66	.51	56	.33	64	.38	61	.33	35
37	.34	56	.31	53	.49	52	.38	58	.39	56	.49	56
38	.04	33	.04	35	.06	36	.28	23	.26	21	.29	26
39	.29	43	.18	42	.32	50	.18	34	.28	44	.21	34
40	.38	44	.40	50	.36	50	.21	32	.09	33	.27	40
41	.29	40	.30	37	.43	52	.30	41	.32	37	.40	54
42	.40	58	.37	51	.26	46	.40	38	.37	33	.40	31
43	.19	28	.03	25	.18	32	.20	31	.05	19	.19	30
44	.36	50	.31	46	.27	40	.15	54	.11	52	.21	54
45	.31	57	.28	54	.32	45	.34	54	.28	53	.38	49
46	.32	35	.36	31	.26	34	.28	46	.26	43	.26	40

Note: Discrimination measured by corrected item-total correlation.

Another difference has to be discussed. It is the overall mean. Within Form A all values reported for the three countries are more or less equal whereas within Form B the German-speaking group is ending up with about one more raw point. Looking at Table 11.6 one can see that there are partially large differences between the percentages of correct responses on Form A as well as on Form B. Again, the general reason for this has to be searched for in the different curricula and, to some extent, also in the differences of cultures and languages (Beck and Krumm, 1991, pp. 17-19). As to Form B, the German-speaking students come off a little bit worse with the questions on the fundamental and the international economic concepts (items 1-12 and 40-46). But this loss seems to be overcompensated by their relative gains with questions on micro- and macroeconomic economics concepts summing up to the difference of one raw point mentioned above. So, under a formal aspect it has to be stated that the WBT Form B is somewhat easier than Form A. It is true that the difference of one point is not very large; but comparisons between the outcomes of Form A and Form B whether national or international have to consider this difference.

Looking at the standard deviations of the means in Table 11.5, the finding that the values of the WBT are a little bit lower than those of the TEL seems to be an indicator for the greater homogeneity of the German-speaking samples (see Section I). The standard errors of measurement (S.E.M.) of both versions are nearly the same. This is because the lower reliability coefficient of the WBT is compensated by the lower standard deviation.

Now, looking at the construct validity we can state that the means of the different groups of German-speaking students develop roughly in the expected direction. On Table 11.7 the ranks estimated and the ranks drawn from the data are found in the last three columns. For Forms A and B there is one mutual change at a time for Austria (ranks 2 and 3) and Germany (ranks 2 and 5) comparing the empirical outcomes with the number of MCG-matchings. In both countries the students of school type 1 (GSS) rank higher than we expected from the analysis of the curricula (see Table 11.3). This indicates that the members of this group are presumably profiting directly and indirectly by their higher intelligence level. They seem to gain more economic knowledge from the daily discussions and the mass media than the other groups. Working on the WBT items they exploit their better logical abilities and more elaborated sense for subtle verbal differences.[2]

Of course, making hypotheses on the bases discussed above is not as precise as one has to wish. This becomes obviously by comparing the empirical ranks with the ranks drawn from the hours of instruction. The two patterns coincide only in one of the five rank places. Obviously, the gap which has to be bridged by estimation is broader if the bases of the hypothesis is not a syllabus plan but the amount of hours of instruction. Moreover, predictions would be improved if we were able to extend the concept of match-counting on a second dimension: the cognitive levels of objectives and of the test-items. Again it is true that between both lies the reality of teaching and learning. We don't know whether the teachers do precisely what the syllabus plans prescribe. But the more books and other learning aids are developed on the basis of syllabus plans the closer the connection between aims and item-responses should be. Therefore one of the next steps of investigation will be the analysis of the most important books under the aspects of content and cognitive level. Besides this, looking again at Table 11.6 it can be said that the WBT is an instrument which measures fairly the same as the TEL does with sufficient accurateness.

Communities and Differences Between Austrian, German, and U.S. Students

Comparing the TEL and the WBT outcomes a first finding is that in each country the mean values are only moderate. Even the best groups solved only between 50 percent to 60 percent of the 46 items on a test which is not very difficult and which is rated by experts as a good indicator of economic literacy. When the results of the TEL were published in the U.S.A. in 1988 many journalists, politicians, and scientists felt that they are shockingly bad (Walstad & Soper 1988; *The New York Times*, Dec. 29, 1988). Looking at the findings of our studies we have to state now that these feelings are also in order with respect to Austria and Germany. The German-speaking students fail to reach the objectives formulated in the curricula provided for them in the same way as the American high school students. Though these curricula are not identical with the

TABLE 11.7: Comparisons Between Students in Austria, Germany, and the United States by School or Course Type

No.	Group	Mean	S.D.	N	Rank: hrs. of instr.	Rank: MCG matches	Rank: emp. data
Austria			*Form A*				
1	Gen.Sec.Sch.	22.34	6.01	513	5	3	2
2	Sen.Voc.Sch.	25.33	5.97	655	1	1	1
3	Int.Voc.Sch.	19.68	6.23	164	2	2	3
5a	Dual Voc./Ret.	14.30	4.91	169	4	5	5
5b	Dual Voc./Ind.	15.58	4.32	55	3	4	4
Germany							
1	Gen.Sec.Sch.	24.34	6.14	671	5	5	2
2	Sen.Voc.Sch.	25.14	5.55	716	1	1	1
3	Int.Voc.Sch.	15.02	4.92	711	2	3/4	5
5a	Dual Voc./Ret.	15.90	5.53	757	3	3/4	4
5b	Dual Voc./Ind.	23.80	6.49	632	4	2	3
United States							
6	Economics	23.57	8.5	2,585			
7	Consumer Ec.	21.70	8.0	309			
8	Soc. Studies	22.85	8.7	259			
Austria			*Form B*				
1	Gen.Sec.Sch.	23.12	6.44	516	5	3	2
2	Sen.Voc.Sch.	27.59	6.16	670	1	1	1
3	Int.Voc.Sch.	21.53	5.20	161	2	2	3
5a	Dual Voc./Ret.	15.77	4.56	343	4	5	5
5b	Dual Voc./Ind.	15.89	3.57	55	3	4	4
Germany							
1	Gen.Sec.Sch.	25.85	5.81	661	5	5	2
2	Sen.Voc.Sch.	27.13	5.55	682	1	1	1
3	Int.Voc.Sch.	16.79	5.09	691	2	3/4	5
5a	Dual Voc./Ret.	17.78	5.79	761	3	3/4	4
5b	Dual Voc./Ind.	25.81	6.42	625	4	2	3
United States							
6	Economics	25.55	8.9	1,930			
7	Consumer Ec.	18.07	7.0	405			
8	Soc. Studies	22.14	7.6	430			

Source: Soper and Walstad, 1987, pp. 20-21, for U.S. data.

MCG, our analyses reported in section I showed that the students in Austria and Germany should also arrive at substantially higher scores than they actually do.

It is true that the Austrian students on both forms gain the highest ranks and that the American high school students "with economics" range in the average two points beyond the German and the Austrian highest-scoring groups. And it has to be added that in the German-speaking countries we measured the extent of economic literacy of students who will stay for one more year at school. Some of them will be taught in economics more intensively only in their last year of schooling. But even if they score then, let's say, about 30 raw points, on average, this score is not enough looking at the problems mentioned in the first section.

To get a clue about the national differences and similarities between the groups of students who answered the test questions look at Table 11.8. It shows that the German and Austrian students are more similar than the German-speaking and the American students.[3] Going into more detail one can see that the weakest group in the United States is still better than the weakest groups in Austria and Germany. However, the best group in the United States is worse than the respective groups in the two German-speaking countries. This result is mirrored by comparing the differences of ranges between the best and the worst group in each country. In Austria and Germany these differences are at least two times larger than in the United States. We suppose that this is partly a consequence of the different school systems. The comprehensive system in the United States seems to produce more homogeneous results than the divergent school branches in Austria and Germany. Another reason for this finding may be found in the difference of influences on economic knowledge by sources from outside the schools (i.e., cultural differences in a broader sense of the word). We can imagine (and we will examine in further studies on our data) that the habits of information reception by the people as well as the styles of information presentation by the mass media are showing divergent profiles in our three countries and therefore are influencing our populations with different consequences for their status of economic knowledge. It can't be excluded that the large differences in the percentages of correct responses to the items of the TEL or WBT stem also in part from this source of special cultural conditions.

TABLE 11.8: Ranges of Achievement Between the Different Groups Tested in Each Country

	Form A		Form B	
	means	diff.	means	diff.
Austria	14.3 - 25.3	11.0	15.8 - 27.6	12.0
Germany	15.0 - 25.2	10.2	16.8 - 27.1	10.9
U.S.	21.7 - 23.6	5.2	18.1 - 25.6	7.5

Source: Data from Soper and Walstad, 1987, pp. 20-21.

NOTES

1. The numbers reported for "Germany" in Table 11.2b are somewhat rough estimators because there are different syllabus plans for the 16 states of the Federal Republic of Germany. For this analyses we draw on the figures for Bavaria where about one third of the students of our sample are living. The other two thirds come from Hessen, Northrhine-Westfalia, and Saarland.

2. This supposition is supported by the results of administering a verbal subtest ("Analogien") of a general intelligence test (IST-70 by Amthauer 1973; see also Conrad 1983, 160-172) where this group (GSS) is achieving the comparatively highest scores.

3. This result is confirmed by an analyses of test bias on the bases of items. It seems that the German-speaking students can be regarded as one group which is different from the group of American students (Krumm 1992). We are not considering this bias problem for the comparisons dealt with in this chapter.

REFERENCES

Amthauer, R. (1973). *Intelligenz-struktur-test* (IST-70). Goettingen: Hogrefe.

Beck, K. & Krumm, V. (1989). Economic literacy in German-speaking countries and the United States: First steps to a comparative study. *Economia, 1*(1), 17-23.

Benner, H. (1992). Zur neuordnung der ausbildungsberufe im berufsfeld wirtschaft und verwaltung. *Wirtschaft und Berufserziehung, 11*, 326-340.

Conrad, W. (1983). Intelligenzdiagnostik. In K.-J. Groffmann & L. Michel (Hrsg.), Intelligenz- und leistungsdiagnostik. *Enzyklopaedie der Psychologie, B II 2*, 104-201. Goettingen: Hogrefe.

Gilliard, J. V., et al. (1989). *Master curriculum guide in economics. Economics: What and when. Scope and sequence guidelines, K-12*. New York: Joint Council on Economic Education.

Krumm, V. (1992). Probleme der interkulturell vergleichenden schulleistungsmessung mit dem test of economic literacy. In F. Achtenhagen & E. G. John (Hrsg.), *Mehrdimensionale lehr-lern-arrangements. Innovationen in der kaufmaennischen Aus- und Weiterbildung* (pp. 584-611). Wiesbaden: Gabler.

Soper, J. C. & Walstad, W. B. (1987). *Test of economic literacy: Examiner's manual* (2nd ed.). New York: Joint Council on Economic Education.

Walstad, W. B. & Soper, J. C. (1988). A report card on the economic literacy of U.S. high school students. *American Economic Review, 78*(2), pp. 251-256.

CHAPTER 12

ECONOMIC LITERACY IN THE REPUBLIC OF KOREA AND THE UNITED STATES

Kyung-keun Kim

It is widely accepted that a firm knowledge of economics fosters, in youngsters, a highly useful way of thinking which could be applied for the rest of their lives. That is, studying economics can provide young adults with the knowledge and skills they need to address economic questions and make decisions as consumers, workers, and voting citizens. Of greater importance is the fact that the lasting effects from an economics course may be far greater than initially thought. This is so because economic reasoning is a transferable skill which is applicable to a variety of issues, as well as a variety of subjects (see Brenneke and Soper, 1985). For high school students, whether or not they go on to college, economics should thus be viewed as a vital subject worth taking.

Recognizing the value of teaching economics to high school students, Korean high schools offer a mandated course in economics. Specifically, high school students are required to take the course entitled "politics and economy" before graduation. Usually, high school students take the course for four semesters, and those attending vocational high schools for at least two semesters before they graduate. Note that only one textbook for this subject is in use and it is compiled by the state. The economic contents are contained in the latter half of the textbook of the politics and economy course.[1] Besides the politics and economy course, an economics course called "practical economics" is offered in some high schools as an elective.

Although this amount of required economic education in high schools is offered, economists and educators believe most Korean students have less than the expected level of economic understanding. They suspect that high school students may not possess a high level of economic understanding due to an array of problems plaguing economics instruction in high schools, which will be discussed later. To fully realize the scope of the problem, we need more information about what students know and what concepts students understand to address this question, which will in turn allow us to develop effective economic education programs in high schools.

The level of economic understanding among high school students has never been assessed in Korea. Although it is certainly worthwhile to investigate the level of economic understanding among students, a standardized instrument for use in high schools is not available in the country. Therefore, I decided to translate the *Test of Economic Literacy* (TEL) (Soper and Walstad, 1987). It was expected that the data collected by administering the Korean version of the TEL (henceforth, KVTEL) to Korean students would permit me to conduct a comparative study.

This chapter seeks to describe results from the translations and administration of the TEL in Korea. It begins in the next section with a discussion of the translation of the TEL into Korean and some of the problems I encountered in making the test items as equivalent as possible in the KVTEL. In the second section, I briefly describe the norming procedure for the Korean sample. In the third section, basic findings, including the norming data are presented and, if applicable, some comparisons are made with the U.S. data. Finally, the chapter suggests actions that should be taken to enhance the status of economic education and hence, improve economic understanding of students in Korea.

I. TRANSLATION OF THE TEST OF ECONOMIC LITERACY

As is well known, the TEL has two forms, A and B; it covers basic economic concepts considered to be the most important for students to know before they graduate from high school. Through careful examination, I found that the main content categories of the test (i.e., concepts of fundamental economics, microeconomics, macroeconomics, and international economics) are fully covered in the textbook of the "politics and economy" course. Therefore, I concluded that the TEL, should it be translated properly into Korean, would also be appropriate for use with high school students in Korea. In preparation for this study, I decided, for convenience, to translate only form A of the TEL into Korean.

Since I wanted to obtain comparable data, the KVTEL was constructed by translating the TEL as literally as possible. Although I made conscious efforts not to alter the conceptual core of the TEL in the KVTEL, certain test items needed to be modified. Otherwise, I reasoned, the KVTEL would not provide the same kind of information in Korea as the TEL was supposed to measure in the U.S. It turned out that about one-fifth of the items had been slightly modified due to various reasons. In the following, some of the reasons that made minor modifications unavoidable are discussed.

First, some items on the TEL make references to the United States, a foreign country or a foreigner's name which might sound unfamiliar to Korean high school students. In order to give students an equal opportunity to provide a correct answer to the test items by helping them feel more comfortable with the items, I decided to replace the foreign idioms by those indigenous to Korea.

In item 1, for example, the Republic of Korea was substituted for the United States, and electronics for wheat. Similarly, Sandy Smith was replaced by Kil Dong Hong, a famous name appearing in Korean folklore, and Korean *won* was employed as a currency unit instead of U.S. *dollars* in item 5. Following the same principle of adaptation, to a varying degree, items 15, 17, 22, 30, 31 and 44 were also modified.

Due to the differences in political and economic systems between Korea and the U.S., I had to modify a couple of other items, as well. Thus, the "government" was used in item 37 instead of the "federal government." For the items that require special understanding of the workings of the U.S. economic system (i.e., items 11 and 20), I omitted any reference to the U.S. in order to induce students to respond in a more general context.

It is extremely important to translate economic terms properly because the accuracy of the solutions could be greatly influenced by how carefully they are worded. Overall, I had experienced relatively little difficulties in translating economic terms into Korean. This might be attributed to the fact that economics is an imported discipline in Korea, primarily from the U.S. As a matter of fact, a majority of Korean economists in academic circles were educated in the U.S. As a result, little differences seem to exist between Korea and the U.S. in economics syllabi at the higher education level, in particular.

Still, I found that there was no defined term for "general sales tax" (item 24), which Korea currently does not have. On the other hand, value added tax (VAT) is widely used in Korea and hence Koreans are familiar with it. Therefore, I decided to substitute value added tax for general sales tax. Presumably, this alteration would not have affected a chance of giving a correct answer.

II. NORMING THE KOREAN VERSION OF THE TEL

As previously indicated, the TEL has two forms, each consisting of 46 items, with 15 common items. In the U.S., Form A was normed with a sample of 4,235 students and Form B of 3,970 students from a large, representative cross-section of American high schools (Soper and Walstad, 1987). In the U.K., Form A only was normed, with a sample of 7549 students from 162 schools in 1989 (Whitehead and Halil, 1991). In both cases, the samples were composed of students in grades 11 and 12.

In preparation for norming the KVTEL, the test was administered to 4,334 students from 39 Korean high schools in mid-December of 1992. These schools and students were chosen by employing a sampling procedure that could provide a nationwide, representative sample of high school students in Korea. Thus, a contrasting sample was chosen from the target population, with representation given to gender, type of school, type of community, and grade level. As a result, unlike the cases in the U.S. and the U.K., those in the first year of high school were also included in the norming sample.

To some extent, it was inevitable to include those in grade 10 in the norming sample for the sake of international comparisons. It was reported that economics is offered usually as an elective in grade 12 in the U.S. (Walstad, 1992). As indicated earlier, however, Korean high schools offer a mandated economics course which usually lasts for 2-4 semesters. Without including the students in the first year of high school, therefore, it would be extremely difficult to obtain norming data for those without economics in the Korean context. In sum, one of the reasons I adopted a slightly different sampling procedure from that of the U.S. was a problem associated with differences in the economics curriculum between the two nations.

Of the 4,334 students who participated in the test, 1,519 were in grade 10 (35.0 percent), 1,522 in grade 11 (35.1 percent), and 1,293 in grade 12 (29.8 percent). Thus, the students in grade 12 were slightly underrepresented in the sample, which might be attributed to the fact that the KVTEL was administered in mid-December, just before the college entrance examination. Several schools did not allow their college-bound students to take the external test at such a critical time of the year.

Female students numbered 2,156 (49.7 percent), while male students totaled 2,178 (50.3 percent). Those who attended general high schools totaled 2,833 (65.4 percent), while students attending vocational high schools numbered 1,501 (34.6 percent). Stratified by type of community, the number of the students living in Seoul (the capital city) amounted to 1,026 (23.7 percent), those in other large cities totaled 1,055 (24.3 percent), those in smaller cities 1,297 (29.9 percent), and those in rural communities 956 (22.1 percent).[2] The students with economics were 3,025 (69.8 percent) and those without summed to 1,309 (30.2 percent). Note that the classification of students with and without economics was based on students' responses to this statement: "Mark whether you have taken the politics and economy course in your school. Yes ( ), No ( ), In Process ( )." Students who marked "Yes" or "In Process" were classified as with economics. Even those students who marked "In Process" were presumed to have taken the course at least for two semesters.

According to a nationwide survey of teachers of the politics and economics course, about 30 percent of high schools offer the practical economics course, which teaches some economic concepts and knowledge that students need in their everyday lives (Kim, 1992). It is difficult for me to assess how this course is perceived by the students and whether they take the course with enthusiasm, if offered. The effectiveness of this course is rather questionable because it is offered as a non-credit course on an elective basis. Hence, the magnitude of contribution this course has made to economic understanding of high school students is likely to be limited. In general, Korean students seldom show any interest in the subjects irrelevant to the college entrance examination. Besides, in order to make a clear-cut distinction between those with economics and without, I decided to include only those students having taken or were taking the politics and economy course in the with economics group.

III. DISCUSSION OF THE NORMING DATA

In this section, the norming data for Korea are provided and, if applicable, comparisons are drawn with U.S. data. The administration of the KVTEL led to the establishment of norms for various subgroups of high school students in Korea. The norming data from the 4,334 students are thus expected to provide baseline data of economic understanding of high school students against which those using the KVTEL could compare the scores of their students.

Table 12.1 exhibits aggregate statistics for the norming sample in Korea with the comparable U.S. data. Before proceeding further, note here that cautions should be exercised in making comparisons because the U.S. sample differs considerably from the Korean sample. In particular, the samples differ significantly with respect to the exposure to economics instruction. This fact should be taken into account when evaluating the comparisons drawn below.

The Korean overall mean score was 23.77 and the corresponding U.S. mean was 22.06. It appears that Korean students performed a little better than their U.S. counterparts. The Korean mean score for the with economics group was 24.42, which compares with 23.33 for the U.S. with economics group. Thus, the with economics students in Korea had, on average, about one more correct response than their U.S. counterparts. When it comes to the without economics students, however, this picture changes considerably. Korean students without economics performed far better than did American students without economics, with the former having, on average, about 5 more correct responses than the

TABLE 12.1: Comparative Aggregate Statistics for TEL, Form A and KVTEL

Statistics	R.O.K.	U.S.
Sample size	4,334	4,235
Alpha	0.82	0.87
S.E.M.	3.10	3.06
Percent with economics	69.80	74.50
Mean overall	23.77	22.06
	(7.25)	(8.33)
Mean with economics	24.42	23.33
	(7.58)	(8.45)
Mean without economics	22.25	18.37
	(6.18)	(6.71)

Note: Numbers in parentheses are the standard deviations. The U.S. data are from Soper and Walstad (1987).

latter. As a result, the differences in the mean scores between the students with and without economics were 4.96 points in the U.S., while the corresponding differences in Korea proved to be only 2.17 points.

The data in Table 12.1 indicate that there were significant differences in economic understanding between those with and without economics in the U.S. The difference of 4.96 points on form A of the TEL show that economics instruction raises TEL scores about 27 percent when scores are computed using the mean scores of those without economics as the starting level (Walstad and Soper, 1991). However, employing the same computing procedure, the differences of 2.17 points on the KVTEL suggest that economics instruction increases KVTEL scores only about 10 percent.

It might be too premature at this juncture to speculate on the specific reasons for the relatively small difference in the mean scores for the Korean students with and without economics. The TEL has been proven to possess the capacity to distinguish between students with more economic knowledge and those with less (Soper and Walstad, 1987). It might therefore be illogical to refute the validity of its Korean version, the KVTEL. What, then, gives rise to the unique results of the Korean sample?

Several factors could be considered in the context of the Korean case. For one thing, lack of incentive to take an external test seriously when it does not count for a grade might decrease the size of score differences. In addition, previous exposure to economics instruction of those without economics might contribute to their relatively strong performance. A majority of those without economics in the Korean norming sample were students in their first year of high school, accounting for about 79 percent of the total without economics demography. However, all junior high school students are required to take "social studies" for three years before graduation, during which the same economic concepts taught in high school are covered in grades 8 and 9, albeit in less sophisticated and simpler forms. Strictly speaking, therefore, even the without economics students in the Korean norming sample might have some formal background in economics.

Still, I believe that the most important reason behind the relatively small spread between scores of the with and without economics groups involves the ineffectiveness of economic education in high schools. Most evident is the reality that the final level of achievement is anything but impressive. Aside from previous exposure to economics instruction, Korean students can provide correct answers to only about half the questions on the KVTEL even after more than two semesters of economics courses. Furthermore, economics instruction appears to make little difference in the economic literacy of high school students. All this raises questions about the effectiveness and quality of the economic education students receive in high schools.[3] It is widely recognized that economics instruction in high schools is confronted with various problems. These problems will be discussed briefly later.

Finally, the Cronbach alpha reliability was .87 for form A of the TEL and .82 for the KVTEL. In addition, the standard error of measurement (S.E.M.) was 3.06 for the former and 3.10 for the latter. Whatever the reasons may be, the KVTEL turned out to be a somewhat less reliable test than the original TEL, form A.

Table 12.2 provides percentile norms obtained from the students with and without economics. Note that a great majority of the Korean students in grades 11 and 12 were in the with economics group (i.e., about 92 percent), while the opposite holds true for the students in grade 10. A student in grade 11 with economics who obtains a raw score of 29 on the KVTEL is performing at the 80th percentile. On the other hand, an eleventh grader with economics in the U.S. who scored 29 performed at the 82nd percentile (see Soper and Walstad, 1987). Only 29 percent of the twelfth graders with economics scored more than 29 in the U.S., compared with 40 percent of their counterparts in Korea.

The average percentage of correct responses for each item for Korean students with and without economics, and the overall item discrimination coefficient are shown in Table 12.3. As noted by Soper and Walstad (1987), the item discrimination coefficient (corrected item-total correlation) indicates the ability of a given question to discriminate between those who know economics and those who do not. The closer it is to 1.0, the better the item. In general, an item discrimination coefficient below 0.20 may be seen as a poor discriminator. The total number of items falling in this category on the KVTEL was 3, compared with 7 for the TEL.

TABLE 12.2: Percentile Norms by Economics Instruction: KVTEL

Raw Score	Grade 10 With Econ (N=440)	Grade 10 Without Econ (N=1,079)	Grade 11 With Econ (N=1,292)	Grade 11 Without Econ (N=230)	Grade 12 With Econ (N=1,293)
46					
•					
41					99
40			99		97
39			99		95
38			99	99	93
37	99		97	98	91
36	99		96	97	87
35	99	99	95	96	84
34	98	99	93	95	80
33	97	98	90	94	76
32	96	96	88	91	73
31	94	96	86	89	69
30	92	93	83	86	64
29	89	89	80	82	60
28	86	87	76	77	56
27	82	83	71	72	52
26	77	79	66	67	48
25	71	76	61	63	44
24	66	71	59	58	40
23	61	66	53	52	35
22	54	58	45	47	32
21	47	53	40	40	28
20	41	44	36	36	25
19	36	38	31	32	21
18	30	33	23	28	17
17	25	27	21	23	14
16	20	24	16	19	11
15	15	18	12	16	9
14	10	13	10	12	7
13	7	9	7	9	5
12	5	6	5	6	4
11	3	4	4	4	3
10	2	2	2	3	1
9	1	1	1	2	1
8	1	1		1	

TABLE 12.3: KVTEL Item Discrimination and Percentage of Correct Response

Item	Discrimination (N=4,334)	Overall (N=4,334)	Without Econ. (N=1,309)	With Econ. (N=3,025)
1	.13	76.7 %	73.0 %	78.3 %
2	.48	46.1	31.1	52.7
3	.42	44.0	32.5	49.0
4	.22	30.8	21.6	34.7
5	.20	31.8	29.8	32.7
6	.15	33.8	34.1	33.7
7	.39	57.7	52.9	59.8
8	.15	52.4	49.9	53.6
9	.30	70.0	65.8	71.8
10	.31	42.8	42.5	42.9
11	.33	68.9	64.0	71.0
12	.41	75.0	75.8	74.6
13	.42	64.5	59.1	66.8
14	.27	51.0	44.7	53.7
15	.40	63.8	61.9	64.7
16	.36	70.9	71.4	70.6
17	.34	58.9	56.0	60.2
18	.41	55.8	54.7	56.3
19	.41	76.7	78.4	75.9
20	.25	35.5	34.7	35.8
21	.32	64.8	64.7	64.9
22	.21	34.1	35.2	33.6
23	.29	44.9	46.8	44.0
24	.41	47.1	37.9	51.0
25	.24	31.0	26.7	32.9
26	.39	87.8	87.9	87.7
27	.35	47.3	45.5	48.0
28	.45	51.5	44.7	54.5
29	.43	44.1	37.2	47.0
30	.42	67.5	67.2	67.6
31	.35	41.9	39.1	43.0
32	.34	33.7	27.3	36.5
33	.31	45.4	42.7	46.5
34	.38	52.0	50.2	52.8
35	.25	37.6	33.9	39.2
36	.45	53.6	49.6	55.3
37	.37	41.5	37.4	43.3
38	.30	36.7	30.6	39.3
39	.26	53.5	50.9	54.6
40	.33	37.3	30.6	40.2
41	.30	49.0	45.9	50.3
42	.43	69.9	68.0	70.8
43	.27	40.4	42.1	39.7
44	.29	46.8	46.4	47.0
45	.38	70.9	67.5	72.4
46	.32	39.3	34.9	41.2

Table 12.4 represents the percentage of all Korean students responding to each of the four options for the forty-six items on the KVTEL and the percentage of omitted responses. Of importance is the fact that in some items the proportion of students responding to one of the incorrect options was higher than that of those students giving a correct answer (items 4, 5 and 25). For the teachers, these items appear worth investigating since a substantial proportion of students failed to provide a correct answer.

TABLE 12.4: KVTEL Percentage Response to Each Alternative

Item	A	B	C	D	Blank
1	76.7%*	2.2%	11.1%	9.9%	0.1%
2	5.9	15.5	32.1	46.1*	0.4
3	36.0	9.1	44.0*	10.8	0.0
4	46.8	30.8*	17.1	5.2	0.2
5	6.9	39.0	21.9	31.8*	0.4
6	26.1	13.5	33.8*	25.7	0.9
7	3.6	12.8	26.0	57.7*	0.0
8	29.3	10.6	52.4*	7.5	0.1
9	17.4	6.3	6.3	70.0*	0.0
10	42.8*	8.3	14.8	34.0	0.1
11	68.9*	6.4	16.4	8.3	0.0
12	75.0*	6.6	10.4	7.9	0.0
13	16.3	64.5*	11.6	7.6	0.0
14	10.5	51.0*	14.2	24.1	0.1
15	17.1	63.8*	8.0	11.0	0.0
16	4.9	15.7	8.5	70.9*	0.0
17	17.2	10.2	13.7	58.9*	0.0
18	55.8*	33.9	7.3	3.0	0.0
19	76.7*	11.9	7.0	4.4	0.1
20	35.5*	7.1	31.8	25.3	0.3
21	12.9	5.4	64.8*	16.9	0.0
22	11.7	34.1*	34.1	20.1	0.0
23	19.8	23.0	44.9*	12.3	0.0
24	7.3	33.5	47.1*	12.0	0.1
25	42.3	19.0	31.0*	7.6	0.0
26	4.0	3.2	4.9	87.8*	0.0
27	47.3*	34.7	6.7	11.1	0.2
28	19.1	16.5	51.5*	12.8	0.0
29	44.1*	28.4	17.0	10.3	0.2
30	9.9	11.4	11.1	67.5*	0.1
31	26.9	23.6	41.9*	7.5	0.3
32	15.2	33.7*	27.0	23.9	0.2
33	18.4	7.9	45.4*	28.1	0.2
34	9.1	17.2	21.6	52.0*	0.1
35	20.6	26.0	37.6*	15.4	0.3

TABLE 12.4: KVTEL Percentage Response to Each Alternative Continued

Item	A	B	C	D	Blank
36	53.6*	22.2	10.2	13.9	0.1
37	25.2	17.7	15.3	41.5*	0.3
38	15.2	36.7*	26.2	21.6	0.3
39	14.3	53.5*	10.4	21.4	0.4
40	14.1	35.3	37.3*	12.2	1.0
41	16.0	15.1	49.0*	19.5	0.4
42	8.2	69.9*	13.5	7.9	0.4
43	7.5	40.4*	19.9	31.8	0.4
44	25.3	46.8	14.4*	12.9	0.5
45	8.9	70.9*	8.0	11.8	0.5
46	39.3*	5.1	31.7	23.4	0.5

Note: * denotes correct response. N = 4,334.

Following Walstad and Soper (1991), Table 12.5 shows the areas of relative strength and weakness in student knowledge of economic concepts. The average percentages correct were 53 percent for those with economics and 48 percent for those without economics. As to the percentages correct for the four major *Framework* concept clusters (see Saunders et al., 1984, or Chapter 3), those with economics performed a little better on the fundamental economic concepts (54 percent) and the microeconomic concepts (55 percent) than on the macroeconomic concepts (51 percent) and the international concepts (52 percent). But the magnitude of the differences in the percentages correct across the four major *Framework* concept clusters was relatively small, compared with the data for the U.S. norming sample (see Walstad and Soper, 1991).

Looking at the specific concepts within each broad concept cluster, the data indicate that students have problems with the fundamental concepts. In particular, they seemed to have serious difficulties in understanding the "fundamental" concepts of scarcity, opportunity cost, and productivity. It is also evident that students were poorly prepared to answer questions on such macroeconomic concepts as aggregate supply, inflation and deflation, monetary policy, and fiscal policy. Moreover, high school students revealed a relatively low level of economic understanding on market failure in the microeconomics cluster and comparative advantage/barriers to trade in the international cluster.

Interestingly, all these concepts were identified as the areas of relatively weak student understanding in the U.S., as well. It can be said, then, that teachers of economics courses could enhance economic understanding of their students by focusing on these concepts or concept clusters and providing more instruction in these low achievement areas. By doing so, they might be able to raise overall understanding by a significant degree (Walstad and Soper, 1991).

TABLE 12.5: KVTEL Percentage Correct Across the Concept Categories

No. of Items		Without Economics (N=1,309)	With Economics (N=3,025)
46	All Items	48%	53%
12	Fundamental	46	54
13	Microeconomics	53	55
13	Macroeconomics	46	51
8	International	48	52
2	Scarcity	30	41
3	Opportunity cost/trade-offs	28	40
2	Productivity	42	44
1	Economic systems	53	60
2	Economic institutions & incentives	65	71
2	Exchange, money & interdependence	74	76
2	Markets & prices	51	55
4	Supply & demand	59	62
2	Competition & market structure	67	66
2	Income distribution	50	50
2	Market failures	41	39
1	Role of government	38	51
1	Gross national product	88	88
1	Aggregate supply	46	48
2	Aggregate demand	41	51
1	Unemployment	67	68
2	Inflation & deflation	33	40
3	Monetary policy	38	44
3	Fiscal Policy	43	48
3	Comparative advantage/barriers to trade	42	48
3	Balance of payments & exchange rates	52	52
2	International growth & stability	51	57

Table 12.6 provides some additional descriptive statistics for various groups derived from the Korean norming sample. By and large, the results in Table 12.5 are consistent with the *a priori* expectations. The differences in the mean scores between females and males were not of a noticeable size. The higher the grade level, the better the mean scores. Those attending general high schools performed better than did their counterparts in vocational schools. In general, those living in smaller cities showed higher achievement levels than did those living in other communities. This can partly be attributed to the fact that the former might have

taken an entrance examination for high school and thus received more solid training in economics as well as in other subjects. It is important to note that in Seoul and in other large cities the lottery system for high school entrance is currently at work. As could be expected, the mean scores also tend to rise with the mothers' level of schooling.[4] Finally, those who wished to go on to college performed significantly better than those who intended not to.

Having discussed all this, it is clear that the level of economic education in Korean high schools is inadequate and ineffective. There was a relatively small difference in economic knowledge between those with economics and without. In addition, the students in the with economics group could correctly answer only about half the test questions even after at least two semesters of course work, indicative of the ineffectiveness of economic education in high schools. Many factors are presumed, either separately or in combination, to account for the ineffectiveness of economic education in high schools.

First, the most important factor affecting the status of economic education in Korea is a relatively low proportion of economics items on the college entrance examination. This is so because economics still remains an underemphasized subject in high schools. Currently, economics items account for about 1.5 percent of the total on the college entrance examination. Due to such a low proportion of the total scores, students can afford to refrain from studying economics. Also, few students show interest in the subject, which they perceive as difficult to understand.

Secondly, the limited amount of instruction time relative to the extensive concepts and topics to be covered in the course tends to make economics instruction more or less superficial. Many teachers of the subject complain that even the most useful instructional materials might not be used because of time constraints, although very few supplementary materials for teaching economics are available in Korea.

Thirdly, while the teacher is considered a key factor affecting what is taught in the classroom, most teachers responsible for economics instruction seem inadequately prepared to teach the subject. The data resulting from the nationwide survey of teachers responsible for teaching economics in high schools show that these teachers have taken, on average, about 4 economics courses before they graduate from college. However, a great majority of surveyed teachers (about 81 percent) reported feeling a lack of economic understanding (Kim, 1992).

Finally, professional economists have displayed little interest in economic education at the elementary and secondary level. Also, in the "only" textbook of the politics and economy course, too many topics and concepts are discussed in a superficial, and inapplicable fashion, making the subject even less interesting.

TABLE 12.6: KVTEL Descriptive Statistics for Various Groups within the Norming Sample

	Without Economics			With Economics		
	Mean	S.D.	N	Mean	S.D.	N
Gender						
Females	22.96	5.44	507	24.25	7.05	1,649
Males	21.80	6.57	802	24.63	8.16	1,376
Grade Level						
Grade 10	21.98	5.96	1,079	21.40	5.95	440
Grade 11	23.50	7.02	230	23.06	6.91	1,292
Grade 12	-----	----	-----	26.82	8.00	1,293
Type of School						
General	24.22	6.28	698	25.32	7.84	2,135
Vocational	19.99	5.23	611	22.27	6.44	890
Type of Community						
Seoul	22.51	5.59	404	24.60	7.29	622
Large Cities	21.95	5.98	332	26.30	6.67	723
Smaller Cities	24.48	6.47	366	26.21	7.56	931
Rural Communities	18.27	5.02	207	20.24	7.02	749
Mother's Schooling						
Elementary	20.80	5.90	294	23.01	7.42	812
Junior High	21.55	6.47	422	24.30	7.43	1,006
High	23.09	5.66	481	25.51	7.45	950
College	26.29	6.23	85	26.69	8.66	160
Going on to College						
Yes	23.16	6.16	1,003	25.07	7.54	2,569
No	19.19	5.25	296	20.72	6.65	426

CONCLUSION

Thus far, economics has been a universal subject in Korea regardless of its effectiveness. However, a significant change affecting the status of economics will soon take place. Beginning in 1996, economics will be offered as a separate course on an elective basis. This means that economics will have to compete with other social science courses for the attention of students. Combined with various problems noted earlier, the perceived difficulty of the subject relative to other social science courses are likely to make it less popular than other social science courses as an elective among students.

With this in mind, it is important, then, to make economics more attractive as an elective than other subjects in the social sciences curriculum. Several steps should be taken to achieve this important objective. To begin with, teachers responsible for teaching economics should be more adequately prepared to teach the subject. Attention should be given to inducing prospective teachers to take more economics courses before they graduate from college. Also, deficiencies in teacher knowledge from preservice training should be corrected through the increased use of workshops and in-service courses.

Considering the overwhelming importance in economics instruction in Korea, a wider range of quality textbooks should be produced so that students might have more leeway in choosing the very textbook appropriate for them. In addition, quality instructional materials made available are likely to be instrumental in attracting student interest and reducing preparation time for teachers. Professional economists should assume a more active role in exerting pressure for more classroom time for economics and improving economic education below the college levels. Taken together, all these actions should lead eventually to a significant increase in student achievement levels in economics.

NOTES

I am grateful to William Walstad for encouraging me to undertake this study and for providing me with various background studies.

1. As a matter of fact, though in a somewhat limited and condensed form, economic contents in the textbook of the politics and economy course are similar to the contents of a typical college principles textbook.
2. The classification of type of community was made primarily on the basis of the number of inhabitants. Thus, large cities are defined as ones with populations of over 1 million, smaller cities with populations of 50 thousand to 1 million, and rural communities with populations of less than 50 thousand.
3. Obviously, regression analysis should be used to account for many other factors that might influence the final level of students' performance.
4. In Korea, mother's level of schooling can be viewed as a proxy for family income level or IQ level.

REFERENCES

Brenneke, J., & Soper, J. C. (1985). Economics in the secondary classroom. In M. C. Schug (Ed.), *Economics in the school curriculum, K-12* (pp. 60-74). Washington, DC: National Education Association and Joint Council on Economic Education.

Kim, K. (1992). Current status of economic education in high schools and policy suggestions for its improvement. *Current status of economic education in Korea and tasks ahead* (pp. 3-40). Seoul: Center for Economic Education, Korea Development Institute.

Saunders, P., Bach, G. L., Calderwood, J. D., Hansen, W. L., with Stein, H. (1984). *A framework for teaching the basic concepts* (2nd ed.). New York: Joint Council on Economic Education.

Soper, J. C., & Walstad, W. B. (1987). *The test of economic literacy: Examiner's manual* (2nd ed.) New York: Joint Council on Economic Education.

Walstad, W. B. (1992). Economics instruction in high schools. *Journal of Economic Literature, 30*(4), 2019-2051.

Walstad, W. B., & Soper, J. C. (1991). Economic literacy in senior high schools. In W. B. Walstad & J. C. Soper (Eds.), *Effective economic education in the schools* (pp. 99-116). Washington, DC: National Education Association and Joint Council on Economic Education.

Whitehead, D. J., & Halil, T. (1991). Economic literacy in the United Kingdom and the United States: A comparative study. *Journal of Economic Education, 22*(2), 101-110.

CHAPTER 13

HIGH SCHOOL ECONOMICS IN AUSTRALIA

Kevin McKenna

In Australia, education is the responsibility of the state governments (there are eight, including two territories) and state governments have a strong tradition of defending their independence and resisting any attempts by the federal government to impose uniformity. Consequently, there is a wide diversity of approaches to educational systems, structures and syllabi. For example, some states have seven years of primary school followed by five years of high school, where others have six years of primary, four years of high school and two years in a separate secondary college.

About one third of final year high school students go on to universities or colleges, and in all states the focus of the final years of high school is on preparation for competitive entry into tertiary study. Students will normally study five or six subjects in years eleven and twelve, at least four of which are examined rigorously and combined to produce their "tertiary entrance score." For example, in Western Australia, there are 70 year-long units available in the final year of high school. Only English is compulsory and 28 of these units may be counted towards the tertiary entrance score. (The others are for interest or for students who do not intend further study.)

I. ECONOMICS STUDY

A student who studies economics at high school in Australia would normally be expected to spend about one sixth of his time for two years in a reasonably rigorous study of the subject. This is far more time than a typical American student would spend, but less than a student going for "A" levels in the United Kingdom.

About 25 percent of final year high school students in Australia study economics. However, tertiary entrance procedures and the pattern of subjects vary considerably from state to state, so there is considerable variation between states in the proportion of students taking economics. Currently, between 15 percent and 30 percent of year-12 students in any state study economics. By way of comparison, in 1990 about 21 percent studied history and 17 percent studied geography.

The percentage of students studying economics has been declining over recent years. One reason for this, in some states, is that competing subjects such as business studies and legal studies have been introduced in recent years. Further, with increasing retention rates, more lower-ability students are staying on to year 12, and economics seems to be perceived as a more theoretical subject than alternatives such as history, geography or business studies.

High school teachers in Australia, as a general rule, have either three or four years of tertiary education, with either a three year degree in teaching or a three year specialist degree (e.g., Bachelor of Science) followed by a one year Diploma in Teaching. First degrees in Australia in disciplines such as science, social sciences or arts are three year courses, generally lacking the broader components of a U.S. four year course. Economics in junior high school is perceived as an arm of "social studies" and may be taught by generalist teachers with degrees in history, geography, etc. However, upper school economics is seen as a specialist subject and teachers of upper school economics in Australia tend to be relatively well trained, with the majority of them having an Economics degree or an Arts degree with a major in economics.

II. THE ECONOMICS SYLLABUS IN AUSTRALIA

Education authorities in each state set syllabi for the tertiary entrance subjects and either assess them through externally set and marked examinations or arrange procedures for internal assessment which is externally moderated. In all states economics is one of the tertiary entrance subjects.

Consequently, as in the U.S., there is a multiplicity of high school syllabi. This chapter does not seek to give comprehensive details on the economics content taught in each state from K-12, but rather to give an outline of the current state of economic education.

In general, there is very little economics content which is compulsory, even in junior high school. In Western Australia, for example, students are given a range of choice within subject areas and economics has to compete with other social sciences for students. In lower secondary (years 8 to 10) they can choose three economics units, where eight units make up one semester's work. These are consumer economics (budgeting, credit, loan interest, etc.), introductory economics (scarcity, supply and demand, role of government, etc.) and comparative economic systems.

At present syllabi in the various states differ considerably, though there is a tentative move towards a standard syllabus. Although state governments resist any attempt by the federal government to impose its requirements in any area, including education, they sometimes agree to discuss moves towards uniformity where this is clearly to their own individual advantage, e.g., uniform labelling standards for food. The current move towards uniform syllabi is still in its early stages and may well come to nothing. One difficulty in making such a change can be seen from an examination of Table 13.1, showing the divergence of syllabi for macro-economics in the various states. This table clearly shows that some states, such as Tasmania, have a very light syllabus compared to states such as Victoria, New South Wales and Western Australia.

In some states, where the syllabus is structured over two years with year 12 building on year 11 work, the content and level approaches the equivalent of a U.S. first year college course and students use college texts as references. Topics such as crowding out, the permanent income hypothesis and the basics of monetarism are included in some syllabi. These states would come close to English 'A' level standard. Other states, which allow students to do only one year of Economics for tertiary entrance, do not have such a high standard.

III. TEST OF ECONOMIC LITERACY

This disparity between the syllabi of the various states suggests that there should be quite a variation in the level of economic knowledge also. This has been investigated, using a standard instrument, the *Test of Economic Literacy* (TEL) (Soper and Walstad, 1987). This test is becoming widely accepted as a benchmark instrument. Following Walstad and Soper's (1988) investigation in the U.S., Whitehead and Halil (1991) have used the TEL in the U.K., and Beck and Krumm (1991) translated it and administered it in Germany and Austria.

The TEL has two parts, each of 46 questions, with 15 common items, for use in pre- and post-tests. Part A was normed in the U.S. in 1985 and 1986 with a sample of 8205 students from a large, representative cross-section of high schools. An overlapping sample of 6570 students was used to norm Part B. In the U.K., Part A only was normed with a sample of 7549 students from 162 schools in 1989. In both cases, the samples comprised students from both of the

TABLE 13.1: Macroeconomics Syllabi by State

	WA	Qld	NSW	Vic	Tas	SA
Circular Flow model	*Y*	*Y*	*Y*	*Y*	*Y*	*Y*
'leakages/injections'	Y	Y	Y	Y	Y	Y
national accounts	Y	Y	Y	Y	Y	Y
GDP	Y	Y	Y	Y	Y	Y
GNE	Y	Y			Y	
national income		Y			Y	Y
domestic factor incomes		Y				
price indices			Y	Y		Y
equilibrium	Y		Y	Y	Y	Y
components of expenditure	Y	Y	Y	Y		Y
permanent income			O			
ex-post & ex-ante savings & investment	Y		O			
multiplier	Y	Y	Y	Y	N	Y
paradox of thrift			O			O
accelerator	Y	Y	O		N	
determinants of consumption	Y		Y	Y	Y	Y
determinants of investment	Y		Y	Y	Y	Y
inflationary/deflationary gaps	Y		O	Y		Y
Business Cycle						
inflation	Y	Y	Y	Y		Y
unemployment	Y	Y	Y	Y		Y
stagflation	Y	Y	O	Y		Y
Philips curve			Y			
Government economic policies						
economic objectives of government	Y	Y	Y	Y	Y	Y
links & conflicts between goals	Y		Y	Y		Y
Fiscal policy						
effect on economy	Y	Y	Y	Y	Y	Y
effectiveness	Y	Y	Y	Y		Y
automatic stabilisers	Y	Y	Y			
tax regimes						
public debt		Y	Y			
PSBR			Y			
crowding out			Y			O
Monetary policy						
money supply	Y	Y	Y	Y	Y	Y
credit multiplier	Y		Y			Y
determinants of interest rates	Y	Y	Y	Y	Y	Y
nominal vs real	Y		Y		Y	
operation of monetary policy	Y	Y	Y	Y	Y	Y
effectiveness	Y	Y	Y	Y		Y
basics of monetarism	Y	Y		Y		Y

TABLE 13.1: Macroeconomics Syllabi by State Continued

	WA	Qld	NSW	Vic	Tas	SA
Incomes policy						
objectives	Y	Y	Y	Y		Y
effectiveness	Y	Y	Y	Y		Y
Trade						
comparative advantage	Y	Y	Y	O		O
terms of trade	Y	Y	Y			O
forms of protection	Y	Y	Y	O		O
effects of tariffs & subsidies	Y			O		O
effects of quotas	Y			O		O
External policies						
balance of payments	Y	Y	Y	O		Y
'fixed' & 'floating' exchange rates	Y		Y			Y
'appreciation' & 'depreciation'	Y	Y	Y	O		Y
effects of ER on economy	Y	Y	Y	O		Y
measures to reduce CAD	Y			O		Y
foreign investment arguments	Y			O		O
significance of foreign debt	Y					
Growth						
measurement	Y	Y	Y	O		Y
costs & benefits	Y	Y	Y	O		Y

Note: Y = required by the syllabus; O = optional, students may alternatively study other areas in economics (e.g., environmental economics); N = specifically excluded by the syllabus.

last two years of high school. In both cases, also, students who were not studying economics made up a substantial proportion of the sample.

This test was used in Australia in 1992 with 939 students from the upper two years of high school. Only minor modifications have been made in the test. As in the U.K., different words were chosen to more accurately depict the same concept, e.g., trade union for labor union. The concept tested in the question was altered only in one case, where the way of expressing the exchange rate was changed from the "price of foreign currencies in U.K. sterling" to the "price of Australian dollars in foreign currencies", the more usual mode in Australia.

It was decided to follow a sampling procedure similar to the ones used in the U.S. and the U.K., namely to spread the sample over type of school, location and gender. Initially nearly 100 schools were approached and asked to participate in the test. Thirty-two schools agreed to take part. Of these schools, 11 were private and 21 were public (i.e., government schools). Sample sizes ranged from 4 students from one small country high school to 112 in a large city school.

Students completed the test in September or October, towards the end of the academic year and before their final exams.

As in the U.S. and U.K., students from both year 11 and year 12 were chosen. However, it was decided that requiring schools to give the test to students who were not studying economics would lower the response rate unacceptably, so schools were asked to administer the test only in economics classes. Australian results can still be accurately compared with the "with economics" results of the other studies.

In Australia, education through to age 15 is compulsory and the retention rate to year 10 is 99 percent. However, only 86 percent finish year 11 and by the end of year 12 the retention rate has dropped to 71 percent, made up of 66 percent of males and 77 percent of females (Australian Bureau of Statistics, 1991). This probably results in the average ability levels of Australian year 12 students being below that of the U.K. students, who were studying economics at the advanced level, a level which is restricted to the top 25 percent of the ability range (Whitehead and Halil, 1991). On the other hand, it may be above that of the U.S. final year students included in Walstad and Soper's (1988) sample, where there was a broader range of ability levels.

Another factor in this international comparison is the amount of time which students had spent studying economics. The U.S. students sampled had generally been exposed to only one semester (half a year) of economics. In Australia, as in the U.K., most students study economics for two years. The Australian sample covered both years, with 40 percent of students being in year 11 and 60 percent in year 12. Results are given for both years for Australia and the U.K. to see the effect of the extra year of economics study (though this is confounded with the extra year of maturity). For the U.S. the year 12 results generally do not reflect the effect of extra study in economics. Comparison with the U.S. results is difficult then, given that U.K. and Australian students had either twice as much or four times as much time spent studying economics as the U.S. students.

The results from each study, for students studying economics (i.e., ignoring the "without economics" groups from the U.K. and U.S. samples) are shown in Table 13.2. It is clear from these results that the Australian students scored, on average, 5 to 7 points (10 to 15 percent) higher than U.S. students in the same grade, but about 5 points (10 percent) lower than U.K. students. This ranking is to be expected, given earlier comments about relative ability levels and school retention rates.

TABLE 13.2: Aggregate Statistics for TEL, Form A, Year 11 and 12 Students Studying Economics

Nation	Year	Means	S.D.	N	Range
Australia	11	26.90	6.40	368	9-42
	12	31.11	7.16	571	10-45
U.K.	11	31.84	5.82	2,169	9-46
	12	36.87	4.74	1,814	11-46
U.S.	11	21.26	7.99	2,067	-------
	12	24.04	8.47	2,168	-------

Source: Whitehead and Halil, 1991, for U.S. and U.K. data.

Comparative percentile norms for students studying economics are given in Table 13.3. These expand on the results in Table 13.2. As expected, the U.K. students outrank the U.S. and Australian students at every level. A comparison between the U.S. and Australian students is interesting, though, as in both year 11 and year 12 the upper scores are very similar, despite the fact that Australian students would generally have had more economics teaching. Below the very top scores, however, it is clear that Australian students are scoring considerably higher than U.S. students in the same grade. For example, a mark of 37 or above was scored by the top 3 percent of year 11 students in both countries, while a mark of 27 or above was scored by 51 percent of Australian students but by only 24 percent of U.S. students.

Looking in a little more detail at the Australian sample, the difference in results of Australian students attending private schools compared with those attending government schools is given in Table 13.4. While there is virtually no difference between government and private schools at the year 11 level, students in year 12 at private schools scored significantly higher than those in government schools. This could be due to a greater emphasis in private schools on preparation for the tertiary entrance examination.

Information was also collected on the sex of students in the Australian sample. Table 13.4 also shows an analysis of scores by gender. The small, though statistically significant difference in favor of males, is a result which is very similar to the U.S. and U.K. findings (Whitehead and Halil, 1989).

TABLE 13.3: Percentile Norms for Students Studying Economics

	Year 11			Year 12		
Score	Australia	U.S.	U.K.	Australia	U.S.	U.K.
46						
45						99
44						98
43			99			95
42			98	99	99	90
41			97	97	98	84
40	99	99	94	96	97	76
39	98	98	92	93	97	67
38			87	90	96	58
37	97	97	83	86	94	50
36	94	95	77	82	92	41
35	90	94	71	77	90	33
34	87	93	65	73	87	26
33	84	91	59	67	84	21
32	80	90	51	62	81	16
31	75	88	45	59	78	12
30	70	84	38	55	75	9
29	64	82	32	49	71	6
28	55	82	25	43	68	5
27	49	76	21	38	64	4
26	45	73	17	34	61	3
25	40	70	13	29	57	2
24	35	67	10	25	53	
23	30	64	8	20	50	1
22	25	61	7	17	46	
21	22	57	5	15	42	
20	18	54	4	12	38	
19	13	49	3	9	35	
18	10	45	2	8	30	
17	8	40		6	26	
16	5	34	1	4	22	
15	3	29			18	
14	2	23		3	15	
13		18		2	12	
12	1	13		1	8	
11		8			5	
10		5			4	
9		2			2	
8		1			1	

Source: Whitehead and Halil, 1989, for U.K. and U.S. data.

TABLE 13.4: TEL Scores of Australian Students by School Type

Year	Type/Sex	Mean	S.D.	N	*p*
11	Private	26.75	6.97	166	
	Government	27.02	5.91	202	.68
11	Male	27.56	6.65	208	
	Female	26.03	5.97	160	.02
12	Private	32.08	6.51	246	
	Government	30.37	7.54	325	.005
12	Male	32.28	7.43	247	
	Female	30.21	6.82	324	.001

IV. INNOVATIONS IN ECONOMICS TEACHING

In general, economics teaching in Australian high schools follows a traditional "chalk and talk" format. The typical upper school student would have five classes every week, each of 45 minutes to an hour, over two years.

Over recent years there have been two major innovations introduced to economics classrooms across Australia, the *Sharemarket Game* and the *Managing the Australian Economy* Competition. In the *Sharemarket Game* syndicates of students invest a notional $50,000 in a selected range of stocks and bonds. They buy and sell shares over eight months, aiming to maximize the value of the portfolio by the end of the game. It is generally used with year 11 students as means of introducing them to financial markets and giving them an understanding of the operations of the Sharemarket and the investment industry. Further, it helps develop analytical skills and promotes decision-making in small groups. This exercise is organized and managed by the Australian Stock Exchange with a range of additional sponsors.

The *Sharemarket Game* was introduced by a West Australian teacher in 1974 after he had seen a similar exercise running in Scotland with great success. It immediately appealed to high school teachers and students and soon became a national program. By 1980 some 500 schools were involved. In 1992 a total of about 30,000 students from were involved in the Game.

The other major national innovation in economic education in Australia is *Managing the Australian Economy*, a macro-economic computer simulation which is used in a competition for final year high school students. Heats are held in 35 cities across the country, covering all states. In 1991 over 450 schools took part (i.e., over 20 percent of high schools in the country).

The econometric model behind *Managing the Australian Economy* is based on one developed for the U.K. by Keith Lumsden and Alex Scott of the Esmee Fairbairn Research Centre at Heriot-Watt University, Edinburgh (Lumsden and Scott, 1982, 1983-1988). The model was first translated to reflect Australian economic conditions in 1983 then revised in 1987 (McKenna, Lumsden and Scott, 1988) and again in 1992 (McKenna, 1992).

Though the Competition involves senior high school students, the econometric model is based more on intermediate macro theory, and the package is used extensively in university and executive development courses. The model is a dynamic growth model with four control variables: government spending on goods and services, the average income tax rate, the average sales tax rate and the level of interest rates. The model generates the values of 26 other economic variables, such as inflation, unemployment, investment, balance of payments, etc.

Students initially are provided with a manual which explains the economic relationships built into the model. It also gives an eight year "history" of the economy. This is a set of annual data which has been generated by the model for each of the eight years together with a discussion of the policies followed and the response of the economy over this time. This data closely resembles that for the Australian economy over the period 1984-91.

Minor complications are added each "year," when students are presented with exogenous shocks either constraining their use of the policy variables or affecting some other variable in the economy, for example exports. The competition can be varied by varying the data for economic conditions at the commencement of the start year and by varying the exogenous shocks. The model is sufficiently complex so that no amount of practice can produce rules for optimum play.

The objective is to maximize the sum of a specified welfare function over the ten "years" of the simulation. The welfare function varies, but typically involves positive points for GDP growth and negative points according to some function of inflation and unemployment and, perhaps, budget or balance of payments deficits.

The competition began at Curtin University of Technology in Perth, Western Australia, in 1982 with 6 schools, using a much simpler model. In 1984 the first version of the current model was used, with 10 schools. It has grown considerably since then and details of participation are given in Table 13.5.

In 1985 the first national final was played using computer and telephone link-ups, with each state finalist team competing from their own state, all playing simultaneously. From 1988 Mobil Oil sponsored the competition, so that the eight state finalist teams, plus teachers, are flown to the national capital, Canberra, for the national final (as well as some entertainment and sightseeing). This sponsorship from Mobil (just under $1 million over six years) has been essential to the growth of the competition. The support of the Economic Society of Australia has also been a vital factor.

TABLE 13.5: Managing the Australian Economy Competition (Number of cities, states, and schools)

Year	Cities	States	Schools
1984	1	1	10
1985	5	5	75
1986	5	5	120
1987	6	6	140
1988	12	8	176
1989	20	8	293
1990	26	8	375
1991	26	8	445
1992	35	8	455

Heats of the competition are held in July, the middle of the academic year, in a number of cities throughout the country, mainly in tertiary institutions. Each participating school sends a team of four students. The competition itself takes two hours. There is always a high level of excitement, as the welfare scores for all teams are displayed after each round, then the next exogenous shock is announced. Members of the winning team at each heat are presented with minor prizes, and the team with the highest score in each state wins a trip to Canberra for the national final at the Australian National University, as well as a computer for their school.

Success in the version used in 1992 was measured by a welfare function which was, for the first few rounds:

$$\text{WELFARE} = 10 * (C^{.6} * I^{.2} * G^{.2}) - 2 * U^2 - INF^2 - 10 * \text{Budget Deficit}$$

To test the students the welfare function was varied several times during the final. For example:

$$\text{WELFARE} = 10 * (C^{.6} * I^{.2} * G^{.2}) - 2 * U^2 - INF^2 + 10 * BOT$$

So, teams lost points for a Balance of Trade Deficit (BOT), but gained points for a surplus. The point to these shifts in the welfare function was not to have the students suddenly start manipulating the economy aiming to maximize trade surpluses, but to require them to make judgments on trade-offs and to manage their economy in the light of these judgments.

For each of the ten decision rounds the students were also presented with one or more exogenous shocks. Sometimes these acted as constraints on decision variables, e.g.:

> One of your Ministers is proven to have connections with the Mafia drug trade in Australia and extensive holdings of gold bullion in safety deposit boxes in a Swiss bank.
>
> Opinion polls show that support amongst the electorate has plummeted, and you lose an important by-election.
> Your Cabinet decides that you must cut income taxes by 4 percent this year.

Other shocks involved events affecting other economic variables, e.g.:

> Economic development in Eastern Europe accelerates.
> Some foreign investment, previously targeted for Australia, now goes to Eastern Europe, so capital inflow into Australia is now $0.5 billion lower than otherwise, as is private investment spending.
>
> In addition, some major Australian companies see opportunities in Eastern Europe and invest there. This has the effect of reducing net capital inflow a further $1 billion. Some of this investment takes the form of Australian machinery and expertise, so exports are $0.5 billion higher than otherwise.

The primary purpose of using the simulation with students is to stimulate interest in, and understanding of, economics, particularly the subject matter of macroeconomics. The competition has a second objective, which is to stimulate interest in economics as a tertiary course of study and as a profession, and to demonstrate to students that economics is an exciting and challenging field in which to work.

Although no evaluation has yet been carried out on the second objective (stimulating interest in economics as a tertiary course of study and as a profession), informal evidence indicates that it is having a significant effect. Experience shows that the national finalists include many of the best economics students in the country. Many of these students, however, are outstanding in their other subjects also, and casual surveys of these students indicate that most of them intended to go on to study mathematics or science at university. After the national final, however, a significant number indicate that they will change their university applications and will now enroll in economics courses.

After the 1991 competition a major survey of high school economics teachers was carried out. This survey clearly showed that teachers were very enthusiastic towards the simulation: (1) 98 percent of the teachers who participated had a positive attitude to the competition; (2) 92 percent described the software as "an excellent teaching tool"; (3) 97 percent stated that the simulation "assists students to really understand macro economics and to see its application"; and, (4) 91 percent said it "substantially improved student motivation."

V. CONCLUSION

While economics plays a strong role in education in secondary schools in Australia, the number of students it has been attracting over recent years has tended to decline slightly. The reasons for this are uncertain, but it is probably related to the introduction, in some states, of competing subjects (e.g., business education) and to the perception among the increasing number of lower ability students that economics is a relatively rigorous subject.

In Australia the organization of education, including subject syllabi, is a state responsibility and the content of the economics syllabus varies widely from state to state. Nevertheless, there is core of material which is generally common throughout the country. A student studying economics would normally spend one fifth or one sixth of his time on the subject for both of the final two years of high school.

It is not surprising, then, that on the *Test of Economic Literacy* Australian students on average score considerably higher than U.S. students. That they do not do as well as U.K. economics students may be due more to the lower retention rates and consequent higher ability levels of the U.K. students than to any difference in the quality of the teaching. Teachers of upper school economics in Australia would normally be expected to have a first degree with a major in economics.

Two major national innovations have been introduced to economics teaching in recent years. The *Sharemarket Game* is played by the majority of year 11 students in the country as a means of introducing them to concepts associated with investment and the stock exchange. The *Managing the Australian Economy* competition is played in over 20 percent of schools at year 12 level, as a means of familiarizing students with some of the complexities of macro economics. Both simulations are highly valued by teachers who participate in them as exercises which motivate and educate economics students.

REFERENCES

Australian Bureau of Statistics. (1991). *Schools Australia* (Catalogue No. 4221.0). Canberra: Australian Government Publishing Service.

Beck, K., & Krumm, V. (1991). Economic literacy in German speaking countries and the United States: First steps to a comparative study. *Economia, 1*(1), 17-23.

Lumsden, K. G., & Scott, A. (1982, 1983-1988). *Running the British economy*. London: Longmans Micro Software.

McKenna, K. (1992). *Managing the Australian economy, 1992*. Perth, Western Australia: Curtin University of Technology.

McKenna, K., Lumsden, K., & Scott, A. (1988). *Managing the Australian economy*. Perth, Western Australia: Curtin University of Technology.

Soper, J. C., & Walstad, W. B. (1987). *Test of economic literacy: Examiner's Manual* (2nd ed.). New York: Joint Council on Economic Education.

Walstad, W. B., & Soper, J. C. (1988). A report card on the economic literacy of U.S. high school students. *American Economic Review, 78*(2), 251-256.

Whitehead, D., & Halil, T. (1989). The test of economic literacy: Standardisation in the U.K. *Research Papers in Economics Education.* London: Institute of Education, University of London.

Whitehead, D., & Halil, T. (1991). Economic literacy in the United Kingdom and the United States: A comparative study. *Journal of Economic Education, 21*(2), 101-110.

CHAPTER 14

THE CHANGING FACE OF ECONOMICS INSTRUCTION IN RUSSIA

Francis W. Rushing

One of the most historic events in the last half of the twentieth century was the shattering of the Union of Soviet Socialist Republics into 15 independent states. Russia has now set forth on a more radical reform movement, attempting to create a decentralized market-based economy. The reforms do away with the old centralized command institutions. New commercial structures are encouraged and some spontaneous market activity has emerged, particularly in Moscow with the Kiosks. Market-based trade has expanded within Russia, and between Russia and the rest of the world (Lipton and Sachs, 1992).

Although full of promise, the reforms do not provide immediate success. The transition brought about higher unemployment, increased uncertainty as to the availability of economic inputs, declining outputs, and continuing shortages of food, shelter, and clothing. Russia's financial conditions have led to rapid (almost hyper) inflation, which threatened the potential for full democracy and the transition to a market economy. The absence of good data, and the confusion over a steady stream of new laws and revisions of laws, make an assessment of the progress of the reforms difficult, providing ideal conditions for critics to question the wisdom of the entire process. The opposition to the reforms has been centered within the parliament, which is composed of many hard-liners who seem intent on slowing, if not reversing, the transition to a market economy. These conditions led David Lipton and Jeffrey Sachs (1992) to write:

> Many observers are deeply pessimistic about Russia's long-term economic prospects. They fear that the reforms initiated this year [1992] simply cannot be sustained. A number of reasons are offered. Some claim that the short-term dislocations of the economy are so great as to guarantee a political backlash or even social explosion. Others claim that Russia's distinctive history and the character of its people will prevent the efficient operation of a market system. Our own concerns lie elsewhere: with the risks for political instability as a result of the partial nature of Russia's political and institutional reforms. (p. 249)

Although the old order has collapsed, a new order is slow to evolve. There is no road map to provide the Russian leaders with directions for going from a command system to a market system. Indeed there is little real enthusiasm by many of the government officials to take the trip at all. Events, however, seem to have closed the road back to Communism, and now transforming the economy into some form of market-oriented system is the most likely choice. This chapter will look at one aspect of the transformation: preparing the Russian people to become full participating members of a market economy by learning how the market works and how all individuals are important in their roles as producers, consumers, and citizens. The chapter will focus on what is happening in Russia in teaching about the market, and will explore various strategies for putting economic education into the curricula of the pre-university institutions.

Section I will describe the organization and curriculum of the former Soviet Union's educational system, since it is the foundation of the now evolving Russian educational system. Section II will explore what evidence there is about the attitudes of the Russian people toward a market system, and whether or not the attitudes may be barriers to implementing economic education programs in Russia. Section III discusses the kinds of programs and the concepts which should constitute the core of an economic education curriculum. Section IV will explore how the curriculum might be taught, and how to prepare the instructors to be effective implementors of the curriculum. The next section (V) describes what economic education activities are occurring. The conclusions in section VI will summarize some of the key points made in the chapter, and discuss some of the problems and prospects of economic education in Russia.

I. THE EDUCATIONAL SYSTEM OF THE USSR: THE POINT OF DEPARTURE FOR REFORMS

The rationale of the old Soviet system had been one of functional education, designed to integrate individuals into productive work and occupational roles in employment (DeWitt, 1980). The Soviet leadership had perceived that specialized education was the most effective means of fostering the productive contributions of the individual for the good of the system. Students had four options upon completion of the ninth grade. They could continue in the upper secondary level of the general education day school. This was the path most students pursued who desired and were qualified to enter institutions of higher education. A second option was for the student to enroll in a specialized secondary school, where the student was provided with two to three additional years of specialized training after completing the final two years of the required curriculum. Vocational-technical schooling was a third option. In these schools the students completed the required curriculum and received occupational training for positions as skilled workers in a variety of specialties. This program might take three to three and one-half years to complete. Finally, the youths might enter the workforce or become homemakers. These persons had the opportunity to attend evening classes or take extension courses to earn the equivalent of the general education curriculum (Ailes and Rushing, 1991).

One of the distinguishing features of the old Soviet educational system was that it attempted to provide a universal and relatively uniform curriculum for all Soviet youths up to the completion of the secondary school process. This curriculum was the last in a series of educational reforms that occurred in the Soviet Union after the second world war. The Soviet educational curriculum had several features which are important to note. First, the curriculum was uniform in content and in presentation. Secondly, it had far more math and sciences and languages than one would find in the typical U.S. school system. This reflected the Soviet belief in preparing students for the work force, which would require math and scientific knowledge. Languages were important, first to establish a national language – Russian – in a union with many different nationalities and languages, and secondly, to prepare the best linguists to function in a multilingual world.

Another contrast with the typical U.S. curriculum was the number of hours devoted to the social sciences. Social studies appeared in the 10th and 11th grades but only for 2 hours per week at most. History was important in grades 5 through 11, and focused on the history of the Soviet Union and its antecedent – the Russian Empire. Geography was fairly prominent in grades 6 through 10, and was one of the disciplines where "economics" was taught. One has to be aware that Marxian ideology and party dogma were infused throughout the curriculum, but were taught to legitimatize the regime and not to prepare individuals for economic analysis and decision-making (Ailes and Rushing, 1991).

Beatrice Szekely noted in 1987, upon reviewing the new social studies curriculum, "The two-year social studies course teaches a blatantly ideological curriculum that interprets social reality from the Marxist-Leninist perspective of the current Communist Party leadership with underpinnings of social science" (p. 5). This analysis is supported by the content topics in the curriculum: "Imperialism-Monopoly Capitalism. The General Crisis of Capitalism"; "The Spiritual-Intellectual Culture of Socialism"; and "The Individual in Socialist Society: Nurturing the New Socialist Man" (Kondakov, 1987).

History in the Soviet curriculum spanned grades 5 through 11. A look at the curriculum, however, shows that history, like social studies, was presented to the Soviet student from the Marxist-Leninist interpretation of history, i.e., dialectic materialism. All history – Russian, European, and world – was subject to the Marxian dialectic. For instance, topic 3 in grade 6 was "The Establishment of a Slave-Owning Order in Ancient Egypt"; topic 7 was "Aegean Greece and the Origins of Classes Among Greeks"; in grade 9 the content included "The Development of Capitalism and the Shaping of the Industrial Proletariat in Russia, 1860's-1890's"; in the eleventh grade "The USSR's Economic Development" filled the history classroom hours. A significant aspect of the history content was the economic interpretation of history embodied in it. The Soviet teacher was not to teach the students how to analyze or interpret history, but students were to learn it as the book presented it without questioning its factual or political correctness (Soviet Education, 1987a).

The geography curriculum in grades 8 and 9 had the role of geographical science in addressing the country's economic and social challenges. In grade 9 the topics turned to a general description of the economy, including the geography of the most important interbranch complexes and branches of the economy, such as machine-building, fuel, the agri-industrial complex, the consumer and service sectors, and transport. Thirty hours of class time were devoted to instruction in the economic and social geography of the Union republics and major regional subdivisions. In these hours the students were taught about the economic features of the major regions, and finally about the economic development and the social progress of the Soviet Union.

The 10th grade focused on the "economic and social geography of the world." This was virtually a new course in the reformed geography curriculum of 1984-86, and focused on the geography of global natural resources and ecological problems. The instruction included descriptions of socialism, capitalism, and three socioeconomic country systems (socialist, developed capitalist, and developing). Four countries were examined separately – China, Japan, the United States, and India (Soviet Education, 1987b). This instruction consisted of descriptions of various economic systems, without any in-depth discussion of the theoretical underpinning for the systems.

The curriculum was designed to make the student familiar with the structure of the Soviet economic system as directed by the planners and the party. The curriculum focused on facts, not analysis; rote, not thinking; and taught by instruction, not discovery. These instructional characteristics applied to the other disciplines as well.

One feature of the old curriculum stands out as important with respect to the future of economic education. The science and math curricula were both spiral and integrated across disciplines. For instance, if one looks at biology, physics, and chemistry, they were taught at multiple grade levels and in most years concurrently. A review of these curricula by a team of U.S. experts led them to conclude that the Soviets had effectively provided their students with the discipline content at appropriate grade levels, and had used the concept of building blocks within the discipline. These blocks were then utilized at the appropriate time in other scientific disciplines (chemistry and physics). Mathematics curricula manifested similar characteristics and were also integrated into the sciences (Ailes and Rushing, 1989). One might ask if this approach in the old Soviet curriculum will make infusing market-oriented economics into the curriculum of Russian schools more or less difficult.

The curriculum described above has been undergoing changes since the breakup of the Soviet Union, although some important changes had already been initiated prior to the breakup. The most important changes were to provide the regions and the local schools greater autonomy over a portion of the curriculum, particularly what is known as the electives. A revised state basic curriculum was introduced in 1990. This curriculum retained a core for all Union Republics, but permitted the republic levels to design the elective and specialized courses as well as the optional and extra classes. In addition, this curriculum reduced the number of hours and encouraged greater diversity in methods of instruction as well as content (USSR State Committee, 1990). This general direction of educational reform has continued since 1990, and in fact there is evidence that even more of the Russian curriculum is determined at the local district and school levels than in 1990, particularly in cities like Moscow and St. Petersburg.[1] Decentralization of educational decision-making seems to be paralleling the trends in the economic and political arenas.

II. HISTORICAL ATTITUDES AND BEHAVIOR: ARE THEY ROAD-BLOCKS TO TEACHING MARKET ECONOMICS?

In a *Washington Post* article, Peter Reddaway (1992) declared that shock therapy cannot work in Russia because the Sovietized political culture is so unsuited to free markets, entrepreneurship, privatization, and the rule of law that it will take a decade or two to overcome this culture even with sustained assistance from the West. Can this be true? Is Russia's past to be a principal barrier to developing private markets in the future?

Robert J. Shiller, Maxim Boycko, and Vladimir Korobov have undertaken some interesting research on differences in attitudes between the former Soviet Union and the United States; they extended the study to Russia, Ukraine, and East Germany of the former Soviet block, as well as Japan and West Germany. The initial research consisted of telephone interviews with individuals living in Moscow and New York. These interviews focused on the respondents' attitudes toward and understanding of markets, the functions of prices, and income equality. The second stage expanded the scope to include economic behavior as well as opinions, and greatly expanded the sample in terms of numbers and geography.

The first survey was taken when the Soviet Union was still intact but had a declared intent to move toward a market-like economy. The findings are quite interesting with respect to the Reddaway hypothesis. According to Shiller, Boycko, and Korobov (1991)

> Soviets appear to be no more concerned with fairness of prices than U.S. citizens. Further, Soviets appear to be no more concerned with income inequality, and they appear to have the same or even [a] stronger appreciation of [the] importance of incentives.... We did find some evidence that there is such a resistance toward exchange of money and less warm attitudes toward business; we found also that there may be more of a concern that the government may later nationalize private enterprises. This evidence is of great concern in assessing the long-run outlook for the level of prosperity of the Soviet Union. Still, these differences do not seem so large as to be considered the prime suspects in the annoyingly tangible and immediate problems of today, like that of the soap shortage. (p. 399)

The lack of significant differences in the responses to many of the questions in the Moscow and New York survey may result in part from a lack of economic understanding on the part of the Americans. A Gallup poll has revealed that Americans are not very informed about the workings of their own economy, even though they have grown up under the market system (Walstad and Larsen, 1992).

The second study by Shiller, Boycko, and Korobov (1992) was more complicated, as it attempted to distinguish between attitudinal and situational factors as guiding people's behavior. Attitudinal factors relate to psychological traits, personality, and culture while situational factors relate to people's perceptions of their economic situations. Situational factors include institutions that affect people, their economic expectations, and their expectations about how other people will react to their own actions. The authors conclude that

> ...attitudinal factors are less important than situational factors in influencing how successfully ex-communist countries will make the transition to market

> economies. The biggest obstacles to a successful transition do not seem to lie in the basic attitudes and psychological traits held by people in the ex-communist countries.... Our research has consistently confirmed that some problems worthy of concern exist for the ex-communist economies of Russia and Ukraine. These problems are situational, not attitudinal. People trust current institutions relatively less in the ex-communist countries and are less likely to expect their own efforts to succeed. Because of these problems, Russia and Ukraine exhibit a tendency for short-term outlook and behavior. (pp. 179-180)

The authors conclude that these situational barriers will gradually fall as a kind of "social osmosis" occurs, i.e., as people learn by observing what others are doing. Assumptions upon which decisions are made change at varying speeds: rapidly through migration to a capitalist country, but more slowly as relationships and behaviors change within a country. What is somewhat striking is that the authors did not suggest that the social osmosis might be accelerated in Russia by combining economic education with the government's creation of legal and judicial systems to produce a fertile environment for private enterprise. As people observed how the system works, the process would accelerate.

It should be noted that there have been significant changes in Russia. For instance, through January of 1992, 8,900 small-scale privatizations had occurred; the number of joint ventures had risen to 5,000; and there were 600 commodities exchanges operating. The share of the labor force in private organizations, joint stock companies, leased enterprises, and joint ventures rose from 5.8 percent in 1990 to 10.4 percent in 1991 (Lipton and Sachs, 1992). If the privatization process accelerates, the "social osmosis" will also.

How can economic education help accelerate the process? Gunnar Knapp (1993) of the University of Alaska-Anchorage reports on an experience of teaching economics to a group of 34 Russian students between the ages of 17 and 20. The intensive course in "Fundamentals of Market Economics" was one week in duration. The students attended the Magadan International Pedagogical University in Magadan, Russia. Professor Knapp used some of the same survey questions used in the Shiller et al. survey of Moscow and New York. What is interesting about the responses of the survey is that the answers by the Russian students and the University of Alaska economics students were different from the responses of the general populations of Moscow and New York. For instance, on the question "On a holiday, when there is a great demand for flowers, their prices usually go up. Is it fair for flower sellers to raise their prices?" the four groups responded as follows:

Group	*Yes*	*No*
New York: general population	32%	68%
Moscow: general population	34%	66%
Magadan students	78%	22%
Anchorage students	94%	6%

The preliminary analysis of the student responses to the questions suggests that economics students in both countries are considerably more sympathetic toward market mechanisms than the general populations of Russia and the United States, and may be more receptive to the transition to a market system because of less indoctrination in the past. A second, and perhaps equally important, hypothesis is that instruction in economics may change attitudes as well as enhance knowledge. Even though these are university-age students, one might extend the generalization to the secondary-age students in Russia.

A survey in January 1992 on Russians' attitudes toward private ownership and privatization by Irina Boeva and Vlacheslav Shironin lends further evidence to the notion that the youth are more disposed toward economic reform than the population in general, even though the majority of the sample support the fundamental actions to transform the economy (Lipton and Sachs, 1992). Table 14.1 shows these conclusions.

Question 1 presents a clear inter-generational contrast. In the over-59 age group, over fifty percent still see state ownership as the best way to run a business, in contrast to sixteen percent of the under-30 group. These data should be encouraging to educators who hope that their economic instruction will not have to overcome strong prejudices against market economics.

Another interesting research project was conducted surveying high school students from Beijing, China and northern California (Shen and Shen, 1993). The students were surveyed on knowledge, attitudes, and values. The authors observe that the Chinese students appeared to be capable of applying their observations from the real world to modify their outdated and ideologically constrictive classroom instruction. The study also showed that Western economic ideas, although generally not sanctioned by the Chinese leadership, have a hold on student thinking and have (among the youth at least) spawned attitudes and values which are receptive to private enterprise systems.[2]

The findings have relevance in the context of the Russian case, in that once again there is evidence to refute the general assumption that there are inherently negative and insurmountable attitudes toward markets in countries that were previously Communist. Secondly, it tends to support the observation that youth, both Russian and Chinese, are receptive to transforming their economies to be more market-oriented. Finally, there is some evidence, although not strong in the above studies, that teaching economics can impact on values, attitudes, and knowledge, particularly among youth.

TABLE 14.1: Russian Attitudes Toward Private Ownership and Privatization: January 1992 (Responses in Percentages)

Question	Age Group			
	Under 30	30-59	Over 59	Total population
1. State ownership is the best way to run a business.	16	32	52	31
An enterprise is best run by entrepreneurs producing goods people want.	82	64	43	65
Don't know.	2	4	4	4
2. What effect will the following have on your own family situation if/when the government:				
a. Sells state enterprises to private owners?				
Better off	75	57	37	58
Worse off	11	24	40	23
No difference	12	16	22	16
Don't know	2	2	2	2
b. Allows foreigners to buy shares in state enterprises?				
Better off	70	52	26	52
Worse off	15	28	50	29
No difference	13	14	20	15
Don't know	2	5	4	4
c. Allows most farming to be done by private owners or on private land?				
Better off	86	75	61	75
Worse off	5	11	19	11
No difference	8	12	17	12
Don't know	1	2	2	2

Source: Lipton and Sachs, 1992, p. 252.

III. WHAT SHOULD THE ECONOMIC EDUCATION PROGRAMMING BE?

The American experience can be helpful in considering the question of what economic concepts should be included in Russian pre-university economic education. The *Framework for Teaching the Basic Concepts* (Saunders et al., 1993), which has evolved over the last 15 years under the auspices of the National Council on Economic Education is a useful guide and resource for an economic education initiative in Russia.[3] The *Framework* is generally accepted by economists and educators in the United States and has been widely adopted as a guide to what to teach in economics. However, it must be adapted carefully to the learning environment in Russia because the experiences that the Russian student brings to school are different. A list of economic concepts for a beginning program is suggested in Table 14.2 below.

American students experience the market economy from a very early age, whereas the Russian student will require another approach. For example, many Russians typically put much more emphasis on equity and security than Americans and view competition with suspicion if not with some condemnation. Prices are typically considered solely as a method of distributing goods to consumers, and most feel that they should be used to ensure that everybody gets their fair share. In the Russian experience most of what is produced faces a seller's market, and there is little recognition that competition can result in lower prices and better quality products. Much of Russian business is conducted on a basis of personal favor or patronage, and the idea of an impersonal market that allocates without discrimination is not typically understood.[4] Because of these differences, a very careful groundwork must be laid for teaching about markets and prices.

TABLE 14.2: Basic Concepts for an Economic Education Program for Russia

1. Scarcity
2. Opportunity Cost and Tradeoffs
3. Economic Resources, Including Entrepreneurship
4. Productivity, Savings, Investing, Capital Formation
5. Economic Institutions (Private Property) and Economic Incentives (Wages, Profits)
6. Specialization
7. Exchange, Money, and Interdependence
8. Markets and Prices
9. Supply and Demand
10. Competition and Structure of Markets
11. Income Distribution (Relationship Between Income and Resource Productivity)
12. Government
13. Inflation, Unemployment
14. International Economy and Trade

Source: Modified from Saunders et al., 1993.

The fundamental economic concepts as they are set forth in the *Framework* might be included as the starting point for any economic education program. Understanding of scarcity, choice, and opportunity cost lays the foundation for the subsequent development of both micro and macro concepts. The universal condition of wants exceeding the resources necessary to satisfy them, and the consequent necessity of making choices, is certainly in the Russian students' experience. With this starting point, students will explore the nature of economic wants, limited productive resources, and rational decision-making. Effective decision-making requires consideration of opportunity cost, tradeoffs, and marginalism. Concrete student-centered activities can develop this understanding among students as they relate these concepts to their own experiences.

Understanding production that is necessary to satisfy wants entails consideration of specialization and division of labor, productivity, investment in both physical and human capital, and technology. The concept of investment is especially important, and the students will need to understand that the first step toward capital formation and enhanced production is saving. Savings and foregone current consumption are necessary for future increases in productivity. Appreciating the crucial role of incentives where individuals are free to make their own decisions is important to understanding how markets work. Workers, consumers, producers, savers, and investors are all motivated to be productive by the incentives inherent in a market system.

Specialization in production necessitates exchange, interdependence, and the need for money. Students will understand that free exchange benefits both parties to the transaction and that one person's prosperity does not subtract from, but may benefit, others. The importance of financial institutions and a sound system of money will also be part of the students' fundamental understanding.

Microeconomic concepts as they are outlined in the *Framework* should comprise a large portion of the curriculum in economics for several reasons. Because markets and competition are largely outside the experience of most Russian students, these concepts will take considerable time and effort to develop. Also, the economic transformation taking place in Russia makes an understanding of these micro concepts by citizens crucial to their participation in it. Students will need an understanding of supply and demand, equilibrium prices, and the roles of relative prices. The basic concepts can be related to street markets, but the role of prices as decision information between consumers and producers, in the allocation of resources, and in achieving flexibility is less apparent. A discussion of market structures will naturally follow. Among the micro concepts that should receive special emphasis are the roles of relative prices, the entrepreneurial function, and the function of profits.

Of particular importance is the introduction to the Russian student of the role of the entrepreneur in the dynamics of an economic system. Future growth will depend to a large measure on activating the entrepreneurial spirit, which has been suppressed during the Soviet era. The entrepreneur is one of the factors of production in contemporary economics, and entrepreneurship should be integrated with the other concepts associated with the generating of ideas for new goods and services and combining the resources necessary to get them to the marketplace with prospects for making a profit. The concepts associated with entrepreneurship should be taught in the context of economics, but be distinct in the treatment of the role of the entrepreneur in the dynamics of an economy. Also, the students should have their creative senses stimulated and learn about risk-taking, gain-making, failure, and success (Kent and Rushing, 1991). The Russians have begun to research the characteristics of the Russian entrepreneur, not only developing case studies, but also relating the role of the entrepreneur to job creation and economic growth (Dynkin, 1993).

In this initial effort, macroeconomic concepts should be pared to a minimum. There is a danger of overloading teachers and students so that the entire learning experience is jeopardized. At this stage in the Russian economic transformation, micro concepts are more relevant. However, it will be necessary to develop some understanding of inflation, unemployment in structural changes, and the international economy.

IV. IMPLEMENTING AN ECONOMIC EDUCATION CURRICULUM

The initiation of an economic education program in Russia should begin with a limited number of fundamental concepts; the concepts should be taught and retaught in a spiraling fashion throughout the grade levels; they should be taught as content with assigned hours in the curriculum and be infused in a meaningful way with other content, especially history, geography, math, social studies, and career training. The method which has the greatest promise of success under the current socioeconomic conditions and the traditional curriculum would be experience-based instruction.

Research in the United States has shown that the content, grade level, and method of instruction of economics is important to the learning outcomes of the educational process. This is especially true in Russia for the following reasons. First, both the student and the instructors have never lived within a market-oriented society. Second, there is no contemporary economics in the curricula of the country. Third, there are no indigenous student or teacher materials from which the curriculum can be taught (although some translations of foreign materials are being introduced; these are discussed in the next section). Fourth, there is no cadre of teachers who have been trained in contemporary economic concepts or their application at the personal or societal levels.

A number of researchers in economic education have reported that students can learn economic concepts beginning at the pre-school ages.[5] What seems mandatory in the case of Russia is that the student be introduced to the fundamental concepts early in his/her formal education. The literature further shows that the student can have the sophistication of those early concepts expanded, and new and more complex fundamental and microeconomic concepts can be introduced as the student goes through what would be grades 5 through 9 in the old Soviet educational structure.

Finally, the content of the General Secondary, Specialized Secondary, and Vocational-Technical curricula should incorporate not only microeconomic concepts but also some instruction in international economic interaction, entrepreneurship, and perhaps for those entering the work force, some consumer economics or personal decision-making.

The actual number of hours devoted to the specific content of the curriculum at each grade level will have to be determined by those revising the Russian curriculum. Since more of the curriculum hours will be determined at the local level, the decision should be based upon their own educational objectives and the unique socioeconomic profile of the students. It seems reasonable for economics to appear first in the model curriculum in grades 1-4 for perhaps 1 hour per week. These hours should increase during grades 5-9 to ensure universal exposure to market concepts before students diverge onto various paths after the incomplete secondary grades.

Economics should not be thought of as a stand-alone course at one grade level or another, but rather taught at all grade levels with considerable infusion into the other social studies, particularly history and geography. This approach would be consistent with the historical interfacing of disciplines across grades and courses in the former Soviet Union. What it does come into conflict with is the research in the United States which shows that students learned more economics when taught in a stand alone-course called "economics" in the curriculum (Walstad and Soper, 1991). Many economic educators have felt intuitively that infusion of economics across the curriculum should yield significant learning outcomes. This hasn't happened in the United States, perhaps because the U.S. educational curriculum is so structured that neither the teacher nor the student pays much attention to concepts of the infused discipline within the core subject area. The Russian teachers and students have had much more experience in cross-fertilization of ideas, particularly in math and science. Perhaps Russia will provide a new experiment in the impact of infusion of economic concepts into other disciplines.

Given the conditions described above, it can be argued that one of the most effective means of teaching economics is through experience-based instruction. Arguments for this approach are not new in the literature on economic education in the United States (Kourilsky, 1974). However, they take on new significance in the context of newly budding market economies. The students would need the hands-on aspects of experience-based instruction in order to put the economic concepts within a context or structure. The teacher would find that such an approach requires less in the way of printed student materials; it would also permit novice economics instructors to reinforce their understanding of how the concepts interrelate with the whole. Teachers can learn from their coordinators how to conduct an activity and how to debrief the students to ensure that the learning objectives are achieved. This approach also is more concrete for both the teacher and the students.

One instructional program which demonstrates this point, and which has potential for introduction in Russia in the pre-secondary grades, is that of the *Mini-Society* and *KinderEconomy* (Kourilsky, 1974 and 1992). These programs have been quite successful with early learners, and achieve a whole variety of positive learning outcomes – economic concepts, self-assurance, entrepreneurial characteristics, cost-benefit analysis, mathematics, how to start and run a business – in other words, the fundamentals of a market economy plus critical thinking skills. This approach might be a conceptual framework for instructional materials designed by Russians for Russians in grades 5-11.

Other programming might be reviewed for adoption or adaptation in the schools. This would include simulations, either in game form or on the computer. (However, one should be aware that the typical Russian school will not have access to computers for a number of years.) One of the best sources of materials would be the series of curriculum guides that have been developed by the National Council on Economic Education.[6] This series has many activities to teach a number of concepts, and they are designed for different grade levels (principally at the 5-12 levels in the United States). These activities would have to be adapted to the local realities to ensure relevancy for the Russian student. One effective teaching activity is having the students set up and operate a business. This can be done at any grade level, as demonstrated by the *Mini-Society* program.

Teacher and student materials are being developed from scratch in Russia. Even though translation of Western materials is occurring, it is only a stop-gap approach until indigenous materials can be produced. Textbooks were uniform in the old system, and curriculum reform required a complete new set of textbooks. For instance, the 1984 reforms still did not have new textbooks for all content areas when the USSR was dissolved. The reality of the absence of economics course materials almost requires a greater dependence on activities-based instruction than would be true under alternative conditions. The country will undoubtedly have to establish curriculum designers and textbook writers to complete the process of making economic education available to all Russian students.

Where will the instructors come from to teach a new economics curriculum? The best parallel to the conditions facing the transformation of education within Russia is the period in Soviet history (the early 1930s) when universal education became the announced goal of the Communist Party and the central government. At first those persons in society with any education were directed into the classroom, even when they had little more knowledge than their students. Secondly, the government set up a network of pedagogical institutes to train teachers and began to entice, cajole, or direct bright students (mainly female) into these institutes as the future teachers of Soviet children. Thirdly, the government provided extensive in-service training to teachers when the curriculum changed.[7]

It would appear that for the near term, in-service training would be the stop-gap approach. When the new math-science curriculum was adopted in 1984-85, all math and science teachers were required to attend workshops to go over the new curriculum and to be trained for its implementation. The main difference between that situation and the development of economic education programs is that those teachers were already well- trained in their disciplines. The workshops for teachers of economics would have to begin with instruction in the fundamental economic concepts. These concepts could be taught using the same instructional materials the teachers would eventually use in the classroom. This would be the beginning of "operation economic education" and would not be ideal, but it would be a beginning during a period of transition in the educational system. Eventually, contemporary economics would be a content area in the pedagogical institutes and universities, and teachers would learn both their discipline and their pedagogy prior to entering teaching.

V. THE INTRODUCTION OF ECONOMIC EDUCATION PROGRAMS: A BEGINNING

The introduction of privatization to the Russian economy has generated a broad interest in business education (as opposed to economic education). The consequence has been the establishment of a variety of "Business Schools," most of which are private and charge their "students" for instruction. Unfortunately, many of them have staffs with neither a basic knowledge of modern business practices, nor an understanding of the private enterprise system. As O.S. Vikhanskii (1991) states:

> It must be pointed out that literally only a handful of people in the entire country have a fairly adequate grasp of modern business and management, and only a few are able to not only discuss it but also teach it....And yet in this situation we have hundreds and perhaps thousands of business schools, and their number is multiplying constantly.... Beyond all doubt, any normal person would find it absurd if engineers were to undertake to train physicians or artists. (p. 38)

Vikhanskii is somewhat kinder in his analysis of the Moscow State University School of Management, with its programmatic emphasis on the market economy and entrepreneurial behavior; however, he emphasizes the need for quality programs which will require time and considerable assistance from the West. Unfortunately, many teachers have enrolled in the first type of business school, believing they would be prepared to teach the economics of private enterprise in their classrooms. Fortunately, some help has come from foreign economic educators.

Since 1990, many Western organizations and individuals, particularly from the United States, have become involved in the attempt to assist the Russians in the transition to a market system. Perhaps the most influential and financially committed organization is the Soros Foundation, which has funded economic programming for pre-college education. They have done so in partnership with U.S. organizations, such as The National Council on Economic Education and Junior Achievement. In addition, Soros has funded a competition for developing innovative curricula manuscripts for elementary, secondary, and post-secondary schools. The Soros project involves both Russian and Western experts seeking to develop new curricula and to identify and translate Western textbooks. Economics is among the disciplines in the project.

The Soros Foundation has many centers throughout the former Soviet Union. Perhaps the most relevant for our discussion is the Russian-American Center for Economic Education, established in Moscow in 1992 to provide leadership for continuing programs in Russia. Two of the partners, The National Council on Economic Education and Junior Achievement, have conducted workshops in Russia, and each is seeking other partnerships to get its materials into the hands of Russian students. Both are following the economic education strategies they pursue in the United States.

As of mid-1993, The National Council on Economic Education has conducted four economic education workshops for teachers, teacher trainers, and school administrators in Moscow, St. Petersburg, Nizhiny Novgorod, and Novosibirsk. About 200 people have been trained in these workshops. The workshops were two weeks in duration and focused on the content of economics and the methods of teaching economics in primary and secondary schools. The American instructors were paired with Russian instructors so that trainers of trainers were also being produced through the conducting of the workshops. The Soros Foundation and National Council goal is to create at the center a whole cadre of Russian trainers who will then create centers throughout Russia, staffed with knowledgeable and well-trained economic educators. The workshops utilized active (experiential) teaching strategies.

The National Council on Economic Education offers the strategy of developing a cadre of trained teachers through a national network of economic education centers similar to the center in Moscow. This strategy would have advocates for economic education geographically distributed and would seek partnerships with the local school authorities to get economics integrated into the curriculum of the schools. The centers would then provide teacher training and develop materials for the schools.

Junior Achievement has set out to establish a presence in Russia utilizing its U.S. materials, particularly *Applied Economics* and its business simulation

MESE. Although the recipient of Soros grants, Junior Achievement has other U.S. corporate support for printing and disseminating *Applied Economics* in both Russian and English in Russia. In December 1991, a Junior Achievement organization was established in Russia; JA representatives have conducted workshops and/or distributed materials in Moscow, St. Petersburg, Magnitagorsk, the Sakhalin Islands, and Nizhiny Novgorod, to name some. Two hundred thousand Russian-language version *Applied Economics* textbooks have been published, and over 1200 Russian teachers have been certified to teach applied economics.

Among the methods for teaching about economics and business is MESE, a computer simulation. This simulation has been translated into Russian and has proven popular with the Russian students. Student performance in the game has revealed some of the cultural legacy from the socialist regime, e.g., dividing up a fixed pie as opposed to growing a bigger pie for all.

Junior Achievement has been attempting to replicate its U.S. model by finding business consultants in the cities of Russia and training these business-oriented persons to participate in classroom instruction. These "business" contacts then help to influence the use of *Applied Economics* and MESE in the Russian schools. This model, like the National Council Model, is attempting to get economic education into the schools with a bottom-up approach.

In 1992, the European Community entered into an agreement with the government of Russia to establish training centers for teachers. The EC will provide instructors to train teachers of economics. It is anticipated that about 1,000 teachers will get this training after the program has been in effect for one year, and it is hoped that the Pedagogical Institutes will eventually incorporate the economic education training into their curricula. This latter process is anticipated to take two to three years.[8]

There have been some Western-authored textbooks translated into Russian and other East European languages. Professor Paul Heyne's collegiate text, *The Economic Way of Thinking*, has been published in Russia and 100,000 copies were distributed either through sales or through programs sponsored by U.S. organizations. The Institute of Humane Studies, which was primarily responsible for the Heyne translation and publication, is now working on a translation of a high school textbook authored by U.S. economists (Monaghan, 1992). These projects can supply only a fraction of the numbers of good economics text materials that will be needed to support a comprehensive economic education program in Russia.

Another collegiate text has been translated is Campbell McConnell and Stanley Brue's *Economics*, eleventh edition. Under the direction of Anatoly A. Porokhovsky of the Russian Academy of Sciences, the text was translated from English and 100,000 copies were printed. The book sold out rapidly and new printings were ordered. The quick sale of the book lends some evidence that there is a Russian perception of the importance of market-oriented economics.

However, how many of these texts have found their way into use as core materials at the universities or secondary levels in Russian schools is not clear.[9]

The Ministry of Education has authorized the translation and printing of 150,000 copies of J. R. Clark and J. Holt Wilson's text, *Economics: The Science of Cost, Benefit and Choice*. The Russian editors are Andrei Markov and Vadim Ivanov, who adapted the text by using Russian examples in the discussion. The book will be distributed through school and state book stores.[10]

All of the economic education programs to date are only a very small beginning in achieving the objective of integrating economic education into the curriculum of the pre-university educational system in Russia. First, there has not been a commitment by the Russian Ministry of Education to get economics into the mandated curriculum, nor is there evidence that the central government encourages it in the electives that are under the authority of the local schools. There has been an admission by some government officials and some educators that the youth need to learn about economics, but no authority and no funds have been committed to achieve the objective. The Western co-operative programs are an important beginning to provide models for effective economic education programming, but these programs will have to be multiplied several thousand fold to reach the entire student population of Russia. Ultimately, the Russians will have to assume responsibility for the challenge and put their talent and resources into the programs. Foreign participation should be time-bound. Failure to have strong Russian advocacy for economic education when resources are so scarce is to ensure very slow progress toward national economic education.

VI. SUMMARY AND CONCLUSION

The Bolshevik Revolution of 1917 commenced what became known as the "great socialist experiment." For over 70 years the Communist Party attempted to mold a population in the image of the "socialist man." The molding process included the educational system, all modes of public communication, and (if the party's instructions were carried out) the teaching by parents of the virtues of the socialist system. The experiment is over, and the realities of the last three years would assign a grade of F to the experiment. But what is to replace the old system, and by what means will it progress? Russia can be viewed as a possible laboratory in which an effective national economic education program may be designed using the principles of learning theory, curriculum design, and effective training of teachers, and be delivered through a curriculum which achieves the learning objectives. To those educators outside Russia, it is as if there were a blank canvas upon which the educators might apply their artistry. Yet 70 years of Communism have undoubtedly affected those persons who have gone through an educational system devoted to the creation of the socialist man and workers for the great socialist economy. Many of the gatekeepers to the educational institutions are part of the Socialist legacy. Much has to be undone while attempting to replace the old with new ideas and concepts foreign to the people's experiences. The experiment must be started almost from scratch, with very few resources that can be applied immediately to achieve the objectives.

What can be concluded from the discussion above is:

a) The Russian population does have a socialist mentality from the past, but is receptive to ideas of a market economy in its future. The young are particularly receptive to change in their economic institution.

b) The economic concepts that should be introduced into a new economics curriculum should be limited in number, i.e., those which economic educators refer to as fundamental concepts. Primarily, these concepts will be the microeconomic principles within the discipline. Special attention should be given to entrepreneurship in the context of the economics content.

c) These concepts should be introduced and reinforced across all grade levels, utilizing the principles of learning theory and effective scope and sequence for the discipline.

d) The teaching methods should be varied but special attention should be given to utilizing experience-based methods because the students and the teachers have little or no prior experience with markets.

e) Economics should be infused across the curriculum, much as math and science were done in the unified curriculum of the USSR. The old social studies hours might be devoted to economics, while history and geography are content areas for economics infusion.

f) Curriculum materials will need to be developed, but in the near term proven materials from abroad are likely to have to be imported; these need to be simple and activities-oriented. Indigenous economics textbooks are likely to be five to ten years in the writing, publishing, and dissemination. Therefore the curriculum materials will primarily be teacher's instructional materials rather than student materials.

g) Teacher training will need to be initiated to educate the teacher population currently in the work force. The training will have to focus on both economics content and instructional methods.

The Russian educational system will not be without sources of assistance. Economic education in the United States has been formalized since the end of World War II. There are numerous programs, materials, and organizations which have field-tested their approaches and materials over many years. Research in many cases has identified what works (and what doesn't) in the United States. Some of what is known in the United States can be transferred to Russia, and some cannot because of differences in the cultures.

Finally, now is the time to press the case for economics in the curriculum of Russian schools. The educational institutions are in a state of flux. The content is changing to reflect the histories of the Russian peoples. New ideas of how to teach and how to learn are being introduced, with much attention being given to the experiences in the United States (Vaillant, 1991). The curriculum will be under careful review to justify the disciplines to be expanded or contracted. It is necessary that some constituency be established for the inclusion of economics. The energy for economic education has to come from within Russia. Even though a bottom-up approach may achieve the long-term goal of universal economic education, a top-down approach would be traditional in Russia and much faster. If the current opportunity is lost, it may be another decade before future educational reforms will correct the error. That is time which Russia cannot afford to lose.

NOTES

The author expresses appreciation to Professor Thomas McKinnon of the University of Arkansas and to Professor Anatoly A. Porokhovsky of the Institute of the U.S. and Canada Studies, Russian Academy of Sciences, for their comments.

1. Author's interviews in Moscow, October 1992.
2. For more details about this study, see Chapter 16.
3. [*Ed. note*: For further discussion of the *Framework*, see Chapters 3 and 7.] The National Council also publishes a series of curriculum guides. Guides include Strategies for Teaching Economics: Primary Level (Grades 1-3), Intermediate Level (4-6), Junior High School Level (7-9), Basic Business and Consumer Education, Consumer Economics, Economics and Entrepreneurship, High School Economics Courses, International Trade, United States History, World Studies, Using Economics in Social Studies Methods Courses.
4. These observations are the distillation of dozens of interviews conducted in Moscow and St. Petersburg by Thomas McKinnon of the University of Arkansas in 1990 and 1991.
5. See for example, Schug (1991), Banaszak (1991) and Armento (1987).
6. See note 3.
7. See Seymour Michael Rosen, *Education and Modernization in the USSR*. Reading, Addison-Wesley, 1971. John Dunstan, *Paths to Excellence and the Soviet School*, Humanities Press, 1978. *Education in the USSR*. Moscow: Progress, 1977.
8. Author's discussion in Moscow, October 1992, with Ilia Lomakin-Rumaiantsev, Head of the Department of Science, Culture, Education and Technical Policy of the Russian Government Administration.
9. Interview with Dr. Anotoly A. Porokhovsky in Moscow in October 1992.
10. Interview with J. R. Clark, March 1993.

REFERENCES

Ailes, C. P., & Rushing, F. W. (1989). *Science and mathematics education in the USSR.* Summary report prepared for Directorate of Science and Engineering Education, National Science Foundation. Washington, DC: Science Research Institute International.

Ailes, C. P., & Rushing, F. W. (1991). Soviet math and science educational reforms during perestroika. *Technology in Society, 13*, 109-122.

Armento, B. J. (1987). Ideas for teaching economics derived from learning theory. *Theory Into Practice, 26*(3), 176-182.

Banaszak, R. A. (1991). Economics and entrepreneurship education for young adolescents. In C. A. Kent (Ed.), *Entrepreneurship education, current developments and future directions* (pp. 165-181). New York: Quorum Books.

DeWitt, N. (1980). *Current status and determinants of science education in Soviet secondary schools.* Washington, D.C.: National Academy of Science.

Dunstan, J. (1978). *Paths to excellence and the Soviet school.* Atlantic Highlands, NJ: Humanities Press.

Dynkin, A. (1993). Emerging entrepreneurship in Russia: Entrepreneurs' perceptions of their social and economic function. Working Paper, Institute of World Economy and International Relations, Moscow.

Kent, C. A., & Rushing, F. W. (1991). An overview of entrepreneurship in economics. In J. E. Clow et al., *Teaching strategies, economics and entrepreneurship* (pp. ix-xv). New York: The Joint Council on Economic Education.

Knapp, G. (1993). Teaching economics to Russian students: Some preliminary observations. Working Paper, University of Alaska-Anchorage.

Kondakov, M. (1987). New content of education in social studies and humanities as a means of ideological-political pupil upbringing. *Soviet Education, 29*(11-12), 11.

Kourilsky, M. (1974). *Beyond simulation: The mini-society approach to instruction in economics and other social sciences.* Los Angeles: Education Resource Associates, Inc.

Kourilsky, M. (1992). *KinderEconomy.* New York: National Council on Economic Education.

Lipton, D., & Sachs, J.D. (1992). Prospects for Russia's economic reforms. *Brookings Papers on Economic Activity, 2*, 213-265.

Monaghan, P. (1992). Western economics textbook gains many new readers as market systems develop where communism failed. *The Chronicle of Higher Education* (February 26), A39-A40.

Reddaway, P. (1992). Next from Russia: 'Shock therapy' collapse. *Washington Post* (July 12), C7. [As quoted in Lipton and Sachs, 1992].

Rosen, S. M. (1971). *Education and modernization in the USSR.* Reading, MA: Addison-Wesley.

Saunders, P., Bach, G.L., Calderwood, J., & Hansen, W. L. (1993). *A framework for teaching the basic concepts* (3rd ed.). New York: The National Council on Economic Education.

Schug, M. C. (1991). The development of students' economic thought: Implications for instruction. In W. B. Walstad & J. C. Soper (Eds.), *Effective economic education in*

the schools (pp. 137-152). Washington, DC: Joint Council on Economic Education and The National Education Association.
Shen, R., & Shen, T. Y. (1993). Economic thinking in China: Economic knowledge and attitudes of high school students. *Journal of Economic Education, 24*(1), 70-84.
Shiller, R. J., Boycko, M., & Korobov, V. (1991). Popular attitudes toward free markets: The Soviet Union and the United States compared. *American Economic Review, 81*(3), 385-400.
Shiller, R. J., Boycko, M., & Korobov, V. (1992). Hunting for Homo Sovieticus: Situational versus attitudinal factors in economic behavior. *Brookings Papers on Economic Activity, 1*, 127-181.
Soviet Education. (1987a). The history curriculum for secondary general education school. *Soviet Education, 29*(11-12), 22-131.
Soviet Education. (1987b). The new Soviet secondary school geography curriculum. *Soviet Education, 29*(4), 97-98.
Szekely, B. B. (1987). Editor's introduction. *Soviet Education, 29*(11-12), 5.
USSR State Committee for Public Education. (1990). *The State Basic Curriculum.* Moscow: USSR State Committee.
Vaillant, J. G. (1991). *Educational challenges: The nations of the former USSR.* Washington, DC: Atlantic Treaty Association.
Vikhanskii, O. S. (1991). Let's train managers for the market economy. *Soviet Education, 33*(11), 37-44.
Walstad, W. B., & Larsen, M. (1992). *A national survey of American economic literacy.* Lincoln, NE: The National Center for Research in Economic Education and the Gallup Organization.
Walstad, W. B., & Soper, J. C. (1991). Economic literacy in senior high schools. In W. B. Walstad & J. C. Soper (Eds.), *Effective economic education in the schools* (pp. 99-116). New York: Joint Council on Economic Education and The National Education Association.

CHAPTER 15

ECONOMIC EDUCATION AND TRANSITION IN EASTERN EUROPE

George M. Vredeveld

Dimitrina M. Ispirodonova

Eastern Europe is facing one of its most challenging tasks in recent history – to design and implement, after decades of Communist rule, a democratic society featuring the freedom of the individual in the market system. To meet this challenge the Eastern European states have taken the initially painful step of rejecting the key elements of their former societies: a command economy, a closed society and a rigidly structured, hierarchical and all powerful Communist Party. These changes have been abrupt and have created confusion and destabilization of the economic, social and political framework of all the Eastern European states. When the traditional communistic control mechanisms were removed the pent-up forces of national and ethnic chauvinism were released. Religious differences spawned further clashes. Fragmentation, tension and insecurity have been festering in these societies.

Especially in turbulent situations of this kind, it is critical that the people in each country understand their current economic situation and the economic condition to which they aspire. The enlightened support and commitment of a large percentage of the population to these changes will be essential. This becomes a crucial role of education in general and economic education in particular.

This chapter focuses on the role of economic education in a transitory economy, using Bulgaria as a case study. It will describe the educational systems Bulgaria inherited from the Communist era, the difficulties and obstacles Bulgaria now faces in teaching about the free market, and will discuss the economic education activities, programs and curricula that are currently being implemented. It also will explore how economics should be taught and teacher training can be accomplished in the transition period.

I. THE EDUCATIONAL SYSTEM OF BULGARIA UNDER SOCIALISM

The Marxist-Leninist Framework

Education is highly regarded today and has always played an important role in Bulgarian society. Under the domination of the Bulgarian Communist Party (Party), education was used to shape society and to strengthen Party control. The Party required education to serve the State through the teaching of Party dogma and the Marxist-Leninist philosophy.[1] The value of the individual was best measured in terms of his/her allegiance and subservience to the State. The result was an educational system that put a premium on rote learning and conformity to socialist ideals, and harshly penalized individual, analytical and creative thinking.

In 1945 the Party's objective was to create an "ideal" state of freedom, equality and prosperity for all, in which education would play a formative role. But by the late 1950s it was obvious that the ideal society was not being achieved and, in fact, that the country was falling farther behind western nations in establishing a quality life-style for its citizens. It was impossible politically even to suggest that the blame for the lack of success might lie in the *system* of socialism itself. Party leaders would not concede the possibility that socialism, as a political and economic system, could not deliver. To retain its total control, the Party could not utilize the power of individual incentive and the discipline and efficiency of free competitive markets. Rather, the Party focused the blame on the *implementation* and the *management* of the system.

The same shortsightedness also characterized the Party's educational policies. Each Party Congress defined new and increasingly ambitious educational tasks and "radical reforms." The educational system became one of the scapegoats for the failure of socialism to reach its goals. The dilemma facing the Party from 1944 to 1989 was that they wished to achieve for their country many of the successes of western countries, but regarded the means (i.e., free market initiative, individual entrepreneurship and democratic capitalism) to these achievements as unacceptable, if not evil.

The following paragraphs illustrate some of the educational goals and policies of the Party and their effects.

In the early 1950s the Party implemented its first reform of education by radically changing the content and structure of the Bulgarian educational system. The overall goal of that first socialist reform was to eliminate "religion, chauvinism and bourgeois class limitations" and to establish Marxism-Leninism as the theoretical basis of education (Bulgarian Communist Party, 1965). In addition to this overall goal, the educational system was given the task to eradicate illiteracy and provide compulsory education to all children up to the age of fifteen. In support of this goal, the number of general comprehensive high schools increased from 196 to 541, and 15 new universities were established during the first fifteen years of Communist rule.

In spite of the massive expenditures on education, the results did not meet the Party's expectations or goals. The historic Seventh Congress of the Party in 1959 pointed out that education in Bulgaria was lagging far behind "the requirements of socialist way of life" (Bulgarian Communist Party, 1965).[2] In fifteen years, a quality socialistic life-style had not been achieved. Party leaders were becoming aware that it would take more than enthusiastic support for Communist doctrine or the efforts of semi-literate guerilla fighters and ardent Communist reformers.

The Seventh Congress (1959) saw the solution in technology. They decreed that success would be achieved through the "practical implementation of the latest worldwide technical, technological and scientific achievements" (Bulgarian Communist Party, 1965). The Ministry of Education determined that there should be two main types of high schools: general comprehensive high schools and vocational technical high schools, the main difference being the larger amount of specific skills taught in the vocational technical schools.[3] As a result, the emphasis shifted increasingly toward vocational and technical education.

This corresponded to the development of Bulgaria's economy at the time. The State was attempting to develop heavy industry, such as machine-building, chemistry, power generation, ferrous and non-ferrous metal processing. As early as 1961, 60 percent of Bulgaria's GNP was attributable to manufacturing. Agriculture also was changed radically. The vast cooperative farms and the massive migration of the population to the cities led to the mechanization of agriculture and the use of more modern farming methods in order to increase efficiency and productivity. These economic and technological changes increased the demand for a better educated, more productive and skilled work force, especially in industries in which Bulgaria specialized.[4]

Although there was a shift toward a more pragmatic and technical education, the schools still continued to emphasize the ideological socialist development of the young people as loyal "Marxists-Leninists" and good communist citizens. According to the Party General Secretary and the President of the Peoples Republic of Bulgaria, the main civic duty of each and every teacher was "to forge vehement patriots and socialist internationalists, militant combatants for the eternal and unbreakable, life-giving friendship with the Soviet Union."[5]

The Ninth Congress of the Party in 1966 and the Tenth Congress in 1971 defined a principal social and economic task to be "the faster implementation of the achievements of worldwide scientific and technical progress...so as to increase labor productivity, better satisfy the rising material and spiritual needs of the people and heighten their socialist awareness" (Bulgarian Communist Party, 1973). This emphasis again was consistent with the Party's premise that the problem was not the socialist system per se, but rather the management and implementation of socialistic goals. The slogan during this time was to make the Bulgarian nation a "technical nation."

In response to the call for more skill and job-oriented education, the Ministry of Education set up an unified polytechnical high school system that could bring together the two different types of schools that existed until then, namely the comprehensive and the vocational schools. At the same time, the more elitist language schools, art and music schools and schools for gifted children were set up. They brought about the implementation of the George Orwellian notion of "all animals are equal, but some animals are more equal." The more "ordinary" students, nearly always coming from blue-collar families, had to go to the polytechnical schools to learn to become machinists, farmers, electricians, millers, etc.; the nation's "talent," almost always inclusive of the Party officials' children, was being prepared for higher and loftier deeds.

A continuous lifetime training and development system was developed for all white- and blue-collar workers. The youths who entered the work force immediately following an eighth grade education were give the opportunity to attend evening classes or take extension courses to earn the equivalent of the general education curriculum. Expenditures on schools and universities again were increased dramatically. They were provided with more laboratories, modern workshops, libraries, gyms, dining rooms, dormitories, medical centers and recreational grounds and facilities.

The Eleventh Congress in 1976 stated that the main objectives for the period were "to complete the construction of the socialist system as a step toward the transition to communism, and to fully develop man as the main production force" (Bulgarian Communist Party, 1976). At the same time, this Congress, like others before, admitted that socialism was lagging behind in labor productivity and product quality. The growing popularity of travel, television and other media presented graphic evidence of economic and technical successes in the western world. Once again, the Party attributed such successes to superior Western technology. As before, they failed to recognize that the fundamental reason for the superior technology was a more efficient economic system.

Party leaders believed that the system had exhausted its potential for internal technological development and self sufficiency.[6] The only way to keep the economy going and the people satisfied would be to open Bulgaria to "co-operation and mutually advantageous joint ventures" with the rest of the world. Education was given the task of incorporating in its programs the teaching of the latest skills and technical knowledge of the West as well its languages. Specialties like mathematics, computer science, artificial intelligence, cybernetics and robotics, machine languages, systems analysis, etc., received the utmost attention and resources (Bulgarian Communist Party, 1976).

International markets continued to be emphasized by the Twelfth Party Congress (1981). One of the main tasks for the next five-year plan, the Congress stated, was "the intensified and well-balanced development of the Bulgarian economy that will allow it to participate effectively in the international labor and product markets."[7]

The need to compete in competitive international markets increased the significance of economic and social sciences as well. Economics, as a scientific body of knowledge, along with sociology, psychology and political science received more favorable attention from Party leaders. The economists' primary task still was to prove the basic Marxian tenet of the commonality of the individual and collective interests, but they also were required to apply more efficient approaches to central planning, to increase bottom-up decision-making in planning, and to improve horizontal and vertical communication in industrial and social management. This new approach, called the "new economic mechanism" shifted the burden, and hence the blame, to the shoulders of the economists and the top managers of plants and factories.

Managers still had to meet government quotas and requirements, but more discretion was given to them in decision-making. Unfortunately, the freedom and independence given them was greatly restricted by government decrees and policies. Even within this new, less hierarchical and more individualistic approach there were few positive results – only more paperwork and management frustration.

With the shift in focus to some behavioral sciences, the schools provided more flexible curricula with some electives and vocational options. The intention was to create a new type of personnel that was multi-skilled, transferrable and capable of innovation. Computer literacy and joint projects with people renowned in the sciences and arts became a major thrust of the reform. The objective was to increase productivity and diminish the lag between employee hiring and their full utilization by improving the efficiency, versatility and job satisfaction of the labor force. Thus, it was expected, the socialist economy would become more competitive in the global market.

The academic focus on the "new economic mechanism" also affected the structure and management of education. More power and discretion in decision-making were granted to the school management boards and the local administrative education councils. They had to work in close co-operation with the plants and factories, the public organizations, the scientific and research institutions and the parents.

These descriptively democratic goals, however, clashed with the main tenets of the Party. The goals could never be achieved because they always were subject to the main focus in the entire system of education, namely the creation of "ideologically loyal people with a *correct* class and party orientation." The main criterion in selecting teachers, university professors and research workers was their "class and party loyalty." Every product of western civilization, be it of their material or spiritual culture, had to be "carefully analyzed" from Marxist-Leninist criteria. This intellectual intolerance and insistence on Communist ideological supremacy prevented the Eastern European schools from promoting genuinely innovative and analytical thinking. There was a marked tendency to encourage a "black or white" view of the world, the "right" solution always being given from somebody at the top – the teacher, the local party secretary or the General Secretary of the Party. The result was a homogenous education, uniformly functioning, both in terms of content and style of teaching. Compared to American education, there was more focus on facts than analysis, rote learning than thinking, and instruction than discovery. It was preferred that students regurgitate the ready-made "correct" solutions provided by the teachers instead of developing their own critical thinking skills and ability to propose alternative answers.

In spite of its problems, education was generally respected by the population. Even though highly-educated people were seldom rewarded financially for their educational accomplishments, it remained a high priority of the State and of the general population. Admission to prestigious high schools, colleges and universities was very competitive.

The General Structure of Education

The structure of education that exists today was largely determined by Party rule from 1944 to 1989. While there have been many changes in education since 1989, the management of education remains highly centralized. The Ministry of Education has full responsibility for all executive decisions concerning education. It develops the strategy and policies of education, directs how textbooks are to be written and appoints their authors.

The organization of schools in Bulgaria is similar to other European systems. Education begins at age 6 and is compulsory up to 16 years of age. The elementary school includes grades 1-4, the middle or pre-secondary school encompasses grades 5-8 and the high school, depending on the curriculum, goes from 9-11 or 9-12. Grade level requirements consist of a specified number of classes in various subjects. The first eight grades prepare students for entrance examinations to the high school which begins in grade 9.

The Bulgarian system has 4 different tracks for students after they complete the eighth grade: a) the *general education program* of three years, with an option of sitting for university entrance examinations, b) the *vocational program* of three years, with no option for the university entrance examination, c) a variety of prestigious four-year *specialized programs* including schools of economics, mathematics, chemistry and physics, music, arts, languages, and sports as well as technical schools in mechanical engineering, electronics, radio and television, electrical engineering, construction technologies, industrial chemistry, etc., and d) *evening classes* for working youths. The four tracks have a common core course of study of eleven subjects including the Bulgarian language and literature, a western language, mathematics (including computer training), four courses in the sciences, geography, history, and philosophy.

Structure of Economic Education in Bulgaria

Prior to the fall of the Party in 1989, economics was taught in two areas, a basic course at the high school level and an extensive curriculum at the specialized economics schools. All high school students were required to take an 11th grade course entitled "Basics of Marxism-Leninism" designed to provide students with a "reliable, scientific" way of looking at economic and social phenomena. It consisted of three parts: dialectical materialism, political economy and scientific communism which covered the philosophy, economics and history of communist theory and practice. These three areas also were required for all university students and were part of final comprehensive examinations.

In addition to the Marxism-Leninism course, economics was taught in the specialized economics schools. In keeping with the Party's emphasis on *management* and *implementation* of various experimental economic plans, these economic courses had a managerial, applied emphasis. In most instances, an "economics" course did not cover extensively principles of economics, but rather topics normally covered in typical management or general business courses. At the special economics technical schools all students were required to take courses in the theory and practice of bookkeeping, the theory of statistics and statistical applications to commerce, marketing, word and data processing, stenography (including typewriting and correspondence), and economics. While the principles of economics course covered fundamentals of the market system, it was largely a critique of the system, focusing on the contradictions and deficiencies of market economics and its exploitative nature. The failures and disadvantages of capitalism were taught applying the Marxist model.

Another interesting feature of economic education in Eastern Europe, including Bulgaria, was a strong emphasis on an interdisciplinary approach. For example, "economics" was also taught in the history and geography courses. This corresponded fully with Party dogma that the Marxist-Leninist "dialectic" interpretation of the development of civilization should permeate the entire curriculum and especially, social sciences. These subjects were taught concurrently from the 5th to 11th grades in all schools so as to complement each other and reinforce the students' communistic socioeconomic outlook. Therefore, instruction in these subjects focused on descriptions of the social orders and the socioeconomic systems. There was little discussion of the theoretical underpinnings of the various economic systems or any questioning of textbooks' accuracy of interpretation.

II. EDUCATION IN TRANSITION

Philosophical and Structural Changes

Educational reform closely followed on the heels of political reform after the fall of the Communist Party in 1989. The typical features of the totalitarian paradigm previously discussed were officially denounced, including: uniform ideological education, uniform detailed state curriculum and compulsory textbooks, uniform school structure allowing no deviations, state monopoly of schooling permitting no private education, and a hierarchically centralized and uniform management apparatus which excluded local autonomy and discretionary decision-making.

The Socialist Ministry of Education produced a plan in 1991 that attempted to link education reform to the requirements of a democratic society. The report was candid and direct about the effects of a totalitarian regime on the education system.

> The critical analysis of the present state of the education showed that the class-party approach, applied through pedagogical pressure, led to strong ideology, to the disregard of the rights of the individual, to intolerance of other peoples' opinion and even to aggressiveness.... The educational system has been managed by a highly bureaucratic administrative management for a long period of time.
>
> All this requires a completely new social commission as far as education is concerned. The Bulgarian school should reestablish the inmost universal human values, to become more humane and democratic, so the human rights should be restored.... (Ministry of Public Education, 1990)

In that same year, the Ministry proposed a system that would encourage ideological pluralism in public education as a first step towards encouraging free thinking and a democratization of the educational process. The succeeding Ministry of Education (1991), part of the new government headed up by the Union of Democratic Forces, stated in 1992 that their goal was to change the "traditional" Communist values and discover the spirit of the new-age education. They claimed that the achievement of this goal was essential to the process of strengthening a system of new humanistic, ideology-free values that would culturally and spiritually integrate their nation with contemporary civilization.

The Ministry of Education's plan also contained a radical proposal for change in the content and method of education that reflected three basic components. The first was to diversify curricula in order to increase freedom of choice of courses and stimulate all students to work to the limits of their ability. The elimination of curricular totalitarianism was begun by declaring the study of Russian optional and by introducing a number of electives. The second component was to free textbooks and teaching of all remaining Marxist-Leninist bias and to allow students to make independent judgments on major political, social and economic issues. School subjects conveying one-sided ideology were eliminated or replaced by other subjects. A third step was taken when the new Ministry declared that they intended to minimize curricular regulation and give more discretion to teachers and administrators in the selection of textbooks and determination of teaching styles. The state monopoly in education was legally eliminated. The former "three-level" administration consisting of central, regional and local offices was transformed into a two-level structure. Municipalities now are subordinate only to the dispositions of Parliament (implemented by the Ministry of Education) and their decisions can be appealed only in the courts.[8]

It is significant that the Ministry recognized the importance of market mechanisms and competition in the sphere of education. The proposed reforms should produce measurable signs of progress. Yet, the new plan remains highly centralized with the Ministry of Education determining policy and curriculum. The Ministry still prescribes a uniform core curriculum which local authorities implement. Local authorities also enforce attendance and provide facilities, transportation, cafeterias and special support for students.

Changes in Economic Education

If progress is to be made, close cooperation between the West and the new countries in Eastern Europe is of the greatest importance. Today it is possible for joint discussions of common problems and solutions to occur without ideological constraints interfering with an honest exchange of views. The American hands-on approach through an experience-based mode of instruction can be very helpful in considering both the conceptual and methodological aspects of economic education.

In October 1990, the Director of the Center for Economic Education at the University of Cincinnati met with officials of the Ministry of Education to explore ways in which the teaching of economics could be enhanced. A plan was developed, and later a formal agreement between the Minister of Education and the Director of Cincinnati's Center for Economic Education was signed to: (1) design curriculum for grades 1-11; (2) train teachers in basic market economics and in the implementation of the curriculum; and, (3) build a network of centers for economic education throughout Bulgaria. The Minister of Education identified the modernization of economic education as one of his three top goals.

In the summer of 1991, in Haskovo, Bulgaria, five members of the Center's staff conducted a two-week seminar on market economics for high school teachers, modeled after successful summer programs in the United States. Basic market economics concepts were presented along with some suggestions on how they could be taught in the classroom.[9] The Bulgarian students felt most comfortable with descriptive information that was presented, such as how inflation is measured or how central banks are organized. They had more difficulty with abstract concepts. For example, a lecture on the role of profits in allocating resources in a market economy was well received, but not well understood. Many of the Bulgarian participants found it hard to conceptualize the idea that the expectation of profits could attract new resources to an industry and competition would affect prices. Rather, they thought more in terms of what rate of profit the government should guarantee and limits the government should put on profits. About half of the 58 participants were political economy (i.e., Marxism) majors. They felt threatened by the government's new commitment to the teaching of market economics because it would replace their specialty. The other half seemed to look forward to teaching market economics, perhaps because they were not threatened by a loss of their teaching positions.

A basic concern of the American staff was the extent to which Bulgarian teachers would understand and accept presentations on a market economy.[10] Would American teaching styles of discussion, question and answers, and student participation be inhibiting or distracting? Would the personal enthusiasm of the American lecturers be effectively conveyed through simultaneously-translated lectures? Would the Bulgarian teachers be able to "relate" to American presentations and examples?

Many of the concerns turned out to be positive features of the seminar. The teachers took well to American teaching styles and the translators conveyed both literary and attitudinal information.[11] The staff also had the assistance of three Bulgarian teachers who had attended a two-week economics program in Cincinnati the previous summer. These teachers were part of a group of 12 who had been selected by the Bulgarian Ministry of Public Education to attend a variety of economic education programs in the United States. They were able to help with translation of technical words and explain difficult concepts.

Several factors were somewhat limiting to the success of the summer seminar. The sessions were quite long (about 6 hours a day) and a bit tiring, the classroom was crowded and very warm.[12] Furthermore, textbooks in the Bulgarian language were not available. Instead, the staff worked from a translation of the Ohio K-8 Model Course of Study in Economics (a curriculum guide) and a glossary of economics terms.

Following the two-week seminar the American staff helped Bulgarian educators to prepare a curriculum for grades 6-8 and for the high school level. It was based on a typical U.S. model including suggestions for teaching that utilized open discussions, discovery and experimental learning.[13] Many of the techniques were new for the Bulgarian teachers.

Several of the participants taught market economics at the high school level in the Fall 1991. The *Test of Economic Literacy* (form A) was given to 98 of their students in November 1991. They achieved an average score of 38.48 percent correct out of 46 questions compared to the normed American average score of 50.72 percent correct for students with economics instruction (Soper and Walstad, 1987). The Bulgarian students scored nearly as well or better than American students on many of the questions. They scored less well on identifying income determinants (especially in the U.S.), giving examples of factors of production, interpreting consequences of economic growth, and applying the concepts of public goods, aggregate demand, fiscal policy and tariffs. Appendix 15.1 shows average scores on each question.

A second seminar was conducted during the summer of 1992 in Kazanluk, Bulgaria. This time the seminar was open to teachers of grades 6-8 only. Our assignment was more specific – to teach basic economic principles and prepare the 30 participants to implement the new curriculum designed for grades 6-8. The focus helped. The teachers knew they would be teaching economics the following year and were attentive and eager learners. At the end of the seminar an examination was given consisting of 34 questions taken from the TEL. The average score of the teachers was 30.4 out of total of 34 questions – an exceptional accomplishment.

At present all economics school curricula and syllabi are experimental. The new economics program will train and develop people who can make competent, independent economic decisions. To accomplish this, economics will be integrated into the entire educational system beginning in grade one and culminating in the last grade of high school. Thus far, the experimental curriculum has been introduced in grades 6-8 and in the high school.

The economic curriculum for the grades 6-8 contains the following basic components: Knowledge and understanding of the major economic concepts, knowledge of the main economic institutions and industries, the interrelationships of these interest groups, and the application of a critical, analytical approach to economic decision-making.[14] The curriculum is being presented in three modules:

Module 1 (6th Grade) consists of:

- The basic economic problem: limited resources and unlimited wants
- Decision-making
- Economic Systems
- Economic Stimuli

Exchange, Money and Interdependence
Markets and Prices
Demand and Supply

Module 2 (7th Grade)
Limitation of resources
Productivity
Economic Stimuli and Institutions
Exchange, Money and Their Interdependence
Markets and Prices
Demand and Supply

Module 3 (8th Grade)
Limitation of Resources
Productivity
Economic Systems
Exchange, Money and their Interdependence
Markets and Prices
Demand and Supply
Structure of the Market, Competition
The Role of The State
Absolute and Comparative Advantage and Trade Restrictions

The high school curriculum on market economy basics includes 64 teaching hours. It contains the following elements:

Ways of organizing the economy:
Command-administrative economy
Free market economy
Mixed market economy
Traditional economic system
Using economic information for comparison and evaluation
Decision-making process
The problem of the reasonable option
Production and human resources
The laws of demand and supply
Equilibrium between price and volume
Prices controls, production and shortages
Business games in decision-making
Economic cycles
Analysis of the fiscal policy
Foreign currency and international exchange

There are also specialized curricula in management, marketing and economics for the special economics high schools.

III. SOME OBSERVATIONS AND CONCLUSIONS

There are many problems and difficulties that face the Bulgarians as they attempt to reform their curriculum and train their teachers to use it effectively. One difficulty is the potential resistance of the population to a market economy. The Bulgarian people have many reservations about the market economy and privatization. A survey made by Bulgarian Business Service Society Gallup International in March 1993 shows that for 35 percent of the Bulgarians' private ownership of the factories and enterprises is unacceptable, 56 percent recommend confiscation of the properties of the new rich and only 30 percent are ready to participate in privatization. The majority still upholds the communist principle, preached exclusively for fifty years, of the equal distribution of the pie. The concept of looking for ways to enlarge the pie so that everyone can benefit is often rejected or not comprehended.

A second difficulty may lie in the lack of the teachers' commitment to curricular reform. Removing the ideological bias which for decades has heavily dominated all teaching in Bulgarian schools is no small or straightforward task. Rapid changes cannot be forced in this domain, whatever anyone's desire or intention, because the school structure is embodied in the make-up of educational personnel and even in the very design of school buildings. Moreover, the majority of parents and teachers do not welcome structural changes. Teachers feel their jobs possibly may be endangered by any transformations. Some teachers with long and successful professional experience are loyal communists who find it very hard to either abandon or criticize the beliefs cherished for so many years. Teachers also face uncertainty about the new curricula and about how to teach in a way that would keep pace with the changing pattern of economic and social development.

A third challenge to teacher training is the uncertainty that even experienced professional Bulgarian educators may be feeling. The recent and unprecedented political, cultural and economic changes occurring in Eastern European countries have created for their people tremendous trauma and upheaval. Few have escaped the effects. Although the Bulgarian participants in the American economics seminars and curriculum development sessions were competent professionals, it was especially important for the American staff to be sensitive their feelings of vulnerability and insecurity.[15]

It also was important for the American staff not to underestimate the capacity of the Bulgarian educators to understand the market system. Initially, the American staff had a tendency to eliminate a number of concepts from the curriculum or to simplify the material because of time constraints. But the teachers were eager to take on the challenge and in most cases did exceedingly well, in spite of their limited exposure to economics and educational trends in the West.[16]

It is the Bulgarians who must determine the types of curricular changes to make. Except in a few cases, such as in the teaching of some basic market economics concepts, lessons and teaching units cannot be transplanted from the West to Eastern Europe (Gekov, 1993). Incorrect translations then become a problem. It is information about economic conditions specific to Bulgaria that is important to present, especially at the special economics high schools where students receive training for future jobs in the economy. These specialized high schools will require radical reform because of the changes in the economic system, including new economic laws and other bills passed by the Parliament. These schools will require a total replacement of syllabi, curricular and teaching materials.

The new curriculum also should be supported with appropriate textbooks. Unfortunately, almost none exit today. The Ministry of Education estimates that during the next two or three years, more than 100 textbooks should be published with a circulation of about 6,000 each. For a small country in economic crisis, this is a daunting task. Presently, the Ministry is focusing on the following specialties: Industrial business and investment, agrarian economics, economics of tourism and trade, social economics (health care, education and culture), business administration, management of the firm, accountancy and auditing, and information systems.

A final question must be asked. If curricular and pedagogical reform is carried out, can it survive along with more traditional subjects and pedagogy? In the two seminars given by the American team, the Bulgarian teachers had some difficulty with abstract concepts. They were more familiar with a didactic, formal method of presentation. The notions of integration, questioning, critiquing and sharing ideas were "foreign" yet part of the "new way of thinking" that they are being encouraged to adopt and implement in their classrooms. Most responded very positively to a less formal, interactive method. But questions remain. Will the teachers use these "new way of thinking" lessons effectively? And if they do, will the new lessons stand on their own amid other long standing and formerly honored traditional courses and teaching methods? If an economics course is the only one that encourages critiquing and questioning, but the remaining courses discourage it, economics could be mistrusted or even driven out as if it were a foreign virus trying to infect the educational organism.

It is our conviction that economic education can play a prominent role in helping the Bulgarian people understand the new market realities and opportunities. A sound education will assist the legal and judicial system in paving the way for private enterprise.

We feel it is most efficient to concentrate our endeavors on the younger generation of teachers and administrators, many of whom want to take advantage of the more liberal atmosphere, the freedom from bureaucratic constraints and the opportunity to serve the country's children to the best of their ability. "You opened our eyes to the market economy," wrote one Bulgarian participant in the seminar. "I would like longer courses that cover a larger field of economic problems." It would be a tragedy to see them disappointed or to find them joining the vast exodus of experts and highly qualified specialists who can find fulfillment only in other countries.

NOTES

The authors wish to thank Rosamond Vredeveld for extensive comments and assistance with this chapter.

1. The term State is used to describe the government as well as the Bulgarian Communist Party, which was the dominating political and social force from 1944 to 1989. The General Secretary of the Party also was Head of State. The Party appointed members of the Council of Ministers (including the Minister of Education) which was the administrative body of the government. The Party also controlled Parliament since it was the only party represented in Parliament. In essence, the Party controlled all aspects of the State including the executive, legislative and judicial branches.

2. The Seventh Congress was historic because it repudiated the cult of personality, that is, the cult of Joseph Stalin.

3. Over the years, the Ministry of Education has taken on different responsibilities and different names. For example, since 1990, the Ministry has been named the Ministry of Public Education, the Ministry of Education and Science and the Ministry of Education, Science and Culture. This paper uses the more generic term Ministry of Education to refer to that government body responsible for administering policy relative to elementary and secondary (grades 1-12) public education.

4. Areas of specialization were determined by members of CMEA, of which the Soviet Union was the dominant member. The industries in which Bulgaria specialized included computers, chemicals and manufacturing equipment.

5. From an address by Tudor Zhivkov, President of Bulgaria and Party General Secretary to the first Teachers' Congress in 1962 (Bulgarian Communist Party, 1965).

6. Contrary to official statements, the system had much potential for increasing the standard of living through more efficient production and the supply of less expensive and higher quality products. This was difficult to achieve, however, under the planned economy in Bulgaria at that time.

7. The following paragraphs relating to decisions of the XII Congress rely heavily on *XIIth Party Congress, 1981-1984*, (Bulgarian Communist Party, 1981).

8. The system was three-level in name only. In reality, the Party was the only power in education.

9. The concepts included: scarcity, opportunity costs, supply and demand, the role of prices and profits in allocating resources, the role of the government in a market economy, market failures and environmental policies, measurements of economic activity (e.g., GDP and inflation), aggregate demand, aggregate supply, monetary policy and role of central banks, fiscal policy, and economic growth. About two thirds of the seminar time was devoted to presenting content, the rest of the time was used to present teaching activities and methods.

10. It turned out this concern was unfounded. After the two-week seminar the participants evaluated it favorably. A representative comment: "This course entirely changed my outlook. Up to now, I've never thought about the effects of the market upon the consumers and the producers. Everything I learned here will find application in my future work."

11. Comment from a participant in the Haskovo seminar: "I was enriched by your warm personalities and your teaching techniques. I learned that when you teach your lessons, you use examples from everyday life to make theoretical and general conclusions."

12. Comment from a participant in the Haskovo seminar: "Through your methods the information comes easier. It's more exciting and holds my attention. We comprehend everything and don't feel tired after the sessions."

13. Comment from a participant in the Haskovo seminar: "I like most the alternative approach in presenting the lectures, the films, the games, the discussions, etc. It was very interesting and pleasant for me."

14. Inclusion of a critical, analytical approach is dramatically different from the previous method of requiring rote learning. The description of the curriculum is from (Gekov, 1993) and (Ministry of Education and Science, 1992).

15. Comment from a participant in the Haskovo seminar: "You are the first Americans that I see and you gave me the idea of American spirit. I was greatly impressed by the relationships among you, your respect for the individual; your sense of humor. You gave me very much. You also gave me a higher sense of self-respect."

16. Comment from a participant in the Haskovo seminar: "We wished we could go deeper into the problems of the market economy. We need not only to believe and to accept it, but also to know its social consequences."

REFERENCES

Alexandrova, D. (1993). Bulgarians do not intend to participate in privatization (Bulgarite ne vuznameryavat da uchastvuvat v privatizatsiyata). *24 Hours* (March 2).

Bulgarian Communist Party. (1965). *The Bulgarian Communist Party in resolutions and decisions, 1956-1962, Vol. V.* (Bulgarskata komunisticheska partiya v resolyutsii i resheniya). Sofia.

Bulgarian Communist Party. (1966). *Resolution of the IXth Congress of the Bulgarian Communist Party, Nov. 18, 1966.* (Resoljutsiya na devetiya kongres na Bulgarskata komunisticheska partiya). Sofia.

Bulgarian Communist Party. (1967). *Directives of the IXth Congress of the Bulgarian Communist Party, Nov. 18, 1966.* (Direktivi na devetiya kongres na bulgarskata komunisticheska partiya). Sofia.

Bulgarian Communist Party. (1973). *Xth Congress of the Bulgarian Communist Party, April 1971.* (Deseti kongres na Bulgarskata komunisticheska partiya). Sofia.

Bulgarian Communist Party. (1976). *XIth Congress of the Bulgarian Communist Party, March 1976.* (Edinadeseti kongres na Bulgarskata komunisticheska partiya). Sofia.

Bulgarian Communist Party. (1981). *XII Congress of the Bulgarian Communist Party, March 1981.* (Dvanadeseti kongres na Bulgarskata komunisticheska partiya). Sofia.

Bulgarian Communist Party. (1986). *XIIIth Congress of the Bulgarian Communist Party, April, 1986.* (Trinadeseti kongres na Bulgarskata komunisticheska partiya). Sofia.

Gekov, G. (1993). High school economic education: Present state and trends (Crednoto ikonomichesko obrazovanie: sustoyanie i perspektivi), *Az Buki* (January 27), No. 4.

Hunter, W. C. (1993). Banking reform and the transition to a market economy in Bulgaria: Problems and prospects. *Economic Review* (Federal Reserve Bank of Atlanta), *78*(1), 15-22.

Ministry of Education and Science. (1992). *Contents of high school economics education in Bulgaria* (Sudurzhanie ha srednoto ikonomichesko obrazovanie b Bulgaria). Sofia.

Ministry of Public Education. (1990). Development of education 1988-1990: National report of the People's Republic of Bulgaria. Paper delivered to the International Conference on Education, 42nd Session. Geneva.

Ministry of Public Education. (1991). *The school in the Republic of Bulgaria.* Sofia.

Soper, J. C. & Walstad, W. B. (1987). *The test of economic literacy: Examiner's manual* (2nd ed.). New York: Joint Council on Economic Education.

Szebenyi, P. (1991). Change in the systems of public education in east central Europe. *Comparative Education, 28*(1), 19-32.

Tomiak, J. (1992). Education in the Baltic States, Ukraine, Belarus and Russia. *Comparative Education, 28*(1), 33-44.

Appendix 15.1: Results on the *Test of Economic Literacy* (Percent Correct by Item)

Question	Basic Concept/type of operation	Bulgaria	U.S.
1.	benefits of trade (understand)	93%	88%
2.	opportunity cost (apply)	54	53
3.	basic economic problem (define)	55	47
4.	production possibilities (example)	48	44
5.	opportunity cost (apply)	38	35
6.	labor specialization (understand)	42	49
7.	competition/markets (understand)	88	68
8.	capital/labor productivity (apply)	82	64
9.	profits (define)	63	44
10.	incentives/markets (understand)	39	44
11.	labor unions (history/apply)	41	8
12.	functions of money (define)	49	68
13.	real income (define)	65	57
14.	economic demand (define)	40	61
15.	minimum wage (apply)	24	60
16.	demand/price (apply)	57	59
17.	labor supply/income (apply)	48	38
18.	competition (apply)	60	75
19.	monopoly (apply)	64	68

Appendix 15.1: Results on the *Test of Economic Literacy* (Percent Correct by Item) Continued

Question	Basic Concept/type of operation	Bulgaria	U.S.
20.	income determinants in U.S. (define)	13	35
21.	income determinants (define)	74	61
22.	public goods/free riders (apply)	7	32
23.	externalities (apply)	30	38
24.	taxation (examples)	22	60
25.	factor of production (examples)	5	29
26.	gross national product (define)	49	47
27.	production possibilities (define)	31	41
28.	unemployment (determinants)	29	45
29.	aggregate demand (apply)	29	38
30.	interpret graph	51	60
31.	interpret graph	45	41
32.	inflation (example)	48	19
33.	tax policy (apply)	38	35
34.	money supply (apply)	26	41
35.	aggregate demand (apply)	12	33
36.	budget deficit (define)	27	56
37.	tax policy (apply)	40	52
38.	fiscal policy (apply)	4	36
39.	international trade (apply)	44	50
40.	comparative advantage (apply)	35	50
41.	tariffs (understand)	17	52
42.	trade balance (define)	41	46
43.	tariffs (apply)	9	32
44.	exchange rates (apply)	37	40
45.	standard of living (define)	30	45
46.	economic growth (interpret)	7	37

CHAPTER 16

HIGH SCHOOL ECONOMICS IN THE PEOPLE'S REPUBLIC OF CHINA

Ruth Shen

T. Y. Shen

This chapter pursues the dual tasks of examining the contents and the effectiveness of Chinese economic education. Our discussion will be based on a scrutiny of the textbooks used in the high schools and the results of a survey of economic knowledge and attitudes we administered in both China and the U.S. (Shen and Shen, 1993). More specifically we evaluate the success of economic education in three areas, corresponding to the principal goals of high school economic education: the enhancement of economic knowledge, the development of citizenship, and the cultivation of decision making skills.

An important mission of high school economic education is to provide a framework to the students, into which they can position their background knowledge and newly acquired information of different economic activities. In China many of the activities in the economy are planned by a central authority. Although significant elements of a free market have been introduced by reformers in the last fifteen years, the Chinese Communist Party in power has not wavered from its insistence that China is and must remain in the future a socialist country controlled under its dictatorship. Is this accompanied by the formulation of a distinctive framework of economics that differs from the free enterprise economics taught in the "capitalist" United States? How coherent and persuasive is this framework? This is discussed in Section I of this chapter.

Citizenship refers to the performance of polity roles by nationals. In a democratic state citizenship is founded on autonomy and participation. Coupled with a free enterprise economy, there is a harmony enjoyed by the citizens in performing their economic and political roles. In an orthodox socialist regime, on the other hand, citizenship calls for an unquestioning obedience to the authority, whose policies are said to be, tautologically, designed to promote the interests of the citizens. China, of course, never "achieved" such a state of complete totalitarianism. As reform loosens further the hierarchical control, free enterprise has gradually gained a firm foothold. This inevitably leads to a divergence between economic liberalization and political "conservatism." If the market can coordinate economic activities effectively, how does one legitimize the government control imposed on the activities of individuals? Is this contradiction resolved in the Chinese citizenship training? What values are stressed, submission or autonomy? This is examined in Section II of this chapter.

The cultivation of personal decision making skills is another objective of economic education. Mainstream economics in the West is built on decentralized decision making by consumers and producers. The underlying utility maximizing approach accommodates varied attitudes and values held by different individuals. The situation in China is different. The command economy, even though somewhat eroded, is premised on a single set of values (determined by the authority). It has no room for the expression of alternative attitudes or values, and individual decision-making by the subjects is neither required nor welcome. As a result, tools for decision making – utility function, maximization and so on – are not touched in the Chinese economic education. How does this affect the basic decision making process – the guiding values and attitudes and the choice among the perceived options – of the Chinese students in comparison to their counterparts in the United States? This is discussed in Section III of this chapter.

I. THE FRAMEWORK FOR ECONOMICS IN CHINA TEXTBOOKS

Communists triumphed in China in 1949. Since then her economy has gone through four broad phases: socialist transformation from 1949 to 1956, wavering between planning and mass mobilization from 1956 to 1966, a descent toward anarchy from 1966 to 1976, and since 1976, the present reform, built on the piecemeal reintroduction of a market economy. With the flux, no orthodox ideology has taken root. This is in sharp contrast with the presence in the U.S. of a hard core of stable, consensual knowledge on economics. That core serves as the basis for the published guidelines of what economics should be taught in high schools. The guidelines in turn were closely followed by the writers of high school economics textbook (Helburn, 1986).

Without a new, thorough-going ideology to guide them, the Chinese textbook writers start with Marx's economic theory as developed by the Soviets and then add their own *ad hoc* modifications selected from the pronouncements of the current Party leaders. But Marx's theory is largely about the downfall of capitalism as its production relationship undermines class structure and ignites class struggle. The Soviet followers grafted on economic planning, balance equations of demand and supply dressed up in Marxian terms such as labor theory of value. Economics was little more than simple accounting.

Obviously for China, where planning was never in full swing, more must be added if there is to be any glimmer of relevancy. As is to be expected in an authoritarian regime, economic education is directed to rationalize contemporaneous programs; and the programs ushered in by the Chinese reform deviate by a giant margin from the socialist orthodoxy. Since the Chinese authority does not wish to lose its legitimacy as overseers of the socialist enterprise, it – as its predecessors after each metamorphoses – simply issue new interpretations of Marx and the Soviet theories. The textbook writers are carefully chosen followers. The "framework" they produce, sadly, consists of concepts in poorly matched layers piled on each other, pockmarked by damage-control patch work.

To illustrate this we draw on three textbooks. The first (to be referred to as T1 in this chapter) is *Economic Common Sense* (Jing Ji Chang Shi) published by Beijing Normal University, one edition in 1987 and a second, revised, edition in 1988. The latter is currently in use in high schools in Beijing. It was written by a group of university and high school teachers under the guidance of the deputy secretary of the Beijing Communist Party and approved by Beijing Municipal Editorial Committee for "thought education." The second (T2), in two volumes, has the same title. It was compiled by the "Group for the Revision of Teaching Material" of the "Tianjin High School Political Thought Education Committee."[1] It was first published in 1988 and is currently in use in the municipality of Tianjin. The third (T3) is the fourth edition of *Political Economy* (Zhen-zhi Jing ji Xue), published by Siuchuan People's Publishers in 1985. This introductory college text for many of the universities in Southern China is now used as a basic reference book for high school economic instruction in many places. It enjoys a wide circulation: 794,000 copies of the book was printed between 1979 (when it was published) and 1986.

The lack of a socialist economics framework that can accommodate the contemporaneous Chinese economic reform is frankly acknowledged in all three textbooks. In a clever defense, it was stated at the beginning of T3 that socialist economics does not have a fixed model, because – faithful to Marx – "it depends on evolving and complex production relationships."[2] What is good "socialist" economics depends on the country and its stage of development. China is in a "primitive stage of socialist development" and its unique problems require unique solutions. As a consequence, for China there is no "mature, complete, scientific theory" (T3, *Socialism*, p. 10). A textbook selects and arranges the materials based on "pedagogical" considerations.

The password of socialist economics in current circulation is economic development. "The basic task of socialism is to develop the productive power" (T1, p. 2; T2, Vol. 1, p. 15) needed to drive the economy to new heights. Indeed, "anything beneficial to productive power should be regarded as conforming to the fundamental interest of the people and is therefore required and permitted under socialism, while anything that does not contribute to productive power should be deemed as a violation of socialism and thus not permissible" (T1, pp. 10-11).[3] The mistake of the discredited "leftists" before the "correct policy of the current reform leaders" was to emphasize the wrong "conflict" – the conflict between classes – on the Marxian dialectic stage. Because of the "special character" of the Chinese people and her underdevelopment, the "actual" conflict is between people's rising material wants and production (T3, *Socialism*, p. 5). The egalitarian idealism must wait for the final arrival of the advanced stage of communism, when production reaches a higher level than the capitalist West (T3, p. 4).

The central feature of the current Chinese reform is the mix of socialist and capitalist institutions. This was introduced pragmatically to enhance growth, and the textbooks acknowledge it. Mao's mass mobilization program is deemed as the product of "unrealistic" idealism (T3, *Socialism*, p. 7). The former policy makers, pursuing Soviet-style central planning and management are criticized for their rigidity and their insistence on the opposition between (socialist) "planning" and (capitalist) "market" is declared false. Instead, "planning and market complement each other." The precursors also erred in their insistence on state ownership of the means of production. Multiple forms of ownership of the means of production is asserted to be "necessary" for development.

Having swept aside these mainstays of socialist orthodoxy, the textbook writers are confronted with two difficulties. What is the proper mix of capitalist and socialist institutions? More importantly, how can they avoid any hint that the mix suggests an acceptance of capitalism, which is tantamount to treason? On the former, textbook writers revised their texts frequently to reflect the changes in policy orientation.[4] But such revisions are always behind the event – "the direction of the wind" is clear only from hindsight –, so that the textbooks are perpetually outdated. There is also a tendency for the textbook writers (particularly the authors of T3) to huddle in the safe haven of Marx's writings, while leaving many of the reform issues dangling.

The danger of treading too close to the capitalist camp in explaining the introduction of capitalist institutions is stark. To emphatically rebut the tempting thought that the reform represents a transition from socialism to capitalism, the textbooks adopt two approaches. The first approach is to insist on the primacy of socialist economics. Every capitalistic idea or institution adopted under reform is shown to be subordinate to socialism. This may corrupt the meaning of socialism, but used tautologically – or even rhetorically – it is also infinitely flexible. The second approach is to present "capitalist economics" and "socialist economics" in separate volumes. By identifying all the current institutions and policies instituted by the authority to socialist economics and by caricaturing capitalist economics, a clear distinction between the two – the good guys and the bad guys – is achieved.

Of our three textbooks, T1 and T2 employ the first approach. The framework underlying these two books may be compared to that of the U.S. textbooks. The latter normally start from relatively unlimited wants and relatively limited resources. This creates the problem of scarcity and the need for choices. Economic concepts are then developed to answer the questions of "what, how, how much and for whom" to produce (Helburn, 1986, p. 18). At the micro level the major concepts are: economic wants; productive resources; scarcity and choices; opportunities costs and trade offs; economic incentives; specialization, comparative advantage, and the division of labor; interdependence; market demand and supply; and the price mechanism. This culminates in a competitive free enterprise economy coordinated by the market mechanism. Government steps in when there are market failures (public goods, information costs, resource immobility, externalities, and income distribution). At the macro level the major concepts are: aggregate supply and productive capacity; aggregate demand and its associated issues of unemployment and inflation; and the long-run growth problem of saving, investment and productivity.

T1 and T2 incorporate many of the major micro concepts – the building blocks of "capitalism economics" –, but they are grafted to a two-tier schematic framework, based on the slogan pronounced by the supreme leader, Deng Xio-ping: "state adjusts (tiao-jie) the markets, markets guide the enterprises." Free market is equated to anarchy and requires the state to bring it into order: "with refined division of labor, only the state can manage the economy to satisfy people's needs and achieve balanced growth" (T1, p. 165). At the disposal of the state are three major instruments: administrative, legal and economic. Of these the economic instruments are the most important. The state adjusts prices and extends credits with one eye on "value" (as determined by embodied labor) and the other eye on demand and supply. It sets the direction and the strategy for growth. Once the proper price signals are in place and a stable and harmonious environment is provided,[5] the enterprise managers "must" have the autonomy to run the enterprise – this being a lesson "from the past experience" when excessive meddling by the state extinguished their vitality. With given prices and dangling profit incentives, the managers strive for efficiency.

The two tier framework is in fact a weak reed and cannot shoulder the weight of the grafted capitalist theorizing. Even though it portrays the economic reality in China, it has no analytically plausible foundation. In admitting that price mechanism can allocate factors of production, goods and services, why is the market equated to anarchy? Market allocation depends ultimately on consumer demand. The writers of T1 and T2 are careful to avoid any mention of utility analysis, because it is antithetic to socialist labor theory of value. But they observe that "the end of socialist production is to satisfy consumers' material and spiritual needs" (T1, p. 148) and consumers sovereignty should be respected.[6] If this is the case, why must the government step in "to balance supply and demand" and to assure that the rate of growth is "neither too fast nor too slow" (T1, p. 136)? Such contradictions can be resolved only if we assume that party and government leaders are like Plato's omnipotent philosopher-kings, able to pull all the right levers and correct all false starts. This is hardly plausible, and even the textbook writers – who bow to these leaders at every turn – were obliged to point out that decentralization is necessary because the leaders cannot attend to every detail.

The other textbook, T3, follows the second approach of treating capitalist and socialist economics separately to avoid contamination. Its first volume on capitalist economics turns out be a totally anachronistic transcription of Marx's *Capital*, from labor theory of value to the "inevitable" downfall of capitalism. The capitalist economy is portrayed as an anarchy populated by "cannibalistic" exploiters. The second volume on socialism centers on the theme that the economy is a machine that can only be run "as an integral whole" by the government. But this command economy requires the setting of an "advanced socialist economy," beyond the reach of the underdeveloped China. This prepares the stage for the celebrated "theoretical discovery" by Deng Xio-ping of the uniquely Chinese "primitive socialist economy." In this transitional economy, regrettably, not all enterprises are owned and not all prices are set by the state. Hence exploitation such as those in a capitalist economy will take place despite the vigilance of the government in suppressing it (T3, *Socialism*, pp. 472-4).[7] Needless to say a treatise like this – a surviving remnant of Soviet style orthodox economics – is totally out of tune with the enthusiasm towards reform shared by the Chinese leaders and the populace, and provides no insight whatsoever into the real implications of the newly introduced institutions. It is a sad commentary that the text should be used as the principal reference book for high schools in many parts of China.

These texts clearly suggest that high school economics in China is largely political thought education – as indicated by the curriculum listing of the course – rather than an introduction to a "scientific" discipline. The texts distort the realities of reform to fit it into the traditional socialist economics. The key importance of the market to coordinate allocation in a system based on profit incentives is left in a grey zone. The major contributions by entrepreneurs and foreign technologies are ignored. Even the truly remarkable feat of keeping down the population increase by the party authority is not mentioned, presumably because of its ambiguous impact on the central objective of increasing total productive power for the sake of growth. Omissions and contradictions like these are so blatant that it is difficult to believe that they do not undermine learning.

II. CITIZENSHIP AND HIGH SCHOOL ECONOMICS

High school education helps prepare students to fulfill their future citizenship roles. In the West, the aim is to rally the support of the students for a participatory democracy and a decentralized economy coordinated by markets. The system allows them to make free decisions. In China the population are supposed to fall behind the banner of the four "Cardinal Principles": Party leadership, Proletariat Dictatorship, Socialism and Marx-Lenin-Mao Thought. Citizens are expected to be loyal and obedient, so that they perform the tasks assigned to them. This leaves no room for independent thinking or action.

One is tempted to conclude from this that economic education for citizenship training relies on open discussion and analysis in the West and on indoctrination in China. But, on the other side of the coin, Marxist socialism has always prided itself on its "scientific" – as opposed to utopian" – roots. The textbooks used in high school economic education are therefore expected to lay a reasoned foundation for the Cardinal Principles, in order to legitimize the demand for loyalty and obedience. In addition, reform in China has steered the economy towards decentralization. Rationing of consumption is phased out, and private enterprises are proliferating. Blind obedience needs to be reconciled with the need for independent thinking that accompanies the increase in autonomy. Is a new balance struck in the Chinese citizenship training between indoctrination and reasoning?[8]

Under the circumstances, just as the textbook writers have chosen Marx as the starting point for their economic analysis, they attempt a reasoned defense of the Cardinal Principles as the foundation of citizenship training. In essence the issue is the legitimacy of the right to perpetual monolithic dictatorship by a Communist Party now in the hands of a reform leadership.[9] The defense is built on two premises. First, socialism is good. The alternative to socialism is capitalism, which is not only bad but also (according to the authority of Marx) inevitably doomed. Second, the policies of the present Communist party leadership are consistent with socialism. Good citizenship is to support what is good, i.e., the leadership and its policies. Since policy decisions are made by the leaders, only obedience is required of the citizenry.

The development of these two premises, rather than the teaching of economic principles, is in fact the focus of the texts. The establishment of the first premise is accomplished by reviewing historical records and by enumerating its merits. The relative poverty of China is attributed to feudalism, colonialism and bureaucratic capitalism that held back Chinese economic development prior to the arrival of Communist saviors in 1949. The growth record since the takeover, a growth rate of "social production" of 8.6 percent from 1953 to 1987, is indeed sterling and is credited to the practice of socialism (T2, Vol. 1, p. 6). The still higher growth rate of 9.7 percent since 1978 is regarded as a proof of the superior wisdom of the reform leaders, who have managed to correct the mistakes of "Lin Biao and later the Gang of Four." This record is then compared to the stagflation and unemployment of the capitalist West in the last two decades.[10]

The superior merits of socialism follow the populist solution of the puzzle of how an economy is held together when there is division of labor. As we have already mentioned, the texts portray a capitalist economy as both an anarchy and an animal jungle, where decisions are made independently by numerous capitalists who cannibalize each other in pursuit of profits (T2, Vol. 2, p. 11).[11] Socialism is then obviously superior because a centralized government is there to keep everyone in check and to coordinate production and consumption. Above all, since the socialist government by definition represents the interests of all workers in a classless economy, its policies inevitably are directed for the pursuit of general welfare.

The texts are also concerned with the second premise, defending the legitimacy of the present leadership. The driving force comes in from two sources. First, there are still many conservatives – some in powerful positions in the party – who are not at ease with the reform program. The text writers (at least of T1 and T2) appear anxious to draw a line between themselves and the conservatives. Second, since most if not all of these writers are economists brought up under the older Soviet tradition, they are as much the newly released inmates of a conceptual cage inhospitable to most of the reform programs as the reform leaders themselves. They have a strong need to persuade themselves that the current reform policies are proper socialism.

It is inevitable that citizenship education based on these premises would be difficult for many students to swallow. On the first premise, the performance of socialist China pales in comparison with the still superior growth records of capitalist Japan and the four "tigers" – Taiwan, Korea, Hong Kong and Singapore – next door. At the same time, socialist economies of Eastern Europe and the former Soviet Union are known to have failed. The argument that capitalist economies are anarchies is also unconvincing as the increasing exposure to the West has actually given the Chinese an exaggerated view of its prosperity. The disingenuous distortions of the contributions of the capitalist institutions to the success of reform reduces the credibility of the texts, and the absence of an open debate on the relative merits and weaknesses of the different economic systems only breeds cynicism.

The heavy stress on the second premise further weakens the integrity of the texts. The rationalizations are akin to the defense in a judicial court, except that the rule of game – that, under the four Cardinal Principles, the Communist Party alone has the voice – excludes rebuttals. The arguments that are presented are either assertions that do not square completely with personal experiences or tautologies that stand or fall with faith. They provide no plausible explanation for the success of current policies, and offer no guide as to the future limits – if any – of reform.

The central question of "why obedience" in the end goes back to the pragmatic question of what policies are effective for growth. The convoluted discourse debating whether these policies are socialism or not has no real substance. It would seem that citizenship training in China would be better served if the textbook presentation focuses on actual facts, soliciting support for the reform leaders and their empirically proven policies.[12] The record of the government, particularly in the last fifteen years, is in fact admirable. Population growth has been kept down, standard of living were raised, and much poverty and illiteracy were eradicated. The reform program to pull the economy back from the aftermaths of the disastrous Culture Revolution has also been remarkably successful. Since in China today there is no genuine alternative to the Communist Party, open dialogues in the place of thought control might silence much of the simmering discontent without inaugurating the demise of socialism.

The real reason that such a course is not followed is perhaps found in the preoccupation of the present leaders with their struggle against the conservative opponents. This requires them to present themselves as the true torch holders of Marx-Lenin-Mao socialism. The textbook writers and high school economic education in China are caught in this intramural jostle. The writers of T1 and T2 have taken their side with the reform leaders while the writers of T3 appear to be hedging their bet. With economic education turned into an ideological battleground between two *socialist* rival camps, there is little hope to escape from harangue.

III. RESULTS OF ECONOMIC EDUCATION ON KNOWLEDGE, OPINION, ATTITUDES, AND VALUES

The third objective of economic education in high schools is the development of decision making skills. In the U.S. an algorithm of decision making in economic matters is taught. Based on the utility and the profit functions, different decision structures are presented, encompassing such concepts as constraints, trade-offs, and long-run versus short-run specifications. In the Chinese texts there is no comparable discussion of how individual interests may be promoted or what decision procedures are necessary for their pursuit. The primary goal of economic activities, as mentioned above, is economic growth. It promises to satisfy the material and "spiritual" needs of all nationals in the future. The strategy for the attainment of this goal is left to the party leaders, and good citizenship consists of loyalty and obedience. Thus, as far as economic education is concerned, it handicaps the Chinese students in their decision making in two ways. First, the knowledge they receive in the classes is devoid of the specifics of economic decision making and may in fact confuse them. Second, since autonomy and individual responsibility – the twin bedrocks of decision making – are not encouraged, the students in China may develop attitudes and values, such as blind obedience, which make them inferior decision makers.

To determine whether the differences in economic education in the two countries have an *actual* impact on the students' decision making, let us delve further into the general decision making process. Formally, decision making is to choose among options on the basis of an objective function. It has two components: the perception of options based on knowledge/opinion, and the formulation of an objective function based on attitude/value. *Knowledge* in our context is simply the information available to the students. If the information is subject to a personal interpretation, it is transformed into an *opinion*, "what a person believe[s] to be factually true" (Aronson, 1981, p. 96). Opinion is cognitive and transient, easily revised by new evidence to the contrary.[13] In our context, as the students develop their knowledge/opinion on the fundamentals driving the economy, they become more able to attend to the relevant variables. In China, a wider gap between knowledge and opinion may exist, if knowledge from the classroom is perceived as propaganda, and in actual decision making an individual would be guided by opinion rather than knowledge.

One further step into the information processing network within the mind of a person is *attitude*, which adds an evaluative and emotional component to opinion and is held more tenaciously by the person. Attitude governs the choice among the options. At the core of the network is *value*, formalizing a person's self concept. Value is developed to reduce cognitive dissonance, as the individual attempts to resolve the incompatibilities in attitudes (Aronson, 1981, p. 102). If an individual has developed a deeply held and well integrated value system, his/her attitudes are more predictable and also less susceptible to extraneous influences. His/her objective function is more consistent.

Before we move on to discuss a survey that we have made to analyze these decision making components, some preliminary remarks are in order. On the issue of knowledge/opinion, because both the Chinese students and their U.S. counterparts must take examinations, we expect some regurgitation of their textbooks. It is important to remember, however, that observations of the real world as well as folk wisdom reinforced by life experiences are also sources of economic knowledge.[14] Because of the inadequacies of their course materials, we expect the Chinese students to rely more on these extraneous sources. In addition the reforms now taking place in China must have stimulated more economic thinking among the Chinese students, as verified by our survey of student interest in economics.[15] This raises two questions. Balancing the motivation provided by the environmental stimuli and the disincentive of a poorly constructed economics course, how much do the Chinese students know about their economy relative to their U.S. counterparts? Additionally, if the Chinese students draw more heavily from their life experience and personal observations, what is the quality of their knowledge/opinion?

Attitude/value springs from fashion, personality, life experience, and culture. Accordingly we expect a diversity among both the Chinese and the American students.[16] At the same time, economic education, as a minor part of the students' life experience, can have little influence on their general values. An interesting issue is human nature as manifested in the conduct of economic affairs. Mainstream economists have always assumed a universal "economic man" – relentlessly and rationally pursuing his/her self interest, – quite independent of economic education. Since this is the typical behavior in a free enterprise economy like the United States, course material describing and justifying it should be congenial to American students and reinforce their values in this regard. In China the economic education, as we have seen, attempts to direct the students towards loyalty and obedience. If economic man lies in the breasts of the Chinese students as well, this must lead to a tug-of-war between "natural" self-interest and the value of obedience (or equity, a value stressed during the Cultural Revolution barely a decade earlier). Is the economic man instinct so strong as to defy indoctrination? If not, does the economic education – or more generally, the full span of "political thought education" – induce confusion, apathy or cynicism?

As a step towards the answers of these questions, in 1989 the authors conducted surveys of 873 juniors and seniors from three key high schools in Beijing and one rural school about 20 kilometers away. They all use T1 as the textbook in their economics course. We also made a benchmark survey of a sample of 139 seniors from six high schools in northern California, including two "select" high schools that are more comparable to the Chinese key high schools, a small "necessary" alternative high school and two suburban schools. All of these students also had studied economics or were taking the course.

Knowledge/opinion is tested with questions that we have selected from the U.S. *Test of Economic Literacy*.[17] Since the Chinese text does not focus on these questions, we expect that the Chinese students would do worse than their U.S. counterparts, unless their greater interest and their ability to draw from their experience with the recently developed market economy compensates for weakness in the text. This turns out to be the case: the average Chinese students actually did better than Northern California students. Overall, 66.6 percent of the Chinese respondents gave correct answers to the knowledge/opinion questions, compared with 64.0 percent of the students from the two select San Francisco schools, 54.4 percent of the students from the total California sample, and 61.3 percent of the students from the U.S. national sample. The Wilcox W statistic reveals a significant difference between their scores.

Our attribution of their superior knowledge/opinion to folk wisdom is underscored by the fact that the Chinese students scored higher on questions that are not covered in their textbook. For example, 68.2 percent of the Chinese students correctly defined profits as revenue minus costs, compared with 42 percent of the students in northern California. Similarly, 73 percent of the Chinese students stated that "it is the social purpose of profits" to "get businesses to produce what consumers demand." In California, 65 percent selected this as the correct answer. The first of these questions is not covered at all in the Chinese textbook and the second is given only as a supplementary premise, with the primary purpose of profit stated as an incentive to higher efficiency.[18]

The knowledge generalization we draw is that Chinese students did not slavishly follow their classroom learning and meekly accept indoctrination.[19] In response to the flux in their environment, reinforced by their nimbleness and openness, they form opinions from many sources in the world around them. Even though the institutions in their world were different and often inconsistent, they reached views on the operation of the economy that were surprisingly similar to the views of their American counterparts. In this sense the Chinese students are probably, to a greater extent than their American counterparts, compensating for the deficient formal education by their own observations. If this interpretation is correct, we would expect that their attitudes and values will be even less affected by the course in economics as well.

To ascertain the attitude/value held by the students, the students were asked to choose among answers to evaluative questions. Value is characterized by consistency in the attitudes. To test this consistency, each revealed attitude from a survey question is assigned to an underlying value system. If attitudes registered from the different questions belong to the same value system, then (1) the hypothesis that the student has a well integrated value system is not rejected and (2) that value system can be (tentatively) identified from the attitudes he/she reveals. On the other hand, if the revealed attitudes from different questions belong to different value systems, then the student does not have a developed value system in his/her realm of economic thinking.[20]

To facilitate our analysis, we distinguish three value systems: authoritarian, egalitarian, and liberal. An individual is said to subscribe to an authoritarian value system if he/she believes in economic planning and endorses a dominant role of the government in the economy.[21] For each attitude question, an answer will be referred to as an authoritarian-type if it conforms to such a value system. Similarly, an egalitarian-type answer suggests a preference for equal income distribution and the relief of poverty. Finally, a liberal-type answer reveals abhorrence of state control, faith in the invisible hand driven by self interests.

Next we select a criterion question ("question k") and "type" the answer as A(uthoritarian), E(galitarian) or L(iberal) as follows:

Question: Do you think a government should:

a. plan the production of necessary goods and services
b. be ready to step in only if economic disruptions (such as unemployment) cannot be resolved by the market in a timely fashion
c. be inactive in the economy except for the provision of national defense and police
d. correct for distributional injustices and poverty in the economy

Answer "a" is scored as A, answers "b" and "c" as L and answer "d" as E. Based on this scoring, 32 percent of the Chinese respondents gave A-type answers, 33 percent L-type answers and 34 percent E-type answers to question k. In contrast, 12 percent of U.S. respondents gave A-type answers, 47 percent E-type answers, and 41 percent L-type answers. It is not surprising that many more Chinese respondents feel that the government should plan the production of necessary goods and services, a position that is still practiced and stressed in the Chinese textbook. Nevertheless, the proportion was less than one-third. Even more interesting, a larger proportion of the respondents in China (19 percent) than that in the U.S. (12 percent) chose "c" as the answer. Is this proof that economic man lurks in China, despite the fact that the value system it implies is totally opposed to the official doctrine?

To test the consistency of underlying attitudes, we look into the attitudes revealed by the answers to other questions. Four of them in our survey (questions i, i = 1, 2, 3, 4) are particularly relevant and answers to them are compiled in the same way.[22] If there exists a firmly held value system, we expect full consistency in the respondents' attitudes, i.e., the type classification for each respondent should be the same on all questions. Thus, say, a student chose the authoritarian answer to the criterion question, question k. We designate it as Ak, an authoritarian-type answer A to the kth question. If the same student chose the authoritarian-type A to question 1, we designate *this* answer as A1. Without inconsistencies, the (conditional probability) ratio A1/Ak, calculated by adding up the number of respondents who chose A to the kth question and *then* A again to question 1, should equal to 1.0. If there was inconsistency among some students, the ratio would be less than 1.0. If the value of this ratio falls below 1/2, a respondent typed in one way by the answer to the criterion question, was more likely to choose an answer in another question that signifies him/her to be of a different type. A low value of the ratio thus implies the absence of a well integrated value systems for many of our respondents.

A quick glance at Table 16.1 shows that only those choosing a liberal-type answer to the criterion question were consistent. Less than 10 percent of those choosing an authoritarian answer to the criterion question in both China and in the U.S., for example, have chosen an authoritarian type answer to questions 1 and 2. Furthermore, the switch is common in other instances as well, so that in fact a majority – in approximately comparable proportions – of the respondents in both countries chose the liberal position in their answers to questions 1-4, whatever their answers happened to be for question K. We must therefore conclude the direct reference to "government" in question K has introduced a "framing" phenomenon (Tversky and Kahneman, 1986) which ties an answer more narrowly to context. Allowing for this, based on the answers to questions 1-4, it would seem that a majority of the students in both countries are consistent in their attitudes and share a liberal value.

The conclusion that economic man is universal is unavoidable: the pursuit of individual self-interest appears more deeply rooted in human nature than the impulse for dependency or egalitarianism. Indeed, despite tight thought control, the Chinese students have a moderate and liberal outlook, equal to or perhaps even more exuberant than their counterparts in the U.S. The value bodes well for the reform program; the Chinese students were at least as appreciative as their American counterparts of a market economy. The fact that economic education in China was wrongheaded perhaps only deepens their recognition of the contradictions and complexities of their environment. The dissonance may actually serve to stimulate the development of their values. The goals of economic education may be accomplished without streamlined formal instruction.

TABLE 16.1: Consistency of Attitudes (Conditional Probabilities Based on Percentage of Contingent Responses)

	Questions (i = 1, 2, 3, 4)							
Contingency	(1)		(2)		(3)		(4)	
answers	China	U.S.	China	U.S.	China	U.S.	China	U.S.
Ai/Ak	3	7	7	7	NA	NA	NA	NA
Li/Ak	76	53	90	93	67	27	60	60
Ei/Ak	20	40	3	0	16	60	1	0
Ai/Lk	2	6	13	6	NA	NA	NA	NA
Li/Lk	73	58	84	90	71	38	65	75
Ei/Lk	25	35	3	4	14	44	2	0
Ai/Ek	4	5	15	4	NA	NA	NA	NA
Li/Ek	71	74	81	84	61	39	57	49
Ei/Ek	25	21	4	12	33	54	3	2

Note: No answer (NA) corresponds to the indicated type characterization.

NOTES

1. We have also examined another text with the same title, written by the Beijing Normal University faculty members, published in 1990 and currently in use in Siuchuan. The book turned out to be nearly identical to T2.

2. All translations from the original Chinese in this chapter are by the authors.

3. This, we may note, is a much narrower goal than the set of goals – freedom, efficiency, equity, full employment, price stability, growth and security – normally presented in U.S. texts.

4. For example, T1 was first completed in September 1986, revised in March 1987 and again in February 1988.

5. Cyclical problems and stabilization are ignored, presumably because it is a consequence of the free market "anarchy."

6. An alternative to this is to take the goal of economic growth more seriously, perhaps based on former USSR arguments of national security in a world of rivalry against capitalist states. This line is not stressed in China, where rapid economic growth depends heavily on foreign trade, investment and technology accessible only on terms of cooperation. On the other hand, an emphasis on growth could have provided the Chinese writers with an opportunity to build their textbooks on relatively ideology-free supply side notions such as production factors, and technological change.

7. The flavor of the volume may be illustrated by its discussion on competition (T3, *Socialism*, pp. 258-260). In capitalist economies competition is said to be carried out by any means at the disposal of capitalists, including "violence." In contrast, in a socialist economy firms compete to further both private and social gains, they do not neglect to cooperate with each other and employ only "legitimate" means such as technological change. Labor is not a commodity and therefore the competition does not extend to the labor market. Finally, although there will always be losers in a competition, the state will take "appropriate" care of the losers.

8. The habit of "bowing with the wind" cultivated in the past decades under drifting Communist policies is undoubtedly exacerbated by the Confucian and semi-feudal historical root in China, stressing that every individual has a proper place in society and should not overstep his/her bounds.

9. The insistence on this goal is assured by the representation of party representatives in the textbook writing and its subsequent approval.

10. The psychologically potent force of nationalism is also invoked. If the present growth rate continues, by year 2000 "China will be the sixth greatest economic power in the world, behind U.S., USSR, Japan, Germany and France." Ultimately, trumpet the texts, socialism will enable China to overtake all others. This strong and prosperous China is dangled before the students who are urged to, "through diligent study and hard work, advance along the socialist road and deliver the great victory of socialism!" (T2, vol. 2, final phrase on p. 117).

11. There is a concession that in fact there is an invisible hand that coordinates capitalist decisions. But this invisible hand works "blindly" and government has to step in to correct mistakes and excesses. This correction is necessarily ex-post and is therefore inferior to the ex-ante government coordination in socialism. All this aside is given – literally – in smaller prints in the text (T2, Vol. 2, p. 29).

12. This is of course a difficult if not impossible path for the authority to tread. The real problem is of course fundamental. The government is caught in a contradiction – that socialism is not working yet the monopoly of the power by communist party is legitimized by the banner of socialism it carries. Caught in this vise, the government really would prefer the citizens to simply obey and not to deliberate on the issues. Political education then becomes a pretense, and is generally seen as such by the students.

13. Although opinion represents the "real" belief, students are accustomed to take examinations where they are expected to offer the "raw," untransformed information given to them by their teachers or their textbooks.

14. If the real issue of economic education is effectiveness (Peterson, 1982), it does not and cannot score high because – unlike natural science – it touches a sphere of the targeted person that is not *tabula rasa*, a blank slate upon which economic educators can imprint their own scripts. In this context approaches such as DEEP that attempts integration of economic education from kindergarten through high school may be expected to be more effective.

15. For a complete listing of the survey questions see Shen and Shen, 1993.

16. On the whole, basic human needs and instincts are the same. With broadly similar technologies, the social relationships that have been developed in the two societies are also broadly similar. We may assume that the complexity of a modern society requires a diversity of behavior, generated by a diversity of values.

17. The questions were 3, 7, 9, 10, and 28 from the TEL, form B (Soper and Walstad, 1987).

18. The only question the Chinese students scored less well on was, "which of the following is the most essential for a market economy?" The "correct" answer, "active competition in the market place," was selected by 51.4 percent of the Chinese students, whereas 37.9 percent selected "good government regulations." The latter was consistent with the textbook stricture mentioned before, that "state adjusts the markets, market guides the enterprises." Despite the fact that this slogan is *the* central doctrine in their textbook, only a minority of the students have embraced it.

19. This conclusion is also based on responses to other questions. For a discussion of these results, see Shen and Shen, 1993, p. 76.

20. This criterion of consistency is of course far from definitive, especially with the relatively small number of probing questions.

21. This corresponds in a general way to the "authoritarian personality" in the psychology literature, as characterized by rigidity in beliefs, possession of conventional wisdom, intolerance of weaknesses, punitive, suspicious, and above all reliance on authority (Adorno et al., 1950).

22. The questions and their scoring are as follows:

1. In a market economy, the social purpose of profits is to:
   - A: get businesses to follow government regulations
   - L: get businesses to produce what consumers demand
   - E: provide funds to pay workers better wages
   - E: transfer income from the poor to the rich
2. In a market economy, high wages depend primarily on:
   - A: actions of government
   - A: socially responsible business leaders
   - L: high output per worker

E: minimum wage laws

3. Among the following, which features of the economy is the most valuable?
   L: everyone can choose a career path
   E: everyone is guaranteed food, housing and medical care
   E: no one in the society is too rich or too poor
   unclassified: "average income grows regularly from one year to the next"
4. Do you think private property is:
   L: a natural right of people
   L: needed to promote economic incentives
   E: an evil because it may lead to exploitation
   unclassified: "both good and bad."

REFERENCES

Adorno, T., Frenkel-Brunswik, E., Levinson, D., & Sanford, R. N. (1950). *The authoritarian personality.* New York: Harper.

Aronson, E. (1980). *The social animal.* San Francisco: W. H. Freeman.

Helburn, S. (1986). Economics and economic education: The selective use of discipline structures in the economic curricula. In S. Hodkinson & D. Whitehead (Eds.), *Economic education: Research and development issues* (pp. 6-32). London: Longman.

Peterson, W. H. (1982). Introduction. In W. H. Peterson (Ed.), *Economic education: Investment in the future* (pp. 1-10). Knoxville: University of Tennessee Press.

Shen, R., & Shen, T. Y. (1993). Economic thinking in China: Economic knowledge and attitudes of high school students. *Journal of Economic Education, 24*(1), 73-84.

Soper, J.C., & Walstad, W. B. (1987). *Test of economic literacy: Examiner's manual* (2nd ed.). New York: Joint Council on Economic Education.

Tversky, A., & Kahneman, D. (1986). Rational choice and the framing of decisions. In R. Hogarth & M. Reder (Eds.), *Rational choice* (pp. 67-94). Chicago: Chicago University Press.

INDEX